MACROMEDIA® FIREWORKS® 8
REVEALED
DELUXE EDUCATION EDITION

Barbara M. Waxer

THOMSON

COURSE TECHNOLOGY

Macromedia® Fireworks® 8—Revealed, Deluxe Education Edition

Barbara Waxer

Managing Editor:

Marjorie Hunt

Product Manager:

Jane Hosie-Bounar

Associate Product Manager:

Shana Rosenthal

Editorial Assistant:

Janine Tangney

Production Editor:

Summer Hughes

Developmental Editor:

MT Cozzola

Composition House:

Integra—Pondicherry, India

QA Manuscript Reviewers:

Chris Carvalho, Marc Spoto,
Susan Whalen

Text Designer:

Ann Small

Illustrator:

Philip Brooker

Cover Design:

Steve Deschene

Marketing Manager:

Joy Stark

Revealed Series Vision

The Revealed Series is your guide to today's hottest multimedia applications. These comprehensive books teach the skills behind the application, showing you how to apply smart design principles to multimedia products such as dynamic graphics, animation, Web sites, software authoring tools, and digital video.

A team of design professionals including multimedia instructors, students, authors, and editors worked together to create this series. We recognized the unique learning environment of the multimedia classroom and created a series that:

- Gives you comprehensive step-by-step instructions
- Offers in-depth explanation of the "why" behind a skill
- Includes creative projects for additional practice
- Explains concepts clearly using full-color visuals

It was our goal to create a book that speaks directly to the multimedia and design community—one of the most rapidly growing computer fields today.

We feel that *Macromedia Fireworks 8— Revealed, Deluxe Education Edition* does just that—with sophisticated content and an instructive book design.
—The Revealed Series

Author's Vision

The Revealed Series and Fireworks 8 are a perfect match. By combining our unique format and your creativity we have made the process of learning to use Fireworks interesting and sometimes even fun. Because the Web continues to be dynamic, the graphics you can create with Fireworks can compel unique Web art. This book provides comprehensive conceptual information, directed but interesting lessons, and appealing projects—a solid recipe for inspired study in this exciting field.

Continual thanks to the Revealed team at Course Technology for their commitment to quality in this series. In particular, I'd like to thank Marjorie Hunt for always seeing new possibilities and Jane Hosie-Bounar for her unwavering support and for fearlessly guiding this book from jump-start to completion.

I owe Mary-Terese Cozzola very special acknowledgment and an enduring debt of gratitude. Her many creative gifts and developmental skills ensured this book's sparkle. My deepest thanks also to Dave Belden for his contributions and insight.

I happily acknowledge the rich graphic contributions of Anita Quintana and Laura Gutman (*rocket-laura.com*). Thanks also to our Course Technology reviewers, Chris Carvalho, Marc Spoto, and Susan Whalen, and to our Production Editor, Summer Hughes, who never missed a beat no matter how we (inadvertently) tried. I am also grateful to Kirsti Aho at Macromedia for her liaison role.

I would like to give special but always inadequate thanks to my partner, Lindy, who can now reclaim the words, "Just one more thing" as her own. I must also recognize a household of critters who keep the fur flying literally and figuratively.

A final note for my mom, Ruth Goodman Waxer, who passed on her love of things new and different. May her memory be a blessing.
—Barbara M. Waxer

Introduction to Macromedia Fireworks 8

Welcome to *Macromedia Fireworks 8—Revealed, Deluxe Education Edition*. This book offers creative projects, concise instructions, and complete coverage of basic to intermediate Fireworks skills, helping you to create and publish polished, professional-looking Fireworks documents. Use this book as you learn Fireworks, and then use it later as your own reference guide.

This text is organized into eight chapters. In these chapters, you will learn many skills to create interesting graphics that also include interactivity and animation. In addition, you will learn how to use Fireworks to import and export files.

What You'll Do

A What You'll Do figure begins every lesson. This figure gives you an at-a-glance look at what you'll do in the chapter, either by showing you a page or pages from the current project or a tool you'll be using.

Comprehensive Conceptual Lessons

Before jumping into instructions, in-depth conceptual information tells you "why" skills are applied. This book provides the "how" and "why" through the use of professional examples. Also included in the text are tips and sidebars to help you work more efficiently and creatively, or to teach you a bit about the history or design philosophy behind the skill you are using.

Step-by-Step Instructions

This book combines in-depth conceptual information with concise steps to help you learn Fireworks 8. Each set of steps guides you through a lesson where you will create, modify, or enhance a Fireworks document. Step references to large colorful images and quick step summaries round out the lessons.

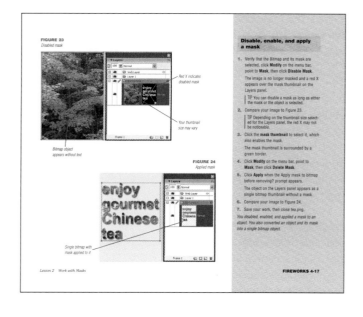

Projects

This book contains a variety of end-of-chapter materials for additional practice and reinforcement. The Skills Review contains hands-on practice exercises that mirror the progressive nature of the lesson material. Each chapter concludes with four projects: two Project Builders, one Design Project, and one Portfolio Project. The Project Builders and the Design Project require you to apply the skills you've learned in the chapter. Portfolio Projects encourage you to solve challenges based on the content explored in the chapter and to create a file for use in your portfolio.

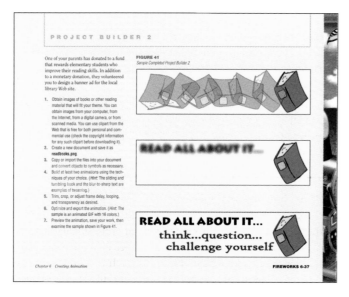

What Instructor Resources Are Available with This Book?

The Instructor Resources CD-ROM is Thomson Course Technology's way of putting the resources and information needed to teach and learn effectively into your hands. All the resources are available for both Macintosh and Windows operating systems, and many of the resources can be downloaded from *www.course.com*.

Instructor's Manual

Available as an electronic file, the Instructor's Manual includes chapter overviews and detailed lecture topics for each chapter, with teaching tips. The Instructor's Manual is available on the Instructor Resources CD-ROM, or you can download it from *www.course.com*.

Syllabus

Prepare and customize your course easily using this sample course outline (available on the Instructor Resources CD-ROM).

PowerPoint Presentations

Each chapter has a corresponding PowerPoint presentation that you can use in lectures, distribute to your students, or customize to suit your course.

Figure Files

Figure Files contain all the figures from the book in bitmap format. Use the figure files to create transparency masters or use them in a PowerPoint presentation.

Data Files for Students

To complete most of the chapters in this book, your students will need Data Files. The Data Files are available on the CD at the back of this text book. Instruct students to use the Data Files List at the end of this book if they need to understand how the files are organized. We also include a list of the Data Files needed for each chapter in the Instructor's Manual.

Solutions to Exercises

Solution Files are Data Files completed with comprehensive sample answers. Use these files to evaluate your students' work. Or distribute them electronically so students can verify their own work. Sample solutions to all lessons and end-of-chapter material are provided.

Test Bank and Test Engine

ExamView is a powerful testing software package that allows instructors to create and administer printed, computer (LAN-based), and Internet exams. ExamView includes hundreds of questions that correspond to the topics covered in this text, enabling students to generate detailed study guides that include page references for further review. The computer-based and Internet testing components allow students to take exams at their computers, and also save the instructor time by grading each exam automatically.

BRIEF CONTENTS

CHAPTER 1 GETTING STARTED WITH MACROMEDIA FIREWORKS

CONTENTS

CONTENTS

xi

CHAPTER 7 CREATING SOPHISTICATED WEB PAGE NAVIGATION

CHAPTER 8 ENHANCING PRODUCTIVITY

Intended Audience

This text is designed for the beginner or intermediate computer user who wants to learn how to use Fireworks 8. The book is designed to provide basic and in-depth material that not only informs, but also encourages you to explore the nuances of this exciting program.

Approach

The text allows you to work at your own pace through step-by-step tutorials. A concept is presented and the process is explained, followed by the actual steps. To learn the most from the use of the text, you should adopt the following habits:

■ Make sure you understand the skill being taught in each step before you move on to the next step.

■ After finishing a skill, ask yourself if you could do it on your own, without referring to the steps. If the answer is no, review the steps.

Icons, Buttons, and Pointers

Symbols for icons, buttons, and pointers are shown in the step each time they are used.

Fonts

The Data Files for this book contain a variety of commonly used fonts, but there is no guarantee that these fonts will be available on your computer.

In a few cases, fonts other than those common to a PC or a Macintosh are used. If any of the fonts in use is not available on your computer, you can make a substitution, realizing that the results may vary from those in the book.

Windows and Macintosh

Fireworks 8 works virtually the same on Windows and Macintosh operating systems. In those cases where there is a significant difference, the abbreviations (Win) and (Mac) are used.

The nature of working with graphics requires detailed work. In Fireworks, this means that you will need to magnify areas of an image. Because monitor sizes and resolution preferences vary, be sure to set the magnification to the setting that allows you to work comfortably. The figures shown in this book are displayed at a monitor resolution of 1024 x 768.

Windows System Requirements

Fireworks 8 runs under Windows® 2000 or Windows XP. Fireworks 8 requires an Intel® 800 MHz Pentium® III or equivalent processor, 256 MB RAM (1 GB recommended to run more than one Studio 8 product simultaneously), and 880 MB of disk space (1.8 GB if you are installing the complete Studio 8). Monitor resolution of 1024 x 768, 16-bit display required (32-bit recommended).

Netscape Navigator, Mozilla Firefox 1.0, or Microsoft® Internet Explorer 5.0 or later recommended.

Macintosh System Requirements

Fireworks 8 runs under Mac OS X® 10.3 or 10.4. Fireworks 8 requires a 600 MHz PowerPC® G3 processor or later, 256 MB RAM (1 GB recommended to run more than one Studio 8 product simultaneously), and 320 MB of disk space (1.2 GB if you are installing the complete Studio 8). Monitor resolution of 1024 x 768, thousands of colors display required (millions of colors recommended). Safari 2.0 or Mozilla Firefox 1.0 recommended.

Data Files

To complete the lessons in this book, you need the Data Files on the CD provided with this book. You can store these files on a hard drive, a network server, or a USB storage device. The instructions in the lessons will refer to "the drive and folder where your Data Files are stored" when referring to the Data Files for the book.

Creating a Portfolio

The Portfolio Projects and Project Builders allow students to use their creativity to come up with original Fireworks designs. You might suggest that students create a portfolio in which they can store their original work.

GETTING STARTED
WITH MACROMEDIA FIREWORKS

1. Understand the Fireworks work environment.

2. Work with new and existing documents.

3. Work with bitmap images.

4. Create shapes.

5. Create and modify text.

chapter

1 GETTING STARTED
WITH MACROMEDIA FIREWORKS

Understanding Fireworks

Fireworks is a graphics program intended specifically for the Web. Both Web enthusiasts and professionals can create, edit, and optimize files, and then add animation and JavaScript-enabled interactivity to those optimized files. Many Fireworks tasks are compartmentalized so that graphic artists can enhance or create designs without disturbing the programming added by developers, and vice versa.

In Fireworks, you can also work with files created by other graphic design programs, and save and export files you create in Fireworks to other programs. Fireworks is an integral component of Macromedia Studio 8, and integrates seamlessly with other Macromedia

applications, including Macromedia Flash, Dreamweaver, FreeHand, ColdFusion, and Director. In addition, you can use other applications, such as Flash or Dreamweaver, to edit Fireworks images using the Fireworks interface from within the host application. Fireworks also allows file sharing with other applications, such as Adobe Photoshop.

In this book, you will learn to use the tools and apply the concepts that make Fireworks a comprehensive Web graphics program. In addition to creating files that can be used in other programs, you will create sample Web pages and animated graphics.

Tools You'll Use

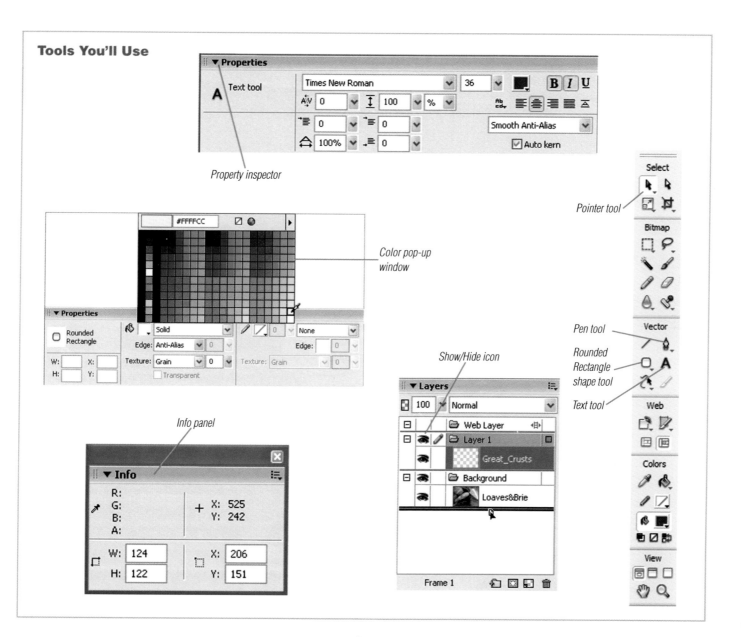

Properties

A — Text tool

Times New Roman · 36 · **B** *I* U

AV 0 · I 100 · %

0 · 0 · Smooth Anti-Alias

100% · 0 · Auto kern

Property inspector

#FFFFCC

Color pop-up window

Properties

Rounded Rectangle — Solid · None

Edge: Anti-Alias · 0 · Edge: 0

W: · X: · Texture: Grain · 0 · Texture: Grain

H: · Y: · Transparent

Show/Hide icon

Info panel

Info

R:
G:
B:
A:

+ X: 525
Y: 242

W: 124 · X: 206
H: 122 · Y: 151

Layers

100 · Normal

Web Layer

Layer 1

Great_Crusts

Background

Loaves&Brie

Frame 1

Select

Pointer tool

Bitmap

Vector

Pen tool

Rounded Rectangle shape tool

Text tool

Web

Colors

View

UNDERSTAND THE FIREWORKS WORK ENVIRONMENT

What You'll Do

 In this lesson, you will start Fireworks, open a file, and adjust panels, including undocking and collapsing them.

Viewing the Fireworks Window

The Fireworks window, shown in Figures 1 and 2, contains the space where you work with documents, tools, and panels. The overall Fireworks environment emulates the familiar interface in other Macromedia applications. When you open or create a document, the Document window contains four display buttons: Original, Preview, 2-Up, and 4-Up. You can work in your document when you click the Original button; the other three are document preview buttons. You can view the current settings in your document using the Preview button. The 2-Up and 4-Up buttons allow you to select different optimization settings and evaluate them side by side. The main area of the Document window contains the **canvas**.

When you open multiple documents and the Document window is maximized, each open document's title appears on a separate tab.

QUICKTIP

The bottom of each Document window also contains frame control buttons for playing animation.

Tools are housed in the **Tools panel**; other functions are contained in panels such as the Optimize panel, Layers panels, and Assets panel. The Tools panel is organized into **tool groups**: Select, Bitmap, Vector, Web, Colors, and View, so you can easily locate the tool you need. You can modify selected objects and set tool properties and other options using the **Property inspector**. Depending on the

Opening Windows-specific toolbars

If you are using Windows, you can open the Main and Modify toolbars from the Toolbars command on the Window menu. The Main toolbar includes buttons for common tasks, whereas the Modify toolbar contains buttons for modifying objects.

action you are performing, information on the Property inspector changes. For example, when you select a tool, an object, or the canvas, properties specific to the selection appear on the Property inspector.

You can rearrange panels in the Fireworks window based on your work preferences. Fireworks allows you to dock, undock, regroup, collapse, expand, and close panels

or panel groups. To open or close a panel, click the panel name on the Window menu. To expand or collapse a panel, click the panel title or arrow in the title bar. To move a panel to a new panel docking area, drag the **gripper**, the textured area on the left side of the title bar, to the left until a placement preview rectangle appears. To undock a panel, drag the gripper and move the translucent panel copy into the work area. You can resize a

panel by placing the mouse pointer at the bottom of the panel, and then dragging the double-sided arrow pointer. Note that displaying all of the panels at one time can obscure your view of the Document window.

QUICKTIP

You can quickly hide or show all open panels by pressing [Tab] or [F4].

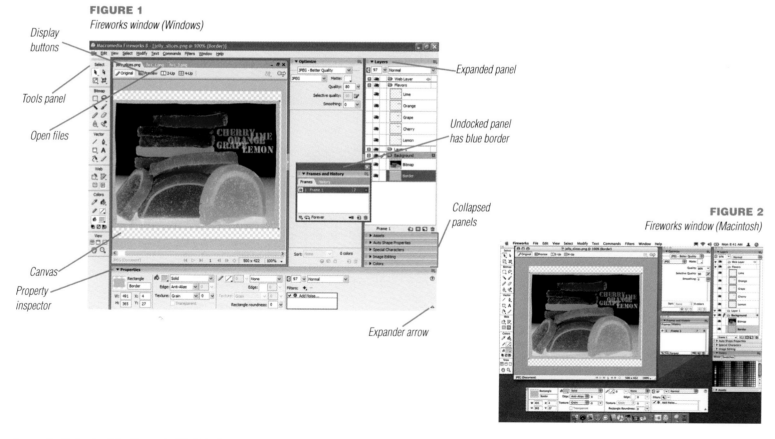

FIGURE 1
Fireworks window (Windows)

Display buttons

Tools panel

Open files

Canvas

Property inspector

Expanded panel

Undocked panel has blue border

Collapsed panels

Expander arrow

FIGURE 2
Fireworks window (Macintosh)

Start Fireworks and open a Fireworks document

1. Windows users, click the **Start button** 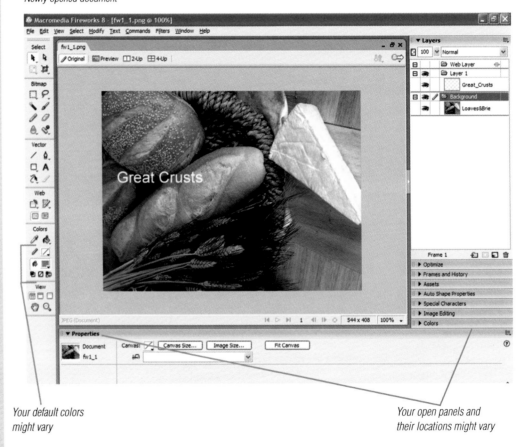 on the taskbar, point to **All Programs**, point to the **Macromedia folder**, then click the **Macromedia Fireworks 8 program icon** (Win).

    Mac users, click **Finder** on the Dock, click **Applications** on the sidebar in the window that appears, click or double-click the **Macromedia Fireworks 8 folder**, then double-click the **Fireworks 8 program icon**. After Fireworks is running, control-click in the Dock, then click **Keep In Dock** (if necessary).

    The application opens with the Start page displayed.

2. Click **File** on the menu bar, then click **Open**.

    TIP   You can also press [Ctrl][O] (Win) or ⌘ [O] (Mac) to open a file, or you can click options on the Start page. To disable the Start page, click the Don't show again check box.

3. Navigate to the drive and folder where your Data Files are stored, click **fw1_1.png**, then click **Open**.

    TIP   If the drive containing your Data Files is not displayed, click the Look in list arrow (Win).

4. Compare your default Fireworks window to Figure 3.

You started Fireworks and opened a file.

FIGURE 3
Newly opened document

Your default colors might vary

Your open panels and their locations might vary

FIGURE 4

Opening panels from the Window menu (Win)

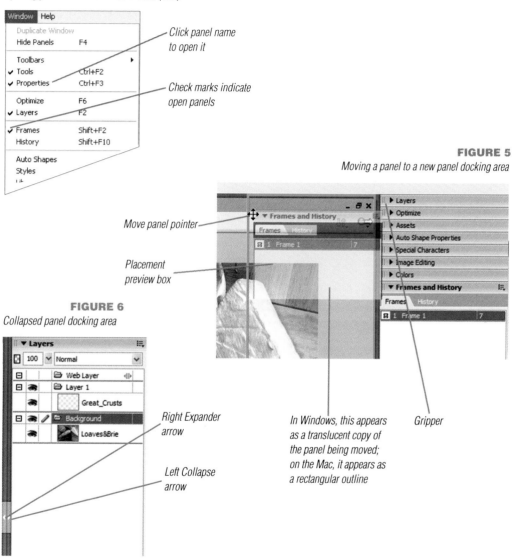

Click panel name to open it

Check marks indicate open panels

FIGURE 5

Moving a panel to a new panel docking area

Move panel pointer

Placement preview box

FIGURE 6

Collapsed panel docking area

Right Expander arrow

Left Collapse arrow

In Windows, this appears as a translucent copy of the panel being moved; on the Mac, it appears as a rectangular outline

Gripper

Open and adjust panels in the Fireworks window

1. Click **Window** on the menu bar, then click to open or close each **panel** until your menu resembles Figure 4.

   TIP Each time you click to open or close a panel, the Window menu closes, so you may need to open the menu more than once.

2. Position the mouse pointer on the top of the **Frames and History panel**, drag the **gripper** ⠿ to the left until you see the placement preview rectangle shown in Figure 5 (Mac users will see a plain rectangle), then release the mouse button.

3. Click the **Frames and History panel title** to collapse the panel, then click the **panel title** again to expand the panel.

   The panel docking area remains open.

4. Click the **Layers panel title** (if necessary) to expand the panel.

5. Click the **Left Collapse arrow** ▶ (Win) in the left side of the Frames and History panel docking area to collapse the area, then compare your image to Figure 6.

6. Click the **Right Expander arrow** ◀ (Win) to expand the panel area.

7. Click the **Options menu button** ☰ in the Frames and History panel, then click **Close Panel Group**.

8. Click **File** on the menu bar, then click **Close**.

   TIP You can also press [Ctrl][W] (Win) or ⌘ [W] (Mac) to close a file.

You adjusted panels in the Fireworks window, and opened and closed a document.

Lesson 1   Understand the Fireworks Work Environment

WORK WITH NEW AND EXISTING DOCUMENTS

What You'll Do

In this lesson, you will set document properties, use the Index and Search tabs of
Help, add a layer, and copy an object
between documents.

Working with Files

Fireworks files are known as **documents**.
When you create a new document, you can
set properties such as the document's size,
resolution, and canvas color. Fireworks
will retain the changes you make to document properties as the default settings for
new documents. A Fireworks document
consists of many **layers**, which you can
use to organize the elements of your document. A layer can contain multiple objects,
all of which are managed on the Layers
panel.

Although you can open or import a wide
range of file formats, the files you create in
Macromedia Fireworks are PNG files and
have a .png extension. PNG files have
unique characteristics that afford you considerable flexibility in working with
images. Different file formats support
images differently. You can divide a document or image into parts and then individually optimize and export them in the
format that best supports the image. For
example, you can save a photograph in
your document as a JPEG and a cartoon

Duplicating options in Fireworks

You can duplicate an object within a document by selecting the object on the canvas,
pressing and holding [Alt] (Win) or [option] (Mac), and then dragging the object to a
new location. However, if you open a document immediately after copying an object
to the Clipboard, Fireworks automatically sets the size of a new document to those
dimensions.

illustration as a GIF. JPEG format compresses color well, and is thus best suited for photographs, whereas GIF format is suitable for line art.

You can also open an existing file or import a file into a Fireworks document. You can copy and paste or drag and drop images or text into a Fireworks document from other documents or applications, or from a scanner or digital camera. Figure 7 shows an object copied from a source document to a target document.

Accessing Help

In Windows, the Fireworks Help system consists of tabs that you can use to access Help topics: Contents, Index, and Search. On the Mac, Help is configured slightly differently but contains similar functionality. In Windows, the Contents tab lists various topics by subject matter. You can type a keyword on the Index tab and access all the topics that begin with that keyword. You can also enter a word or phrase on the Search tab and retrieve a listing of the topics that contain the word or phrase. On the Mac, instead of multiple tabs, Help appears as a single page with an Ask a Question text box and links to additional pages.

In Help, commands on the menu bar help you navigate and print topics. Other commands on the Help menu link you to online support, such as the Fireworks Support Center and Macromedia Online Forums. You can also obtain updates and tips and search for information on the Fireworks page of the Macromedia Web site.

FIGURE 7
Object copied between documents

Open documents

Object is copied to active layer

Create and save a new document

1. Click **File** on the menu bar, then click **New**.

   TIP You can also press [Ctrl][N] (Win) or ⌘[N] (Mac) to open a new file, or you can click an option on the Start page.

2. Type **325** in the Width text box, double-click the value in the Height text box, type **275**, then verify that the resolution is **72**.

3. Click the **Custom option** in the Canvas color section of the New Document dialog box, then click the **Canvas Color box** 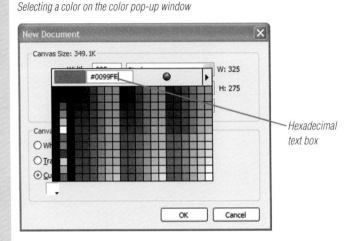.

4. Select the value in the hexadecimal text box, type **#0099FF**, as shown in Figure 8, press **[Enter]** (Win) or **[return]** (Mac), then click **OK**.

   A new Document window appears in the Fireworks window.

   TIP You can also select a canvas color by clicking a color swatch in the color pop-up window.

5. Click **File** on the menu bar, click **Save As**, type **my_blue_heaven** in the File name text box (Win) or Save As text box (Mac), click the **Save in list arrow** (Win) or **Where box list arrow** (Mac) to choose your destination drive and folder, then click **Save**.

6. Compare your document to Figure 9.

You created a new document, set properties for the new document, and saved it.

FIGURE 8
Selecting a color on the color pop-up window

Hexadecimal text box

FIGURE 9
Newly created document

Your document might be maximized

New document settings

FIGURE 10

Getting help on a topic

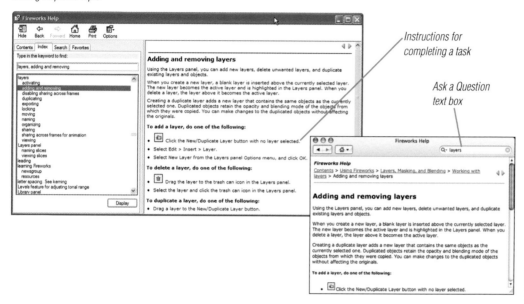

Instructions for completing a task

Ask a Question text box

FIGURE 11

Layer added to Layers panel

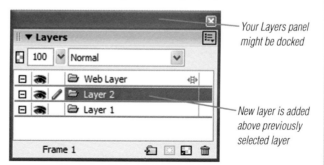

Your Layers panel might be docked

New layer is added above previously selected layer

Get Help and add a layer

1. Click **Help** on the menu bar, click **Fireworks Help**, then click the **Index tab** (Win) (if necessary).

   TIP   You can also open the Help system by pressing [F1] (Win).

2. Type **layers** in the Type in the keyword to find text box (Win) or Ask a Question text box (Mac) at the top of the Help window, press **[return]** (Mac), then double-click **adding and removing** (Win) or **Adding and removing layers** (Mac) in the topic list.

3. Read the instructions on adding a layer, compare your Help window to Figure 10, then click the **Help window Close button**.

4. Click **Window** on the menu bar, click **Layers** to select it (if necessary), click the **New/Duplicate Layer button** on the Layers panel, then compare your Layers panel to Figure 11.

   A new layer, Layer 2, appears on the Layers panel above the active layer.

   TIP   Expand the Layers panel (if necessary) to see all the layers.

You used Help to get instructions for adding a layer in Fireworks, and then used that information to add a layer in the Layers panel.

Use Help to search for a term

1. Open **pool.png**, then resize the Document windows as necessary so that you can see the contents of both open documents.

   TIP If the .png extension is not visible, Windows users can open the file management tool on their operating system, then adjust the settings to display extensions.

2. Drag the **pool.png document** to a blank part of the Fireworks window, then make sure that your view of the documents is unobstructed, as shown in Figure 12.

   TIP Depending on the size and resolution of your monitor, adjust panels and the size of both Document windows as needed.

3. Click **Help** on the menu bar, click **Using Fireworks**, then click the **Search tab** (Win).

4. Click **Options** on the tool bar, then verify that **Search Highlight Off** appears in the menu (Win), indicating that the Search Highlight feature is currently turned on.

5. Windows users, type **Inserting objects into** in the Type in the keyword to find text box, then click **List Topics**.

   Mac users, type **Inserting objects into** in the Ask a Question text box at the top of the Help window, then press **[return]**.

6. Double-click the topic that begins **Inserting objects**, then compare your Help window (Win) to Figure 13.

7. Read the instructions for inserting objects, then close the Help window.

You searched for a term in Help and learned more about inserting objects into a Fireworks document.

FIGURE 12
Open documents in the Fireworks window

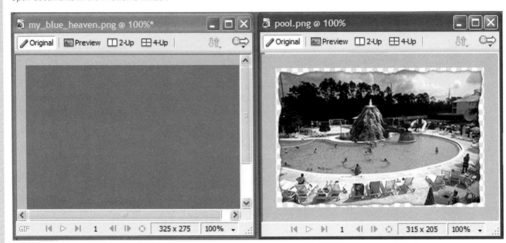

FIGURE 13
Searching for a term in Help

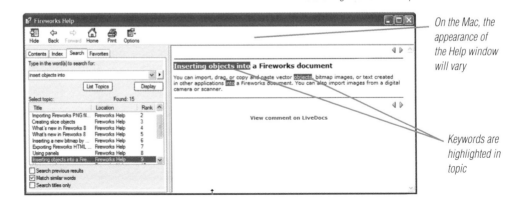

On the Mac, the appearance of the Help window will vary

Keywords are highlighted in topic

FIGURE 14
Object being copied

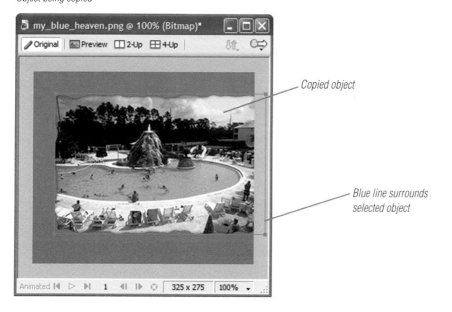

Copied object

Blue line surrounds
selected object

FIGURE 15
Object centered in document

Drag and drop an image

1. Make sure that the **Pointer tool** is selected on the Tools panel.

2. Click the mouse anywhere on the pool image, drag it to the my_blue_heaven document, then compare your image to Figure 14.

   TIP You can also select the object, click Edit on the menu bar, click Copy, position the pointer in the target document, click Edit on the menu bar, then click Paste.

3. Use the arrow keys to center the image on the canvas.

   TIP The arrow keys move an object in 1-pixel increments; press and hold [Shift] to move in 10-pixel increments.

4. Click **Window** on the menu bar, click **Pool.png**, click **File** on the menu bar, then click **Close**.

   TIP If you are prompted to save changes, click No (Win) or Don't Save (Mac).

5. Click the **blank area** around the canvas to deselect the object, then compare your document to Figure 15.

6. Click **File** on the menu bar, click **Close**, then click **Yes** (Win) or **Save** (Mac) to save changes.

You dragged an image from one file to another.

WORK WITH
BITMAP IMAGES

What You'll Do

▶ *In this lesson, you will modify a bitmap image and create and lock a layer.*

Understanding the Layers Panel

Although *layer* is a common term in graphic design applications, a layer's function varies depending on the program. In other applications, such as Adobe Photoshop, you use layers to manipulate **pixels**, discrete squares of color values that can be drawn in a document. In Fireworks, you use layers to position **objects**, which are the individual elements in your document. One function of the Layers panel is to arrange the elements in your document in a logical design order. For example, you can place related elements on the same layer, such as the design elements of a logo, or all the buttons for a Web page. The position of objects/layers in the Layers panel

affects their appearance in your document. Each object is akin to an image on a clear piece of acetate—you can stack them on top of each other and view them from the top. The artwork on the bottom may be obscured by the layers above it, but you can adjust visibility by making some pieces more transparent.

You can place as many objects as you want on a layer, arrange them in any order, and select one or more of them at a time. A document can easily accumulate numerous layers and objects, which can make it difficult to quickly find the ones with which you want to work. You can collapse or expand layers to show all or none of the objects. Figure 16 shows components of the Layers panel.

Customizing your view of the Layers panel
You can select the size of the thumbnails that are displayed in the Layers panel or choose not to display them at all. To change thumbnail size, click the Options menu button on the Layers panel, click Thumbnail Options, and then select the option you want.

An object in Fireworks corresponds to a layer in Photoshop.

Understanding Bitmap Images and Vector Objects

Fireworks allows you to work with both bitmap and vector graphic images in your document. A **bitmap graphic** represents a picture image as a matrix of dots, or pixels, on a grid. Bitmaps allow your computer screen to realistically depict the pixel colors in a photographic image. In contrast, **vector graphics** are mathematically calculated objects composed of anchor points and straight or curved line segments, which you can fill with color or a pattern and outline with a stroke.

Because a bitmap image is defined pixel by pixel, when you scale a bitmap graphic, you lose the sharpness of the original image. **Resolution** refers to the number of pixels in an image. Resolution also refers to an image's clarity and fineness of detail. On-screen resolution is usually 72 or 96 pixels per inch (ppi). (Print graphics require greater resolution.) Bitmap images are, therefore, resolution-dependent—resizing results in a loss of image quality. The most visible evidence is the all-too-familiar jagged appearance in the edges of a resized image.

Because they retain their appearance regardless of how you resize or skew them, vector graphics offer far more flexibility than bitmap images. They are resolution-independent—enlarging retains a crisp edge. Figure 17 compares the image quality of enlarged vector and bitmap images.

FIGURE 16
Layers panel

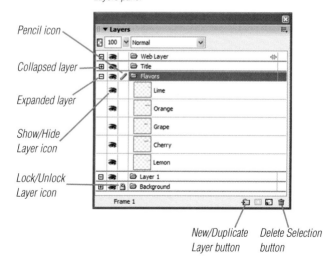

Pencil icon

Collapsed layer

Expanded layer

Show/Hide
Layer icon

Lock/Unlock
Layer icon

New/Duplicate   Delete Selection
Layer button   button

FIGURE 17
Comparing vector and bitmap graphics

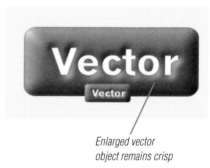

Enlarged vector
object remains crisp

Enlarged bitmap
image appears
jagged and blurry

Open a document and display the Layers panel

1. Open fw1_1.png, then save it as **breads**.

2. Make sure that the Layers panel is displayed and expanded to show all the layers.

3. Click the **Show/Hide Layer icon** 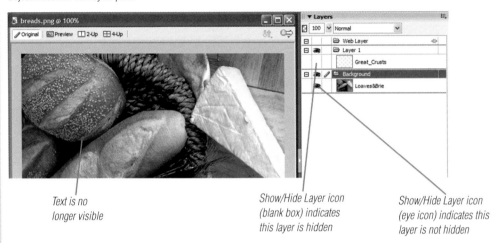 next to the Great_Crusts object in Layer 1 on the Layers panel to hide the layer.

   Notice that the Show/Hide Layer icon toggles between an eye icon and a blank box, depending on whether the layer is hidden or visible.

   | TIP If you do not see an object in a layer, click the Expand Layer icon.

4. Compare your image to Figure 18, then click the **Show/Hide Layer icon** next to the Great_Crusts object in Layer 1.

5. Click the **Great_Crusts object** in Layer 1 on the Layers panel, then drag it beneath the Loaves&Brie object in the Background layer until a flashing double line (Win) or dark black line (Mac) appears beneath the Loaves&Brie object, as shown in Figure 19.

   The Great_Crusts object is now beneath or behind the Loaves&Brie object in the Background layer, so it is no longer visible, although you can still see its blue selection line.

6. Verify that the Great_Crusts object is still selected, then click the **Delete Selection button** 🗑 on the Layers panel.

You hid and displayed an object in a layer on the Layers panel and moved and deleted an object. Moving an object on the Layers panel affects its visibility in the document.

FIGURE 18
Object hidden on the Layers panel

Text is no longer visible

Show/Hide Layer icon (blank box) indicates this layer is hidden

Show/Hide Layer icon (eye icon) indicates this layer is not hidden

FIGURE 19
Object moved between layers

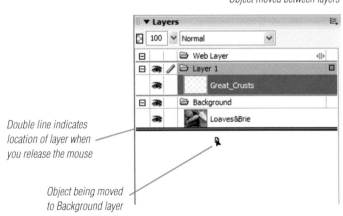

Double line indicates location of layer when you release the mouse

Object being moved to Background layer

FIGURE 20
Brightness/Contrast dialog box

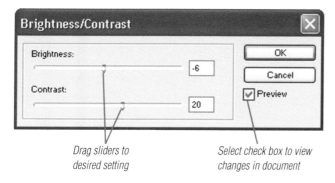

Drag sliders to
desired setting

Select check box to view
changes in document

FIGURE 21
Layer locked on Layers panel

Click pencil icon or
blank box in column
to lock layer

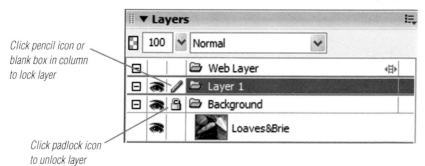

Click padlock icon
to unlock layer

Edit a bitmap image and lock a layer

1. Click the **Loaves&Brie object** on the Background layer to select it (if necessary).

2. Click **Filters** on the menu bar, point to **Adjust Color**, then click **Brightness/Contrast**.

3. Drag the Brightness slider to **–6**, then drag the Contrast slider to **20**.

   | TIP   You can also enter values in the
   | text boxes.

4. Compare your Brightness/Contrast dialog box to Figure 20, then click **OK**.

   The colors in the image appear richer.

5. Click the **pencil icon** 🖉 in the column next to the Background folder icon to lock the layer.

   The padlock icon 🔒 replaces 🖉 in the column.

   | TIP   While it is locked, you cannot edit a
   | layer or its objects.

6. Compare your Layers panel to Figure 21.

7. Click **File** on the menu bar, then click **Save**.

You adjusted the brightness and contrast of the Loaves&Brie object, locked the layer, and saved the file.

CREATE SHAPES

What You'll Do

 In this lesson, you will display rulers and guides, and create and modify a vector object.

Using Rulers, Guides, and the Grid

Rulers, guides, and the grid are design aides that help you precisely align and position objects in your document. Because Fireworks graphics are Web-oriented, where the rule of measurement is in pixels, ruler units are always in pixels. You insert guides from the rulers by dragging them onto your canvas. Guides do not print or export, although you can save them in the original .png document. If you want to specify an exact location, you can double-click a guide and then enter a coordinate. For each open document, you can adjust the grid size to create squares or rectangles and snap objects directly to guides and the grid at any time.

QUICKTIP

To change guide and grid line colors, point to the Grid command or Guides command on the View menu, then click Edit Grid or Edit Guides, respectively.

Sizing and Repositioning Objects

You can use the Info panel and the Property inspector to view information about the position of the pointer on the canvas and selected objects. When an object is selected, the lower half of the Info panel contains the same settings that are in the left corner of the Property inspector. The W and H values show the object's size, while the X and Y values show the object's position on the canvas. You can use the coordinate values to create, resize, or move an object to a precise location. You can also resize and move objects by dragging their sizing handles and moving them on the canvas. The upper half of the Info panel contains the R, G, B, and A (Red, Green, Blue, and Alpha) color values, and the X and Y coordinate values correspond to the area of the canvas where the pointer is currently positioned.

Using the Tools Panel

The Tools panel contains selection, drawing, and editing tools. Although you can use many tools on both bitmap and vector graphics, graphic mode-specific tools are housed in separate sections of the Tools panel.

Some tools have multiple tools associated with them. A small arrow in the lower right corner of a tool button indicates that more tools are available in that tool group. To select additional tools, press and hold the tool, then click the tool you want from the list, as shown in Figure 22. The properties associated with a selected tool are displayed on the Property inspector, although not all tools have properties associated with them. For example, when you select any of the basic tools or Auto Shapes, such as the Ellipse tool or the Arrow Auto Shape, you

can adjust the object's fill and stroke settings on the Property inspector.

Based on the object, layer, or tool, Fireworks automatically determines whether you are editing a bitmap or a vector graphic, and activates or nullifies the tool appropriately. Figure 23 shows the Blur tool (a bitmap tool) actively blurring the floral bitmap image, but the tool can't blur the text because text is a vector object. Bitmap selection tools modify the pixels in a bitmap image, which makes them useful for retouching photographic images.

You can create vector shapes using the tools in the Vector portion of the Tools panel. The shape tool group is divided

into two groups: basic shape tools (Ellipse, Rectangle, and Polygon tools) and Auto Shapes. You can adjust the height, width, and overall size of basic shapes by dragging their sizing handles.

Understanding Auto Shapes

You can create basic or Auto Shapes by selecting the shape and then dragging the mouse pointer on the canvas. For Auto Shapes, you can also click the canvas to create a presized Auto Shape. Auto Shapes are complex vector shapes that you can manipulate by dragging control points. A **control point** is the yellow diamond that appears when you select an Auto Shape on the canvas. When you roll the mouse

FIGURE 22
Selecting tools on the Tools panel

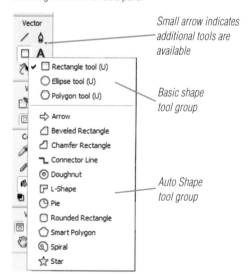

Small arrow indicates additional tools are available

Basic shape tool group

Auto Shape tool group

FIGURE 23
Using a tool on different graphic types

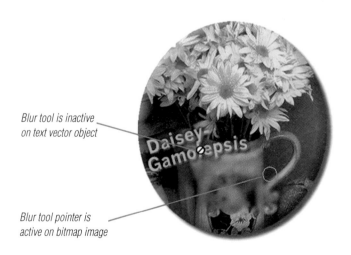

Blur tool is inactive on text vector object

Blur tool pointer is active on bitmap image

pointer over a control point, a tool tip appears, giving you information on how to adjust the Auto Shape. You can adjust individual aspects specific to each shape, such as tips, corners, roundness, the number of points or sectors, and so on. Figure 24 shows the control points for an Auto Chamfer Rectangle and for an Auto Polygon. You can modify an Auto Shape by dragging the control point or by pressing a keyboard shortcut key, such as [Shift], [Alt], and [Ctrl] (Win) or [Shift], [option], and ⌘ (Mac), and then dragging a control point. Figure 25 shows how you can radically alter the appearance of an Auto Shape by dragging control points.

QUICKTIP

To access additional Auto Shapes in Fireworks, open the Auto Shapes panel on the Window menu, and

then drag one of the displayed Auto Shapes to the canvas. To download Auto Shapes from the Macromedia Web site, click the Options menu button on the Shapes panel, and then click Get More Auto Shapes.

Applying Fills and Strokes

You can fill an object with a solid color, texture, or pattern. When you apply a **fill**, you can adjust the following attributes: its color and category (such as solid, gradient, or pattern), and the type and amount of edge of the fill. You can apply a border, known as a **stroke**, to an object's edge. You can set several stroke attributes, including color, tip size (the size of the stroke), softness, and texture.

Anti-aliasing blends the edges of a stroke or text with surrounding pixels so that the edges appear to smooth into the

background. Anti-aliasing reduces the contrast between the edge and the background by adding pixels of intermediate color. When editing a vector shape other than text, you can select one of four anti-alias settings: No, Crisp, Strong, or Smooth, which make the edges look smoother or crisper. When you select a text object, you can also select a System or Custom anti-alias setting. When you select Custom anti-alias, a dialog box appears in which you can set the oversampling rate, sharpness, and strength of the anti-alias.

QUICKTIP

Aliasing can occur when an analog image is represented in a digital mode, such as a graphic image viewed on a computer. The edges of the graphic are discrete rectangles and squares, which do not always illustrate a curve very well.

FIGURE 24
Control points for smart shapes

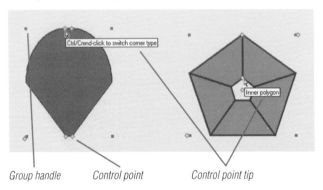

Group handle   Control point   Control point tip

FIGURE 25
Auto Shape variants

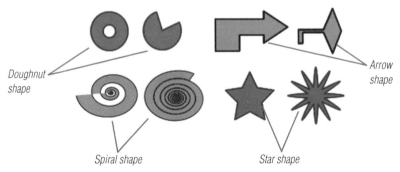

Doughnut shape

Spiral shape   Star shape

Arrow shape

FIGURE 26
Guides displayed

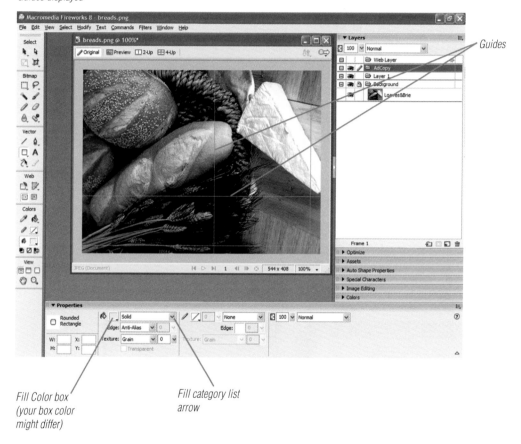

Guides

Fill Color box
(your box color
might differ)

Fill category list
arrow

Display the guides

1. Verify that Layer 1 is active, then click the **New/Duplicate Layer button** on the Layers panel to create a new layer, Layer 2.

2. Double-click **Layer 2**, type **AdCopy** in the Layer name text box, then press **[Enter]** (Win) or **[return]** (Mac).

3. Click **View** on the menu bar, point to **Guides**, then click **Show Guides** (if necessary).

   Horizontal and vertical guides appear in the Document window, as shown in Figure 26.

You created and named a layer, and displayed guides in the Document window.

Create a vector object

1. Press and hold the **Rectangle tool** on the Tools panel, then click the **Rounded Rectangle Shape tool** (if necessary)·

2. Click the **Fill category list arrow** on the Property inspector, click **Solid** (if necessary), then click the **Fill Color box** to open the color pop-up window.

(continued)

3. Click the **rightmost swatch** in the second row from the bottom (#FFFFCC) ✐, as shown in Figure 27.

4. Click the **Edge of fills list arrow**, click **Anti-Alias** (if necessary), click the **Texture name list arrow**, click **Grain** (if necessary), click the **Amount of texture list arrow**, drag the slider to **10**, then click the **Transparent check box** to select it.

   | TIP Fireworks automatically applies the last selected stroke and fill to an object.

5. Click **Window** on the menu bar, click **Info** to open the Info panel, expand the panel, so you can see all the information it contains, then move it out of the way (if necessary).

6. Use the guides to position the pointer ┼ at approximately **300 X/280 Y**, click, then drag the pointer to **520 X/390 Y**, noticing the changing coordinates in the Info panel.

7. Click **Edit** on the menu bar, then click the **Undo Shape Tool** (Win) or **Undo AutoShape Tool (Mac)**.

   The rectangle disappears.

   | TIP You can also press [Ctrl][Z] (Win) or ⌘ [Z] (Mac) to undo a command.

8. Click **Edit** on the menu bar, click **Redo Shape Tool** (Win) or **Redo AutoShape Tool** (Mac), then compare your image to Figure 28.

   | TIP You can also press [Ctrl][Y] (Win) or ⌘ [Y] (Mac) to redo a command.

You set properties for the Rounded Rectangle tool, opened the Info panel, and created a rounded rectangle shape.

FIGURE 27
Selecting the fill color

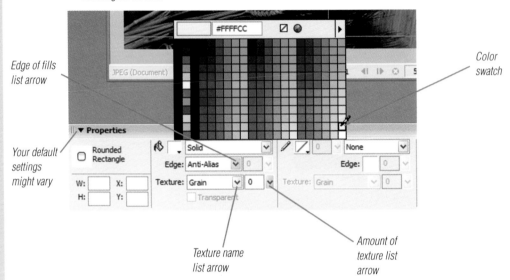

Edge of fills list arrow

Your default settings might vary

Color swatch

Texture name list arrow

Amount of texture list arrow

FIGURE 28
Creating a rounded rectangle

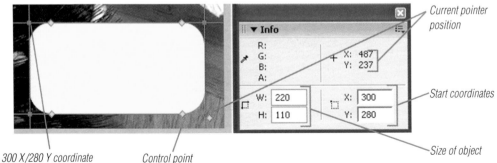

Current pointer position

Start coordinates

Size of object

300 X/280 Y coordinate

Control point

FIGURE 29
Stroke properties

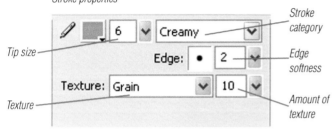

Tip size —

Texture —

Stroke category

Edge softness

Amount of texture

FIGURE 30
Stroke applied to rectangle

Apply a stroke to an object

1. Click the **Stroke Color box** on the Property inspector, type **#FF9900** in the hexa-decimal text box, then press **[Enter]** (Win) or **[return]** (Mac).

2. Click the **Stroke category list arrow**, point to **Charcoal**, then click **Creamy**.

3. Click the **Tip size list arrow**, then drag the slider to **6**.

4. Enter the remaining stroke values shown in Figure 29.

   TIP   To create an ellipse, drag the control points toward the center.

5. Click **View** on the menu bar, point to **Guides**, then click **Show Guides** to turn off guides.

6. Click **Select** on the menu bar, click **Deselect** (if necessary), then compare your image to Figure 30.

7. Save your work.

You fine-tuned stroke properties to add a border to an object that suits the style and mood you want to create. You selected stroke properties, applied a stroke to the rectangle, and turned off the guides. You used the Deselect command so that you could see the results of your work without seeing the selection line.

CREATE AND
MODIFY TEXT

What You'll Do

 In this lesson, you will create text and a path, attach the text to the path, save your document, and then exit the program.

Using Text in a Document

The text features in Macromedia Fireworks are typical of most desktop publishing programs—after you select the Text tool, you can preview the font family and modify properties, including size, color, style, kerning, leading, alignment, text flow, offset, and anti-alias properties. **Kerning** adjusts the spacing between adjacent letters or a range of letters, whereas **leading** adjusts the amount of space between lines of text. You can set other text attributes, such as indent, alignment, the space before and after a paragraph, and baseline shift, on the Property inspector. Figure 31 shows Text tool properties on the Property inspector. You can automatically preview in your document the changes you make to Text tool properties.

After you create text, you can edit the text block as a whole, or edit just a range of text. When you create text, you can create auto-sizing or fixed-width text blocks. **Auto-sizing** means that the text block expands to accommodate the text you enter. If you delete text, the text block contracts. You can spell check text at any time, including selecting multiple text blocks to check their spelling.

QUICKTIP

You can change the orientation of any selected text block by clicking the Text orientation button on the Property inspector, and then selecting an option from the pop-up menu. You can choose a vertical or horizontal text orientation and display the characters left to right or right to left.

Using the Text Editor

You can use the Text Editor to preview fonts and view and modify text that may be difficult to see in your document. To open the Text Editor, select a text block or a range of text, click Text on the menu bar, then click Editor. You can also copy text from the Text Editor and paste it as text into other applications.

Attaching Text to a Path

You can manipulate text by creating a path, and then attaching text to it. A **path** is an open or closed vector consisting of a series of anchor points. **Anchor points** join path segments—they delineate changes in direction, whether a corner or a curve. To create a path, you use the Pen tool to define points in your document, then attach the text to it. You can edit text after you've attached it to a path. You can also edit the path, but only if it is not attached to text. Figure 32 shows text attached to paths.

QUICKTIP

You can also attach text to paths created with a basic shape tool or to paths of Auto Shapes that you've modified with the Freeform tool or the Reshape Area tool.

To edit a path, you adjust the anchor points. To adjust the anchor points, select the path, select the Subselection tool on the Tools panel, and then drag points to new locations on the path as desired. You can also modify the appearance of text on a path by changing its alignment, orientation, and direction. By combining the shape of the path with the text alignment, orientation, and direction, you can create unique-looking text objects that convey the exact message you want.

FIGURE 31

Text properties on the Property inspector

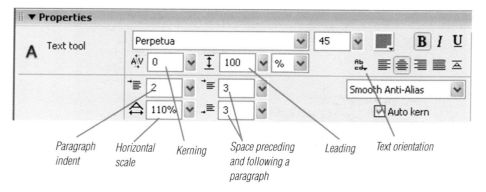

Paragraph indent   Horizontal scale   Kerning   Space preceding and following a paragraph   Leading   Text orientation

FIGURE 32

Text on paths

Image with text attached to paths

Paths visible with text attached

Create text using the Text tool

1. Verify that the AdCopy layer is selected on the Layers panel, then click the **Text tool** [A] on the Tools panel.

2. Click the **Font list arrow** on the Property inspector, click **Times New Roman**, double-click the **Size text box**, then type **36**.

3. Click the **Fill Color box** ■, type **#663300** in the hexadecimal text box, then press **[Enter]** (Win) or **[return]** (Mac).

4. Click the **Bold button** [B] to select it.

5. Click the **Italic button** [I] to select it.

6. Verify that the Center alignment button ≡ and Smooth Anti-Alias option are selected, then compare your Property inspector to Figure 33.

(continued)

FIGURE 33
Setting Text tool properties

Size text box

Fill Color box

Bold button

Italic button

Font list arrow

FIGURE 34
Newly created text

**Upper Crust
Shoppe**

7. Click the middle of the rectangle, type **Upper Crust**, press **[Enter]** (Win) or **[return]** (Mac), then type **Shoppe**.

8. Click the **Pointer tool** 🔧 on the Tools panel, then center the text by dragging it in the rectangle (if necessary).

9. Click **Select** on the menu bar, then click **Deselect**.

    TIP You can also press [Ctrl][D] (Win) or ⌘[A] (Mac) to deselect an object.

10. Compare your image to Figure 34.

Spell check text

1. Click the **Text tool** **A** on the Tools panel, double-click the **Size text box** on the Property inspector, type **24**, then verify that the Bold **B** and Italic **I** buttons are selected.

2. Click the top of the cheese wedge, type **Frehs Daily**, then compare your image to Figure 35.

3. Click **Text** on the menu bar, click **Check Spelling**, then click **Change**.

    The word "Fresh" is now spelled correctly.

    > TIP   If prompted to continue checking the current document, click Cancel. If prompted to select a dictionary, choose an appropriate language. If you have not used the spell checker in Fireworks before now, perform Spelling Setup.

You added text and then checked the spelling of the new text.

FIGURE 35
Misspelled text

Misspelled word

FIGURE 36
Path created in document

Last/selected
path point
created is solid

FIGURE 37
Text on path

Text follows
points on path

1. Click the **Pen tool** 🖊 on the Tools panel.

2. Click the **Fill category list arrow** on the Property Inspector, click **None** (if necessary), click the **canvas** in the locations shown in Figure 36, then double-click when you reach the last point.

   A path appears in the document and the path is complete.

3. Click the **Pointer tool** 🔍 on the Tools panel, press and hold **[Shift]**, then click the **Fresh Daily** text to select both the path and the text.

   TIP To select multiple objects on the canvas at once, press and hold [Shift] while selecting each object.

4. Click **Text** on the menu bar, then click **Attach to Path**.

5. Click **Text** on the menu bar, point to **Align**, then click **Stretched**.

6. Click a blank part of the Document window, then compare your image to Figure 37.

7. Save your work.

8. Click **File** on the menu bar, click **Exit** (Win) or click **Fireworks**, then click **Quit Fireworks** (Mac).

You created a path using the Pen tool, attached text to it, then saved the document and exited the program.

Start Fireworks and open a document.

1. Start Fireworks.
2. Open fw1_2.png.
3. Undock the Layers panel (Win).
4. Collapse and expand the Layers panel.
5. Close fw1_2.png without saving changes.

Create a new document and use Help.

1. Create a new document and set the Width to 200, the Height to 150, and the Canvas Color to #DB7839.
2. Save the document as **pasta_1.png**.
3. Access the Search tab of Help (Win) and search for layers. (*Hint*: Click the Adding and removing layers topic in the Topics found dialog box.)
4. Read the topic on duplicating a layer, then close the Help window.
5. Add a layer to the Layers panel.
6. Access the Search tab of Help (Win) and search for "creating bitmap objects."
7. Read the topic on creating bitmap objects, then close the Help window.
8. Open elbow.gif.
9. Drag the object to pasta_1.png. (*Hint*: You might need to resize the elbow.gif Document window to see the pasta_1.png Document window.)

10. Center the object on the canvas.
11. Close elbow.gif without saving changes.
12. Compare your image to Figure 1-38.
13. Save and close pasta_1.png.

Work with the Layers panel and edit a bitmap image.

1. Open fw1_2.png.
2. Save the file as **pasta_2.png**.
3. Select the Varieties object on the Background layer of the Layers panel.
4. Hide and display the Varieties object on the Layers panel.
5. Move the Ingredients object from Layer 1 above the Varieties object so that it is now in the Background layer.
6. Delete the Ingredients object.
7. Select the Varieties object.
8. Open the Brightness/Contrast dialog box, and set the Brightness to 5 and the Contrast to 25. (*Hint*: Use the Adjust Color command on the Filters menu.)
9. Lock the Background layer.
10. Save your work.

Create a vector object.

1. Display the guides.
2. Create a new layer above Layer 1.
3. Rename the newly created layer **Proper_Names**. (*Hint*: Double-click the layer name.)
4. Select the Rounded Rectangle tool.
5. Enter the following fill color properties on the Property inspector: Color: #66CC00, Fill category: Solid, Edge: Feather, Feather amount: 4, Texture: Burlap, and Texture amount: 20%.
6. Open the Info panel.
7. Drag the pointer from approximately 10 X/250 Y to 90 X/300 Y.
8. Apply a stroke with the following properties: Color: #339900, Tip size: 2, Category: Air Brush Basic, Edge: 100, and Texture amount: 0.
9. Save your work.

Create and modify text.

1. Select the Text tool.
2. Enter the following properties in the Property inspector: Font: Times New Roman, Size: 22 pt, Color: #000000, Bold, and Left alignment.

3. Click the pointer at 20 H/280 V, then type **Rotelie**.
4. Center the text in the rectangle, if necessary, then deselect it.
5. Make sure that the Text tool is selected, then enter the following properties: Font: Impact, Size: 65 pt, Color: #990000, Bold, and Center alignment.
6. Click the pointer above the jars, then type **Pasta Figura**.
7. Deselect the Pasta Figura text.
8. Select the Pen tool, then create a path at approximately 250 X/80 Y, 300 X/65 Y, 350 X/60 Y, 400 X/50 Y, 460 X/60 Y, 500 X/80 Y. (*Hint*: Use the Info panel.)
9. Attach the Pasta Figura text to the path.
10. Change the alignment setting of the text on the path to Stretched.
11. Deselect the text on the path.
12. Turn off the guides.
13. Save your work, then compare your document to Figure 38.

FIGURE 38
Completed Skills Review

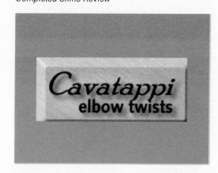

You are in charge of new services at Crystal Clear Consulting. You're preparing to roll out a new Crisis Solutions division, designed to help companies that are experiencing management or financial difficulties. You plan to brief your coworkers on the services at an upcoming company lunch. Each department head—including you—is going to submit a sample introductory Web ad announcing the division. You'll use your Fireworks skills to design a simple ad.

1. Obtain images that symbolize the new consulting service. You will import and copy these images to a layer in the document. You can obtain an image from your computer, from the Internet, from a digital camera, or from scanned media. You can use images from the Web that are free for both personal and commercial use (check the copyright information for any such file before downloading it).

2. Create a new document and save it as **crystal.png**.

3. Access Help, select the Search titles only check box at the bottom of the window (Win), then search for "import an image."

4. Import one of the images you obtained in Step 1 so that it serves as the background.

5. Rename Layer 1 **Background**.

6. Create a new layer and give it an appropriate name.

7. Open another image that you obtained in Step 1 and copy it to the document.

8. Create a new layer and name it **Text Objects**.

9. Create at least one vector object and apply a fill to it.

10. Create at least two text objects. (*Hint*: The font in the sample is Matisse ITC and Eras Demi ITC. You can substitute these fonts with other fonts on your computer.)

11. Attach at least one text object to a path, then rename the object on the Layers panel.

12. Save your work, then examine the sample shown in Figure 39.

FIGURE 39
Sample Completed Project Builder 1

You've just completed your first class in Fireworks. Afterward, you meet with your boss to summarize some of the neat features. She is intrigued by the various ways you can change the alignment of text in Fireworks and has asked you to prepare a few samples for the next staff meeting.

1. Create a new document and name it **meandering_paths.png**.
2. Create a text object that is at least 15 characters long (you can use the font of your choice and as many words as you want).
3. Create a simple path, then attach the text to it. (*Hint*: You can use the Pen tool or a basic shape tool.)
4. Create text that describes the path alignment and the orientation settings. (*Hint*: Refer to Figure 40.)
5. Add a new layer, then copy the text on the path and the descriptive text from the old layer to the new one. (*Hint*: Press and hold [Alt] (Win) or [option] (Mac), then drag the object.)
6. Change the alignment and orientation settings and update the descriptive text accordingly.
7. Repeat Steps 5 and 6.
8. Save your work, then examine the sample shown in Figure 40.

FIGURE 40
Sample Completed Project Builder 2

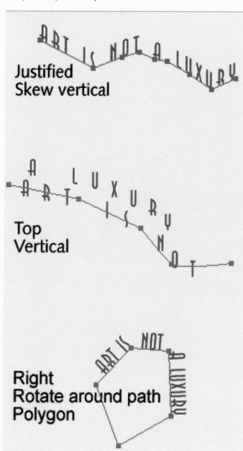

DESIGN PROJECT

You can develop your design and planning skills by analyzing Web sites.
Figure 41 shows a page from the Rock
and Roll Hall of Fame Web site. Study the
image and answer the following questions. Because dynamic Web sites are
updated frequently to reflect current
trends, this page might be different from
Figure 41 when you open it online.

1. Connect to the Internet and go to
   www.course.com. Navigate to the page
   for this book, click the Student Online
   Companion, then click the link for this unit.
2. Open a document in a word processor, or
   open a new Fireworks document, then save
   the file as **rocknroll**.
3. Explore the site and answer the following
   questions. (*Hint*: If you work in Fireworks,
   use the Text tool.) For each question, indicate
   how you determined your answer.
   - What vector shapes does the page
     contain?
   - What fills or strokes have been added to
     vector shapes?
   - Do objects appear to have been manipu-
     lated in some manner? If so, how?
   - Do objects or text overlap? If so, list the
     order in which the objects could appear
     in the Layers panel.
   - Has text been attached to a path?
   - What is the overall effect of the text?

FIGURE 41
Design Project

Your group can assign elements of the project to individual members, or work collectively to create the finished product.

Your team serves on the Education Committee for Cultural Consequence, a cultural anthropology group. The group is constructing a Web site that examines facial expressions and moods in people around the world. The committee is in charge of developing emoticons—a shorthand method of expressing moods—for the Web site. The images will be in the style of the smiley face. You can use the facial expression of your choice in developing the emoticon.

1. Choose an emotion and the emoticon that conveys that feeling.
2. Obtain at least two images for the expression you've chosen. You can obtain images from your computer, from the Internet, from a digital camera, or from scanned media. You can use images from the Web that are free for both personal and commercial use (check the copyright information for any such file before downloading it).
3. Create a new document, then save it as **emoticon.png**.
4. Choose a canvas color other than white.
5. Create a new layer named **Faces** and copy the images you've obtained to the new layer.
6. Create a new layer and name it with the emotion you selected in Step 1.
7. Create the emoticon on the layer created in Step 6 using tools on the Tools panel, and apply fills and strokes to them as desired. (*Hint*: The emoticon in the sample was created with the Ellipse tool and the Pencil tool with a Basic Soft Rounded tip setting.)
8. Create a text object that identifies the expression. (*Hint*: The text in the sample is Pristina.)
9. Save your work, then examine the sample shown in Figure 42.

FIGURE 42
Sample Completed Portfolio Project

2

WORKING WITH
OBJECTS

1. Work with vector tools.

2. Modify multiple vector objects.

3. Modify color.

4. Apply filters to objects and text.

5. Apply a style to text.

2 WORKING WITH
OBJECTS

Understanding Vector Objects

Fireworks offers a number of vector tools you can use to create vector objects. There are many benefits to working with vector objects. For example, you can modify the properties of a vector path at any time—its shape, size, fill, and stroke—without affecting the quality of the image. This editability makes vector objects easy to work with and adds flexibility to your Web graphics.

After you create an object, you can use a variety of features to transform it into a visually interesting graphic. Many of the tools in Fireworks let you alter or enhance the object. You can combine multiple objects to create entirely new shapes using various Combine Path commands. You can also modify a graphic's appearance by adjusting the alignment and grouping of multiple objects. You can change a path's color by filling it with a solid color, gradient color, or a texture, or by adjusting the stroke appearance.

The Stroke, Fill, and Filters sections on the Property inspector maximize your ability to experiment. You can create various combinations of strokes, fills, and filters, and turn them on or off in your document at will. An object's overall appearance varies depending on the order in which effects appear in the Filters list on the Property inspector.

Tools You'll Use

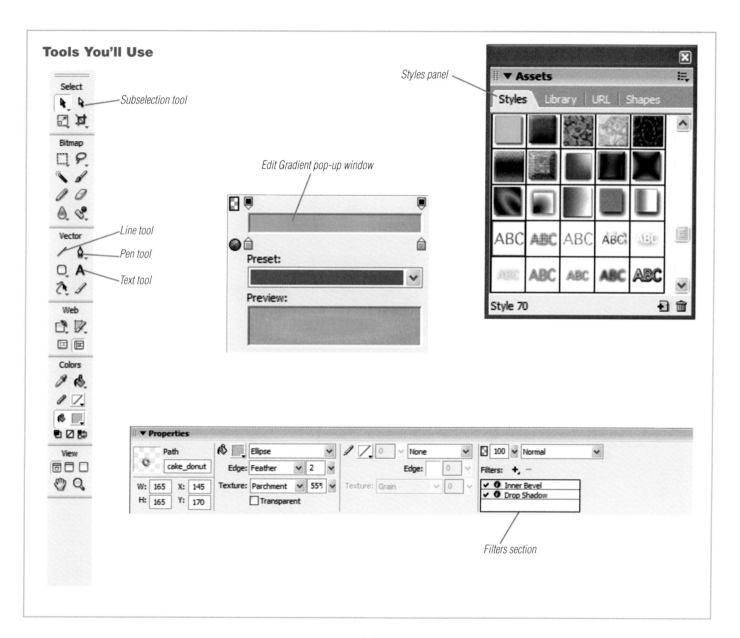

Select

Subselection tool

Bitmap

Vector

Line tool

Pen tool

Text tool

Web

Colors

View

Styles panel

Edit Gradient pop-up window

▼ Assets

Styles Library URL Shapes

ABC ABC ABC ABC ABC

ABC ABC ABC ABC ABC

Style 70

Preset:

Preview:

▼ Properties

Path

cake_donut

Ellipse

Edge: Feather 2

W: 165 X: 145 Texture: Parchment 55%

H: 165 Y: 170 Transparent

0 None

Edge: 0

Texture: Grain 0

100 Normal

Filters: +, −

✔ ❶ Inner Bevel

✔ ❶ Drop Shadow

Filters section

WORK WITH
VECTOR TOOLS

What You'll Do

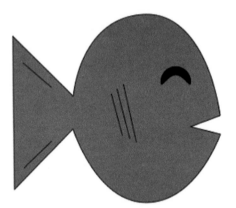

In this lesson, you will create and modify paths and objects using vector tools.

Understanding Vector Tools and Paths

A vector object can be a straight or curved path, or a group or combination of open, closed, straight, or curved paths. When you create a vector object, path segments connect the anchor points of a path. Paths can be open or closed. The points of an open path do not connect; the start and end points of a closed path do connect.

QUICKTIP

The basic Rectangle shape has a Rectangle roundness setting on the Property inspector, which you can use to create a rounded rectangle basic shape.

You can draw free-form paths using the Vector Path and Pen tools. The Pen tool creates a path one point at a time. The Vector Path tool creates paths in one

Making additional points with the Pen tool and Subselection tool

To create a path with the Pen tool, you click the canvas to create corner points. You can create a curve point as you draw the path by dragging the mouse pointer as you click the canvas. If the newly created path is still selected, you can convert a corner point to a curve point by dragging the point with the Pen tool to create a curve point handle. If you want to convert a corner point that is on an existing path, select the path with the Subselection tool and then drag the point until curve point handles are visible.

motion. Fireworks automatically inserts anchor points as you drag the pointer on the canvas. Regardless of its initial shape, a vector object's path is always editable.

If the path of an object has curves, such as a circle, ellipse, or rounded rectangle, the circular points are known as **curve points**. If the path has angles or is linear, such as a square, a star, or a straight line, the square points are known as **corner points**. Figure 1 shows points selected for various objects. When you edit a vector object, you add, delete, or move points along the path; adjust the point handles; or change the shape of the path segment.

Using the Pen Tool and the Subselection Tool

You can add or delete points on a segment using the Pen tool. Modifying the number of points on a path allows you to manipulate it until you have created the exact shape you want. For example, adding points allows you to maneuver the path with greater precision, whereas deleting points simplifies the path's editability. If you want to move points on a path, you can use the **Subselection tool**. You can also use the Subselection tool to select the points of an individual object that has been grouped or to create a curved point.

QUICKTIP

To connect two unconnected paths, select the Pen tool, click the end point of one path, and then click the end point of the other path.

Each anchor point has one or more **point handles**; point handles are visible when you edit a curved path segment, but not when you edit a straight path segment. You can modify the size and angle of a curve by adjusting the length and position of the point handles. You can use both the Pen tool and the Subselection tool to create and modify point handles on curved paths, or to convert curve points into corner points and vice versa.

FIGURE 1
Points on paths

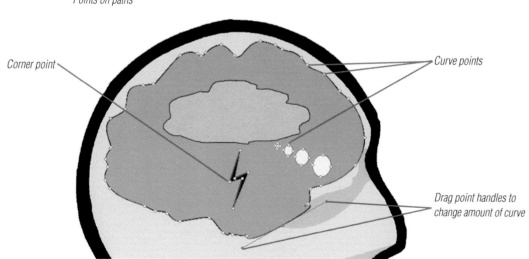

Corner point

Curve points

Drag point handles to change amount of curve

The two-dimensional curves in a vector object are known as **Bézier curves**, named after the French engineer who developed the mathematical formulas to represent three-dimensional (3D) automobile shapes. Figure 2 shows how you can manipulate a vector object by dragging its point handles.

As you become more familiar with using vector objects, you can experiment with more intricate vector modifications using the **Path scrubber tools**, which alter a path's appearance based on the pressure and speed with which you apply the stroke, and the **Reshape Area tool**, which pulls areas of the path to a boundary.

FIGURE 2
Modifying a vector path

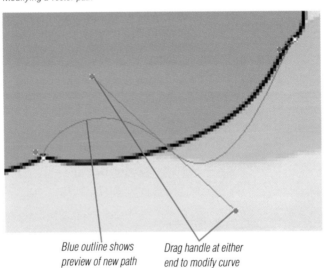

Blue outline shows preview of new path

Drag handle at either end to modify curve

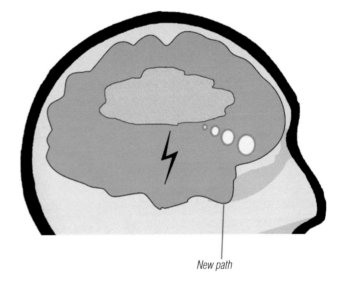

New path

FIGURE 3
Selecting a stroke category

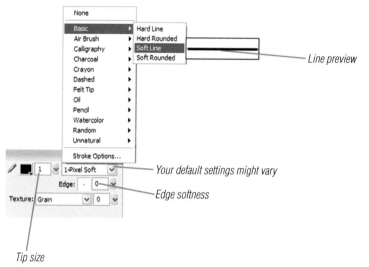

— Line preview

Your default settings might vary

— Edge softness

Tip size

Create an object using the Pen tool

1. Create a new document, set the Width to **300**, set the Height to **275**, verify that the canvas color is white, then save it as **fish.png**.

2. Click **View** on the menu bar, point to **Grid**, then click **Show Grid**.

   TIP You can use the grid to help align objects on the canvas.

3. Click the **Pen tool** 🖋 on the Tools panel.

4. Click the **Fill Color box** 🖤 on the Property inspector, type **#3399FF** in the hexadecimal text box, then press **[Enter]** (Win) or **[return]** (Mac).

5. Click the **Stroke Color box** 🖊 on the Property inspector, type **#000000** in the hexadecimal text box, then press **[Enter]** (Win) or **[return]** (Mac).

6. Click the **Stroke category list arrow**, point to **Basic**, click **Soft Line**, then verify the remaining settings shown in Figure 3.

   TIP You can preview stroke graphics in the Stroke category list.

7. Click the canvas in the locations shown in Figure 4.

   TIP Close the path by clicking your first anchor point.

You created a new document, set properties for the Pen tool, and created a closed path.

FIGURE 4
Creating a shape using the Pen tool

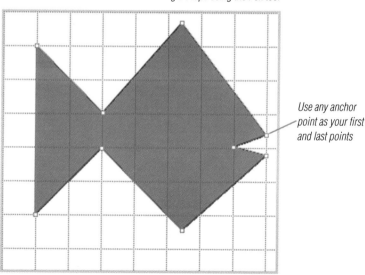

Use any anchor point as your first and last points

Use the Pen tool and the Line tool to modify a path

1. Position the **Pen tool** over the top corner point, then click and drag the point to create a smooth curve, as shown in Figure 5.

   The sharp point smoothes into a curve, and the point handles are visible.

2. Repeat Step 1, but click and drag the bottom corner point, then click a blank part of the Fireworks window to deselect the vector object.

   TIP   Remember that you can undo your changes if you're not satisfied with the results.

3. Press and hold the **Rectangle tool** on the Tools panel, then click the **Ellipse tool**.

4. Click the **Stroke Color box** on the Property inspector, then click the top-left black color swatch in the color pop-up window.

5. Repeat Step 4 for the Fill Color box.

6. Press and hold **[Shift]**, then draw the circle shown in Figure 6.

   TIP   Press and hold [Shift] to draw a perfect square or circle.

7. Click the **Line tool** on the Tools panel, then drag the pointer on the canvas to create the lines shown in Figure 7.

You modified an object using the Pen tool and the Line tool.

FIGURE 5
Converting a corner point to a curve point

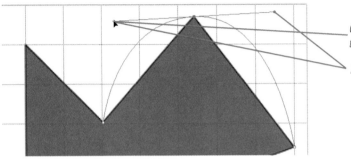

Click corner point and drag handles to create a smooth curve

Point handles

FIGURE 6
Circle object

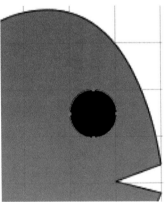

FIGURE 7
Creating lines using the Line tool

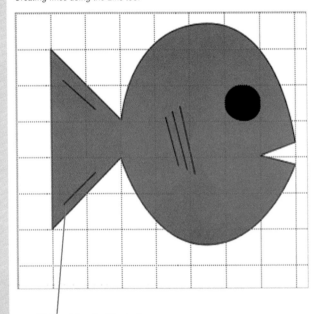

Click and drag the Line tool to create a line

FIGURE 8
Dragging a point handle

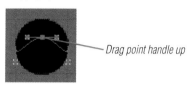

Drag point handle up

FIGURE 9

Modified vector objects

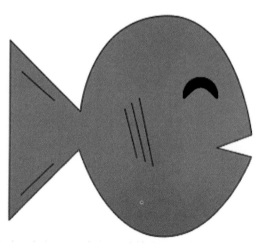

Use the Subselection tool to modify an object

1. Click the **Subselection tool** on the Tools panel, position the pointer over the lower-middle point of the black circle, then click the **point**.

   TIP Click View on the menu bar, then click Zoom In if you want a larger view while you work.

2. Drag the point to the position shown in Figure 8, then click a blank part of the Document window to deselect the object.

   TIP You can also press [Ctrl][D] (Win) or [⌘][D] or [⌘][Shift][A] (Mac) to deselect an object.

3. Click **View** on the menu bar, point to **Grid**, then click **Show Grid** to turn off the grid.

4. Compare your image to Figure 9, then save your work.

5. Close fish.png.

You modified an object using the Subselection tool, and then closed the document.

MODIFY MULTIPLE
VECTOR OBJECTS

What You'll Do

In this lesson, you will create, copy, align, and combine paths of vector objects using the Punch command. You will also group objects.

Aligning and Grouping Objects

Using vector shapes allows you to work with many individual objects at the same time. The Align commands on the Modify menu allow you to align two or more objects with each other: left, centered vertically, and so on. You can open the Align panel to further align, distribute, size, and space multiple objects or to align a vector object's anchor points.

You can also use the Group command on the Modify menu to configure objects on the canvas. The Group command allows you to combine two or more objects to make a single object. You can group any objects in your document: vector images, bitmap images, text, and so on. Fireworks preserves each individual object's shape and its placement in relation to the other objects. After you group objects, you can modify properties of the group as a whole; for example, by changing fill color or by applying a stroke. If you

want to change any one of the objects, you can ungroup the objects, apply the change, and then regroup them. For example, if you want to change the stroke of one object in a group of vector shapes, you must first ungroup the objects before you can modify the individual stroke. However, if the grouped object consists of text and another vector object or bitmap image, you do not need to ungroup the objects to edit the text.

Combining the Paths of Multiple Objects

Fireworks offers six commands for combining paths: Join, Split, Union, Intersect, Punch, and Crop. Each command produces a different result. You must select two or more ungrouped vector objects before you can apply a combination command to them. The Combine Paths commands are described next and most are illustrated in Figure 10.

Join—The Join command allows you to combine the paths of two or more objects to create a single merged object that includes all the points of both paths. If the two objects are both closed, the new path is a **composite path**; if the objects are open, the new path is a **continuous path**. You can also use the Join command to join two open selected points. The first example in Figure 10 shows all four objects joined.

Split—You can split apart the paths of two or more objects that had been combined using the Join command. The Split command creates two or more simple objects and paths. Because the Split command is based on the joined path, and not the original objects, it is not the same as performing Undo.

Union—The Union command creates a path that is the sum total of all the selected paths.

If two paths overlap, the nonintersecting areas are also included. If the selected paths have different fill, stroke, or effects properties, the new path assumes the properties of the lowest object in the stacking order, or the lowest layer on the Layers panel. The union example in Figure 10 shows all four objects combined, with the same properties as the triangle.

FIGURE 10

Sample Combine Path commands

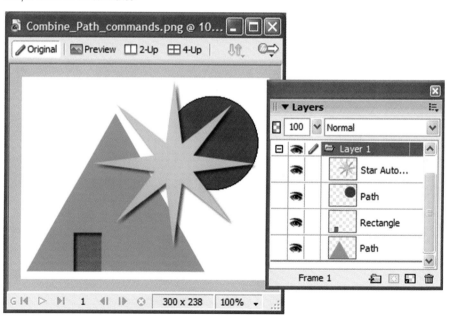

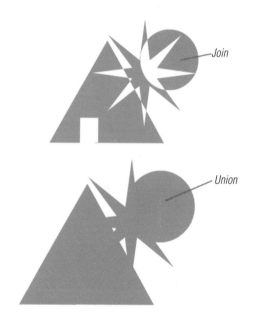

Intersect—The Intersect command creates an object consisting of the area that is common to all of the selected paths. If the selected paths have different fill, stroke, or effects properties, the new path assumes the properties of the lowest object in the stacking order. In the intersect example shown in Figure 10, the intersection is the area shared by the star and the circle hand. The properties are the same as the circle's properties.

Punch—The outline of the topmost object carves through all of the lower selected images. In Figure 10, the *shape* of the star appears to slice through the circle below it. The fill, stroke, and effects properties are unaffected in the areas not being punched.

Crop—The area of the top path is used to remove the areas of the paths beneath it. While the area of the top object defines the object's shape, the fill, stroke, and effects properties of the objects placed further back are retained. In the crop example in Figure 10, the shape of the top object, the rectangle, has the properties of selected path beneath it, the triangle.

> **QUICK**TIP
>
> Use the Group command if you want your objects to maintain independent fill, stroke, and effect settings. If you want to be able to manipulate the paths of two or more objects after you combine them, use the Join command instead of the Group command.

FIGURE 10
Sample Combine Path commands (continued)

Intersect

Punch

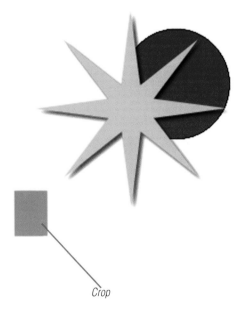

Crop

FIGURE 11
Layers panel and Ellipse tool properties

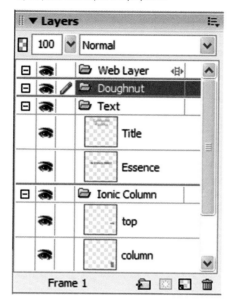

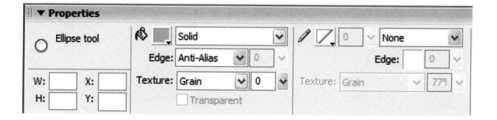

Create a vector shape to an exact size

1. Open fw2_1.png, then save it as **pastries.png**.

2. Insert a layer above the Text layer on the Layers panel, double-click the layer name, type **Doughnut**, then press **[Enter]** (Win) or **[return]** (Mac).

   TIP You can name other objects on the Layers panel in the same manner, or you can name selected objects on the Property inspector.

3. Click the **Ellipse tool** on the Tools panel.

   TIP You can modify the properties of basic shapes on the Property inspector; to modify Auto Shapes properties, open the Auto Shapes panel from the Window menu.

4. Click the **Stroke Color box** on the Tools panel, then click the **Transparent button** on the top of the color pop-up window, if necessary.

5. Click the **Fill Color box** on the Tools panel, type **#E5B900** in the hexadecimal text box, then press **[Enter]** (Win) or **[return]** (Mac).

6. Make sure that the Property inspector is open and that the Edge and Texture values in the Fill section are 0, then compare your Layers panel and Property inspector to Figure 11.

(continued)

7. Display and expand the Info panel, position the pointer ╋ on the canvas at approximately 130 X/170 Y, press and hold **[Shift]**, then drag the pointer until both W and H text boxes on the Property inspector display 165.

   TIP If necessary, you can enter 165 in the width and height text boxes on the Property inspector after you create the circle.

8. Compare your image to Figure 12.

You created a circle and set its diameter.

Copy an object

1. Verify that the circle is selected, click **Edit** on the menu bar, then click **Copy**.

2. Click **Edit** on the menu bar, then click **Paste**.

   A duplicate Path object appears on the Layers panel.

   TIP You can also press [Ctrl][C] and [Ctrl][V] (Win) or ⌘ [C] and ⌘ [V] (Mac) to copy and paste a selection.

3. Click the **Fill Color box** 🪣 ■ on the Property inspector, then click the top-left black color swatch in the color pop-up window.

4. Double-click the **W text box** on the Property inspector, type **44**, repeat for the H text box, then press **[Enter]** (Win) or **[return]** (Mac).

5. Compare your image to Figure 13.

You copied an object and changed its properties.

FIGURE 12
Newly created circle

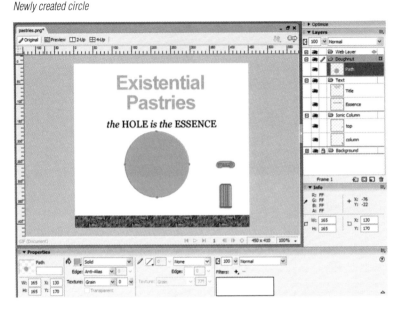

FIGURE 13
Modified object

FIGURE 14
Aligned objects

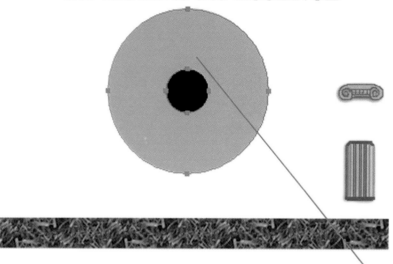

the HOLE *is the* ESSENCE

*Objects are aligned vertically
and horizontally*

Align objects and combine paths

1. Click the **Pointer tool** on the Tools panel, then verify that the black circle is selected.

2. Press and hold **[Shift]**, then click the **yellow circle** to select both objects.

3. Click **Modify** on the menu bar, point to **Align**, then click **Center Vertical**.

4. Click **Modify** on the menu bar, point to **Align**, click **Center Horizontal**, then compare your image to Figure 14.

   The black circle is perfectly centered on the yellow circle.

   (continued)

Cloning, copying, and duplicating

You can replicate any object using the Copy/Paste, Clone, or Duplicate commands on the Edit menu, or by pressing and holding [Alt] (Win) or [option] (Mac) and then dragging the object on the canvas. Each menu command creates an identical object and places it above the original on the Layers panel. The Copy/Paste and Clone commands replicate the object directly on top of the original object on the canvas. The Copy command places a copy of the object on the clipboard, which you can use to paste the object in other open files or in other programs. You can also use Copy/Paste commands to copy items on the Frames or Layers panels. The Duplicate command offsets the copied object 10 pixels down and to the right of the original.

5. Click **Modify** on the menu bar, point to **Combine Paths**, click **Union**, then notice the combined object.

   The black circle is no longer visible.

6. Click **Edit** on the menu bar, then click **Undo Union Paths**.

7. Click **Modify** on the menu bar, point to **Combine Paths**, click **Punch**, then compare your image to Figure 15.

   The paths combine to form a donut.

8. Click the **Edit the object name text box** on the left side of the Property inspector, type **cake_donut**, as shown in Figure 16, then press [**Enter**] (Win) or [**return**] (Mac).

   Fireworks renames the object.

You aligned two objects and then combined their paths. You also undid a Combine Paths command.

FIGURE 15
Objects combined by the Punch command

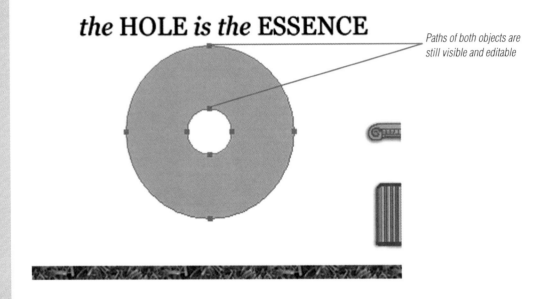

the HOLE *is the* ESSENCE

Paths of both objects are still visible and editable

FIGURE 16
Renaming an object

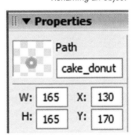

FIGURE 17
Object being moved

FIGURE 18
Grouped objects

*Selection handles for a
single grouped object*

Group objects

1. Verify that the Pointer tool ▶ is selected, then click the **top object** in the Ionic Column layer on the Layers panel.

2. Drag the top object on top of the column object, as shown in Figure 17.

3. Press and hold [**Shift**], then click the **column object** to select both objects.

   The selection handles for both objects are visible.

4. Click **Modify** on the menu bar, click **Group**, then notice that the object on the Layers panel is renamed Group: 2 objects.

   | TIP   You can also press [Ctrl][G] (Win) or
   ⌘ [G] (Mac) to group objects.

5. Drag the grouped object under the circle, as shown in Figure 18.

   The selection handles for a single object are visible.

6. Change the name Group: 2 objects to **full_column**.

7. Save your work.

You grouped and moved objects.

MODIFY COLOR

What You'll Do

Existential Pastries

the HOLE *is the* ESSENCE

In this lesson, you will apply a gradient fill to the cake_donut object, and then modify the fill.

Understanding Fills and Gradients

After you create a vector shape, you can modify its appearance by changing its interior, or **fill**. The Property inspector provides powerful tools for enhancing fills in objects. You can apply several kinds of fills to an object, including solid, gradient, web dither, and pattern. Some of the available fill patterns are shown in Figure 19.

A **solid fill** is the color swatch or hexadecimal value that you specify in the color pop-up window or in the Color Mixer. If you want to ensure that the colors in your document are Web-safe, you can use a **Web Dither fill.** A Web Dither fill approximates the color of a non-Web-safe color by combining two Web-safe colors. **Pattern fills** are bitmap images that have complex color schemes and textures. Fireworks offers dozens of preset patterns from which to choose, or you can create a pattern in Fireworks or another program and then add it to the list. A **gradient** consists of two or more colors that blend into each other in a fixed design. You can select from

several preset gradient fills, which you can apply to an object by choosing a fill category or by selecting the Gradient tool on the Tools panel. The Gradient tool, located as a tool option under the Paint Bucket tool, fills an object with the selected gradient, just as the Paint Bucket tool fills an object with the selected color.

QUICKTIP

You can transform or skew a fill's pattern or gradient by adjusting the width, position, rotation, and angle of the fill handles. The gradient adjusts to the contour of the path.

Whether you select a pattern or gradient as a fill, it becomes the active fill color visible on the Tools panel and on the Property inspector. There may be times when you apply a pattern or a gradient and instantly attain the look you want. You can also experiment by modifying the pattern or gradient, for example by adding a transparent gradient, adding an edge or texture, and adjusting the respective amounts of each. The sophisticated styling you add to objects when you choose a pattern fill type can mimic real-world lighting, surface, and depth, and can have quite a dramatic result, as shown in Figure 20.

You can change gradient colors, including preset gradient colors, at any time without affecting the appearance of the gradient. The Edit Gradient pop-up window allows you to modify gradient colors and the transition from one color to the next by manipulating the color swatches beneath the **color ramp**. The color ramp creates and displays the range of colors in a gradient, including their transparency.

QUICKTIP

You can add a color to a gradient by clicking an area beneath the color ramp; to delete a color, drag it off the color ramp. To adjust gradient transparency, modify the opacity swatches above the color ramp.

FIGURE 19
Pattern categories

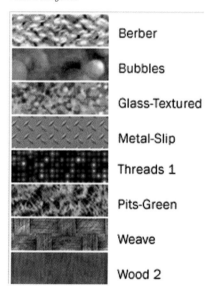

Berber

Bubbles

Glass-Textured

Metal-Slip

Threads 1

Pits-Green

Weave

Wood 2

FIGURE 20
Combining pattern and texture

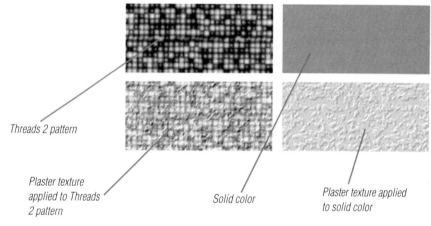

Threads 2 pattern

Plaster texture applied to Threads 2 pattern

Solid color

Plaster texture applied to solid color

gradient to an object

1. ...e **cake_donut object** to select it.

2. ...k the **Fill Category list arrow** on the ...operty inspector, point to **Gradient**, then click **Ellipse**, as shown in Figure 21.

   An ellipse gradient is applied to the object, as shown in Figure 22. Gradient fill handles also appear on the gradient.

3. Click the **Fill Color box** 🖊 ■ on the Property inspector, click the left color swatch beneath the color ramp, type **#E5B900** in the hexadecimal text box, then press **[Enter]** (Win) or **[return]** (Mac).

4. Repeat Step 3 for the right color swatch, but type **#FF8000** in the hexadecimal text box, press **[Enter]** (Win) or **[return]** (Mac) to close the color pop-up window, then compare your color ramp to Figure 23.

5. Click a blank part of the Fireworks window to close the color ramp.

6. Click the **Edge list arrow**, click **Feather**, double-click the **Amount of feather text box**, then type **2**.

7. Click the **Texture list arrow**, click **Parchment**, click the **Amount of texture list arrow**, drag the slider to **55**, click a blank part of the Fireworks window, then verify that the Transparent check box is not selected.

8. Compare your image to Figure 24.

   The new gradient colors and texture are applied to the object.

You selected and modified gradient colors, and applied a texture to an object.

FIGURE 21
Fill and gradient categories

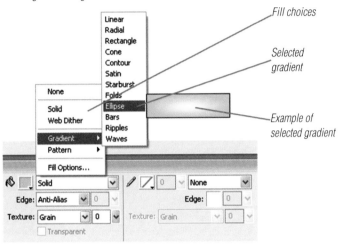

Fill choices

Selected gradient

Example of selected gradient

FIGURE 22
Gradient applied to object

Opacity swatch adjusts transparency

FIGURE 23
Edit Gradient pop-up window

Color ramp shows currently selected gradient colors

Color swatch opens color pop-up window

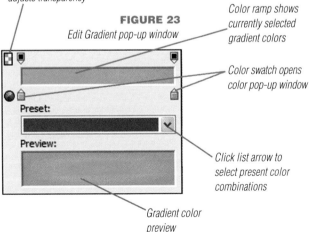

Preset:

Preview:

Click list arrow to select present color combinations

Gradient color preview

FIGURE 24
Texture applied to object

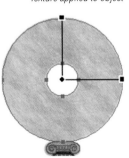

FIGURE 25
Adjusting fill handles

Transform an object and its gradient

1. Verify that the cake_donut object is selected.
2. Click **Modify** on the menu bar, point to **Transform**, then click **Rotate 90° CW** to rotate the object.

   The gradient handles flip position.
3. Drag the fill handles to the positions shown in Figure 25.

   The placement and shading of the gradient is altered.
4. Click a blank part of the Document window to deselect the cake_donut object, then compare your image to Figure 26.
5. Save your work.

You rotated the object and adjusted the fill handles to change the gradient.

Drag round handle to adjust
gradient placement

Drag square handle to
adjust gradient width

FIGURE 26
Modified gradient

the HOLE *is the* ESSENCE

Understanding basic colors in the Color Mixer

The Color Mixer displays the color palette of the values of the active solid color, which you can also view in the Fill Color box or Stroke Color box on the Tools panel or on the Property inspector. You can edit color values to create new colors by changing the values for each color component of a color model. You can define colors in five different models: RGB (red, green, blue); Hexadecimal (Fireworks default), which has values similar to RGB; HSB (hue, saturation, and brightness); CMY (cyan, magenta, yellow); and Grayscale. The color model you choose depends on the medium in which the graphic will appear. Generally, the models Fireworks offers are geared toward screen-based and Web-based computer graphics, with the exception of the CMY or Grayscale models. If you want to use a Fireworks-created graphic in print media, you might want to export the graphic into another program that has additional print-specific color models, such as Macromedia Freehand or Adobe Photoshop. All file formats exported by Fireworks are based on the RGB color model.

APPLY FILTERS TO
OBJECTS AND TEXT

What You'll Do

 In this lesson, you will add filters to objects, including text, and change the order of filters in the Filters list.

Understanding Filters

In addition to using the Fill and Stroke sections of the Property inspector, you can use the Filters section to customize the appearance of objects in your document. The Filters section includes the effects found on the Filters menu, as well as bevel, emboss, shadow, and glow effects. For example, you can sharpen, blur, and add the appearance of depth or dimension to an image. The features in the Filters section are similar to filters, labs, or renders used by other graphics programs, such as Adobe Photoshop or advanced 3D landscaping programs, such as Corel Bryce.

Fireworks calls these **Live Filters** because you can always edit and preview changes to them even after you have saved, closed, and reopened the document. The Filters section lets you experiment with multiple effects. You can add, edit, delete, or hide filters in the Filters list at your convenience. Figure 27 shows the options available in the Filters section.

QUICKTIP

To edit a filter, select the object(s) to which the filter is applied, then click the Info icon or double-click the Filters list in the Filters list to open its pop-up window or dialog box.

Just as you can move objects on the Layers panel to change their appearance in your document, you can modify the overall look of an object by changing the order of filters. Figure 28 shows how changing the stacking order of filters in the Filters list can produce very different results. Each macaw has the same settings and filters applied to it, but in a different order.

QUICKTIP

To move a filter, drag it to a new position in the Filters list.

Using the Filters Menu

The Filters menu contains commands that correspond to many of the features found in the Filters section. However, be aware that some of the effects you add from the Filters menu do not appear in the Filters section of the Property inspector and you cannot alter their settings after you apply them. You can edit or remove these filters only in the current work session—more precisely, you can *undo* these filters, not edit them. After you save or close the document, the Undo actions are lost, and the filter is permanently applied to your document.

Filters and File Size

Although enabled filters generally contribute to increased file size, disabling a filter instead of deleting it does not significantly add to file size. Some filters, such as the Blur, Blur More, and Gaussian Blur filters, may actually decrease file size because blurring an object decreases the total number of colors in the graphic. The fewer colors used in your document, the less storage space required—hence, smaller file size.

Understanding Tr

You can adjust the transpar image or effect in your docum varying its opacity settings. Firew adjusts transparency in terms of perc age, just as it uses percentage settings t adjust the amount of texture in strokes and fills. The **opacity setting** deter-mines if your image is completely opaque (100%) or completely transparent (0%).

FIGURE 27
Filter categories

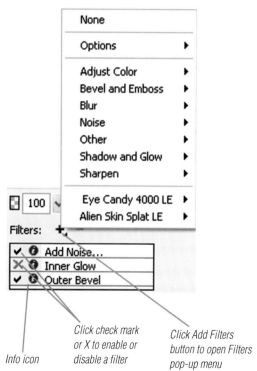

Info icon

Click check mark or X to enable or disable a filter

Click Add Filters button to open Filters pop-up menu

FIGURE 28
Rearranged filters in the Filters list

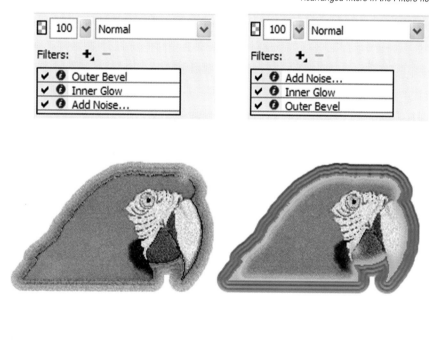

...en click the
...roperty

...en click

...w opens.

3. ...re 29, then press **[Enter]** (Win) or **[return]** (Mac) to close the Inner Bevel pop-up window.

4. Click the **Add Filters button** ➕ on the Property inspector.

5. Point to **Shadow and Glow**, then click **Drop Shadow**.

6. Enter the values shown in Figure 30, then press **[Enter]** (Win) or **[return]** (Mac).

   With these filters applied, the cake_donut object now appears to have depth and dimension.

7. Click the **full_column object**, then repeat Steps 4, 5, and 6.

   TIP To delete a filter, select the effect in the Filters list in the Filters section of the Property inspector, then click the Delete Filters button.

8. Deselect the full-column object, then compare your image to Figure 31.

You applied filters to the full_column and cake_donut objects to give them the illusion of three-dimensionality.

FIGURE 29
Inner Bevel pop-up window

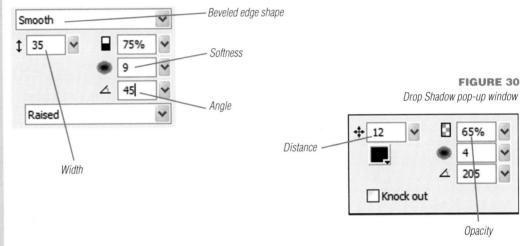

Beveled edge shape

Softness

Angle

Width

FIGURE 30
Drop Shadow pop-up window

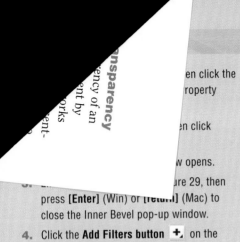

Distance

Opacity

FIGURE 31
Filters, added to objects

FIGURE 32
Rearranged effects

*Drop Shadow effect appears
more subtle*

1. Click the **Title text object**, click the **Add Filters button** ➕ on the Property inspector, point to **Bevel and Emboss**, then click **Raised Emboss**.

2. Press **[Enter]** (Win) or **[return]** (Mac) to accept the default settings in the Raised Emboss pop-up window, then deselect the object.

3. Click the **Title text object**, click the **Add Filter button** ➕ on the Property inspector, point to **Shadow and Glow**, then click **Drop Shadow**.

4. Double-click the **Distance text box**, type **2**, accept the remaining default settings, then deselect the object.

5. Select the **Title text object**, drag the **Drop Shadow filter** to the top of the Filters list, deselect the objects, then notice the difference in the text.

6. Compare your image to Figure 32, then save your work.

You added filters to a text object, and then rearranged the filters in the Filters list to create a more subtle visual effect.

APPLY A STYLE
TO TEXT

What You'll Do

In this lesson, you will apply a style to text and add a new text style to the Styles list.

Using Styles in Documents

Styles are preset attributes, such as color and texture, that you can apply to objects and text. Fireworks manages styles on the **Styles panel**, which you can open from the Window menu. Fireworks comes with two types of styles, text and object. Text styles differ from object styles in that they contain text-specific properties, such as font, size, and style, but you can apply text and button styles to any object. Figure 33 shows a style applied to two different objects. You can create your own style and then save it as a custom style in the Styles panel. When you create a custom style, you can save many of the properties associated with fills, strokes, effects, and text. You can also import or export preset or custom styles.

Figure 34 shows a new style added to the Styles panel. Many text styles change the font style and font size when you apply them.

QUICKTIP

You can apply the attributes from one object to another by selecting the object with the attributes, clicking the Copy command on the Edit menu, selecting the target object, and then clicking the Paste Attributes command on the Edit menu.

Applying a style to a bitmap object

You cannot apply every style to a bitmap object. For example, a bitmap object will not pick up a style that contains certain colors, textures, or strokes. However, if the style contains filters that have color or pixel attributes, such as Noise, Glow, or Inner Bevel, the bitmap will assume those attributes.

Using Plug-ins

A **plug-in** adds features to an application. You can install plug-ins from other software applications into Fireworks. Some plug-ins augment existing features. For example, Fireworks includes a sampling of effects from two Alien Skin products: Eye Candy 4000 LE and Alien Skin Splat LE. (Additional information about Alien Skin plug-ins is available at *www.alienskin.com*.) You need to install the correct plug-ins, software drivers, and modules before you can import files from scanned or digital cameras. Note that plug-ins are platform-specific: for example, the TWAIN module (Win) or Photoshop Acquire plug-in.32 (Mac) are needed to import images from a scanner or digital camera.

Using Adobe Photoshop Plug-ins and Features

Adobe Photoshop plug-ins and other import features are often of interest to Fireworks users. The Fireworks Preferences dialog box allows you to extend the functionality of the program by accessing certain Photoshop features. For example, the Folders tab of the Preferences dialog box contains options for Photoshop plug-ins, textures, and patterns. The Import tab allows you to determine how Fireworks translates Photoshop layers and text—by sharing layers across frames or allowing you to edit text after you import it.

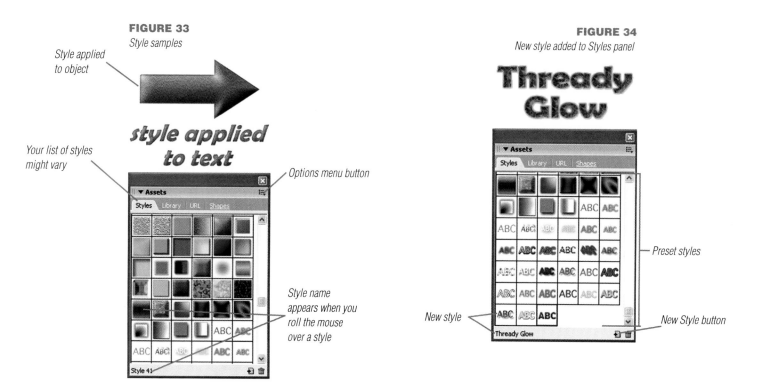

FIGURE 33
Style samples

Style applied to object

Your list of styles might vary

Options menu button

Style name appears when you roll the mouse over a style

FIGURE 34
New style added to Styles panel

Preset styles

New style

New Style button

Apply a style to text

1. Click **Window** on the menu bar, then click **Styles**.

    TIP Make sure that the Styles panel is undocked and expanded or fully visible in a panel docking area.

2. Click the **Text tool** A on the Tools panel, then enter the values shown in Figure 35.

3. Click the middle of the **column**, then type **The cake is commentary**.

    TIP If your text block does not automatically resize to fit the text, drag a blue sizing handle until the words fit.

4. Click **Style 70** in the Styles panel, as shown in Figure 36.

    The text changes size, color, and has a filter applied to it.

5. Compare your text to Figure 37.

You applied a style to a text object.

FIGURE 35
Text properties

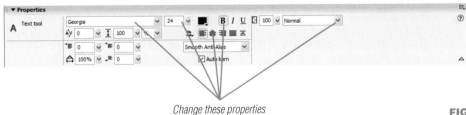

Change these properties

FIGURE 36
Selecting a style in the Styles panel

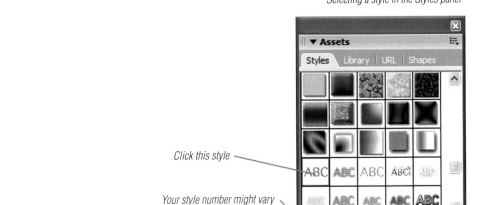

Click this style

Your style number might vary

FIGURE 37
Style applied to text

FIGURE 38
New Style dialog box

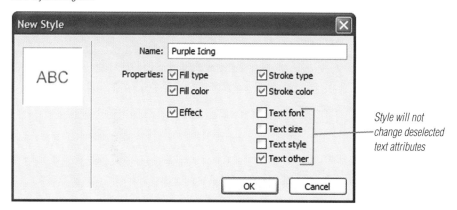

Style will not change deselected text attributes

Create a custom style and align objects

1. Select the object you just created, double-click the **Font Size text box** on the Property inspector, type **20**, click the **Color box** , then type **#9900FF** in the hexadecimal text box.

2. Click the **Add Filters button** ⊞ on the Property inspector, point to **Shadow and Glow**, then click **Glow**, click the **Color box** ⊞, click the white color swatch, press **[Enter]** (Win) or **[return]** (Mac), then deselect the text object.

3. Click the **Options menu button** ⊞ on the Styles panel, then click **New Style** to open the New Style dialog box.

4. Double-click the **Name text box**, type **Purple Icing**, deselect the Text font, Text size, and Text style check boxes, compare your dialog box to Figure 38, then click **OK**.

   A new style, Purple Icing, is added to the bottom of the Styles panel.

5. Click **Select** on the menu bar, then click **Select All**, to select all the objects in the document.

6. Click **Modify** on the menu bar, point to **Align**, then click **Center Vertical**.

7. Click **Select** on the menu bar, then click **Deselect**.

8. Compare your image to Figure 39, save your work, then close the file.

You created a new style and added it to the Styles panel, and then you aligned objects.

FIGURE 39
Customized style applied to text

Create a vector object and modify its path.

1. Open fw2_2.png, then save it as **confection.png**.
2. Select Layer 1, deselect the objects, select the Pen tool, then set the following properties: Fill color: #66CC99 and Stroke: Black Pencil 1-Pixel Soft, 1 px.
3. Using the large white gumdrop as a guide, draw a triangle that approximates the gumdrop's height and width.
4. Convert the corner points to curve points, using Figure 40 as a guide.
5. Use the Subselection tool to increase the height of the object, approximately half the distance to the document border.
6. Drag the object to the lower-left corner of the canvas.
7. Rename the object **Gumdrop**.
8. Save your work.

Align and group objects.

1. Use the Pointer tool to drag the purple circle in back of the multicolored circle.
2. Align the two objects so that they are centered vertically and horizontally.
3. Group the two circles.
4. Move the grouped circles to the top of the right stick, then group them with the stick.

5. Rename the grouped object **Lollipop**.
6. Save your work.

Combine objects' paths.

1. Click the right green wing, then use the arrow keys to move it up and left to merge it with the left green wing.
2. Select both the left and right wings.
3. Combine the paths of the two objects, using the Union command.
4. Rename the combined object **Insignia**.
5. Save your work.

Apply a gradient to an object and modify the gradient.

1. Select the Gumdrop object and apply a Ripples gradient to it.
2. Edit the gradient, and change the left color swatch to #006600.
3. Modify the right gradient by dragging the right fill handle to the lower-right corner of the gumdrop. (*Hint*: The fill handle should resemble the hands of a clock set to 4 o'clock.)
4. Add the following fill properties: Edge: Anti-Alias and Texture: Grain, 25.
5. Save your work.

Apply filters to objects.

1. Select the Insignia object.
2. Apply an Inner Bevel filter with the default settings.
3. Add a stroke with the following settings: Stroke: Black Pencil 1-Pixel Soft, 1 px.
4. Drag the Insignia object to the middle of the Gumdrop object. (*Hint*: Move the Insignia object on the Layers panel, if desired.)
5. Apply an Inset Emboss filter to the Gumdrop object with the default settings.
6. Save your work.

Apply a filter to text.

1. Select the Text tool with the following properties: Font: Times New Roman, Font size: 22, Color: Red, Bold, and Italic. (*Hint*: Change the Fill type to Solid.)
2. Position the pointer in the upper-left corner of the canvas, then type **Sugarless Tastes Great**.
3. Apply a white Glow filter to the text. (*Hint*: Click the Shadow and Glow command on the Filters pop-up window to access the Glow option, then change the color to White and the Halo effect to 1.)
4. Save your work.

Apply a style to text.

1. Open the Styles panel.
2. Select the text.
3. Apply Style 1 to the text. (*Hint*: Substitute a different style, if desired.)
4. Save your work.

FIGURE 40
Completed Skills Review

Add a new style.

1. Change the Font color to #66FFCC and the Font size to 28.
2. Edit the Inner Bevel filter in the Filters section to the following settings: Bevel edge shape: Sloped and Width: 8.

3. Add a new style to the Styles panel, name it **Snow**, and do not have the style affect Text font, size, or style.
4. Compare your document to Figure 40.
5. Save your work.

You're in charge of office security at your business. In the last four months, several employees, including the owner, have neglected to engage their screen savers when they've left their desks for lunch, meetings, and so on. So far, friendly reminders and rewards haven't done the trick, so you're going to e-mail the same obnoxious attachment to everyone. You'll develop a simple, but effective, message using Fireworks vector tools and effects.

1. Create a new document that is 504 × 246 pixels with a white background, then save it as **remember_me**.
2. Create a rounded rectangle that fills the background, and apply the following properties to it: Fill: Pattern: Paint Blue, Edge: Anti-Alias, Texture: Grain, 25, and Stroke: None.
3. Add an Inner Glow filter with the following properties: Width: 8, Color: White, and Softness: 8, then lock the Background layer.
4. Create and name a new layer **Ruler**, then using Figure 41 as a guide, draw a rectangle that has a Linear gradient, then adjust the swatches on the color ramp as follows: Left and Right: #CCCCCC and Middle: #FFFFFF. (*Hint*: Click beneath the color ramp to add a color swatch.)

5. Add a black 1 px Pencil 1-Pixel-Hard stroke and Inner Bevel filter with default settings.
6. Use the Line tool to create evenly spaced hash marks that resemble those on a ruler, then group the ruler objects.
7. Create the following text in the font and filters of your choice: **don't rule out computer security**. (*Hint*: The text in the sample is bold Eras Medium ITC and has a Raised Emboss effect applied to it.)

8. Create **clean up your act** text in the font and color of your choice and apply at least one filter to it using settings of your choice. (*Hint*: The text has Glow and Raised Embossed filters applied to it.)
9. Save your work, then compare your document to Figure 41.

FIGURE 41
Sample Completed Project Builder 1

Impact Potions, a new energy drink aimed at the teen market, is sponsoring a design contest. They want you to introduce the drink by using the design in an ad window on other teen Web sites. They haven't decided on the container yet, so you can create the bottle or can of your choice.

1. If desired, obtain images that will reinforce your message delivery and enhance the vector shapes you will create. You can obtain an image from your computer, from the Internet, from a digital camera, or from scanned media. You can use images from the Web that are free for both personal and commercial use (check the copyright information for any such file before downloading it).

2. Create a new document and save it as **impact_potions**.

3. Create a beverage container using the vector tools of your choice, apply a fill, style, or stroke, and combine paths as necessary. (*Hint*: The side grips on the can in the sample were created using Punch commands.)

4. Create a label for the container, applying fills, strokes, styles, transparency, and filters as necessary. (*Hint*: The label text has been attached to paths.)

5. Create text for the ad applying fills, strokes, styles, transparency, and filters, as desired. (*Hint*: The Aristamp text in

the sample has the Glow and Inner Bevel filters applied to it.)

6. Rename objects or layers on the Layers panel as appropriate.

FIGURE 42
Sample Completed Project Builder 2

7. Experiment with changing the order of filters in the Filters list.

8. Examine the sample shown in Figure 42, then save your work.

One of the many advantages to using Fireworks for your images is the ability to combine vector and bitmap images into one document. For a performance artist, such as the country musician Dwight Yoakam, an official Web site can reinforce both the artistic message and mood. Photographs and Fireworks-generated images combine to convey the feel of an old-time café and street scene. Many images also link the viewer to other pages within the site. Because dynamic Web sites are updated frequently to reflect current trends, this page might be different from Figure 43 when you open it online.

1. Connect to the Internet and go to *www.course.com*. Navigate to the page for this book, click the Student Online Companion, then click the link for this chapter. (*Hint*: Click Two Doors Down Club (Home Page), if necessary.)
2. Open a document in a word processor, or open a new Fireworks document, then save the file as **yoakam**. (*Hint*: Use the Text tool in Fireworks to answer the questions.)
3. Explore the site and answer the following questions:
   - When they were created in Fireworks, which objects could have been grouped?
   - Do objects appear to have been combined?
   - Identify gradients, textures, styles, or other effects applied to objects.
   - Are there objects that appear to be a combination of vector shapes, which include photographic images, objects, or that appear to have an effect applied to them? (*Hint*: Visit the site during the day and during the night and note the differences.)
4. Save your work.

FIGURE 43
Design Project

Your group can assign elements of the project to individual members, or work collectively to create the finished product.

Vintage Wheels, a classic car club, is known for the unusual prizes the club awards to winners of their road rallies. To promote the rallies, the prizes are shown on the group's Web page. Your group has been selected to design and promote this year's grand prizewinner: a custom belt buckle. The only requirement is that the buckle honor a classic car and be large enough to be seen from a distance. You can select the classic auto of your choice.

1. If desired, obtain an image for the buckle. You can obtain an image from your computer, from the Internet, from a digital camera, or from scanned media. You can use images from the Web that are free for both personal and commercial use (check the copyright information for any such file before downloading it).

2. Create a new document and save it as **classic_buckle**.

3. Create two or more vector objects for the buckle and add fills, styles, strokes, or transparency to them. (*Hint*: The ovals in the sample have a combination of Inner Shadow, Inner Bevel, and Outer Bevel filters applied to them.)

4. Apply at least one Combine Paths command to the objects.

5. Create text as desired and apply fills, styles, and filters to them.

FIGURE 44
Sample Completed Portfolio Project

6. Examine the sample shown in Figure 44, then save your work.

chapter

3

IMPORTING, SELECTING,
AND MODIFYING
GRAPHICS

1. Work with imported files.

2. Work with bitmap selection tools.

3. Learn about selection areas.

4. Select areas based on color.

IMPORTING, SELECTING,
AND MODIFYING
GRAPHICS

Understanding Importing

Whether you want to create a simple image or a complex Web site, having the right graphic is crucial to the success of your project. Many times, the graphic you need may have been created in another application. Fireworks makes it easy to access such a graphic—regardless of whether it was created within the Macromedia application suite in a program such as FreeHand, created in another progam, such as Adobe Illustrator, or downloaded from a digital camera or scanner.

Fireworks allows you to import several types of files, including vector and bitmap files, as well as HTML tables. Being able to work with many different file types in the same document has obvious advantages. Fireworks lets you control file size by merging and flattening objects in your document, which combines pixels of different bitmap images or converts vector objects into bitmap images.

After you import a bitmap image, you can use an assortment of tools to select the pixels on that image. You can select pixels based on an area or on color. After you select pixels, you can manipulate them independently. For example, you can select and edit a defined set of pixels or blend a selection into surrounding pixels.

Tools You'll Use

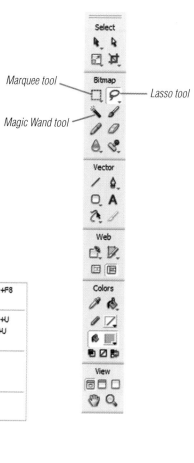

Marquee tool

Lasso tool

Magic Wand tool

WORK WITH
IMPORTED FILES

What You'll Do

 In this lesson, you will import graphics with different file formats into a Fireworks document.

Considerations for Importing Files

If you use mostly vector objects in your documents, you can change their dimensions and appearance without affecting the quality of the graphic. When you import several bitmap images or vector or text objects created in other programs into your document, you may need to weigh the advantages of using the new images against the disadvantage of increasing your file size. In addition to other factors, such as color depth, the number of bitmap images in a document affects file size.

Using Different File Formats

Fireworks offers several ways to acquire an image for use in your document. For example, you have already seen that you can copy and paste or drag and drop images from one native Fireworks .png file to another. Fireworks also has many features that maximize your ability to work with different file formats created in different programs, such as being able to copy and paste a graphic open in a different application into your

Fireworks document. In this example, because the copied graphic is placed on the Clipboard, you can paste it into your document as you would any other copied object. Dragging and dropping a selection from within Fireworks or between applications offers an additional advantage. Whenever you copy a selection, the selection is placed on the Clipboard, which consumes resources from your computer to store it. In contrast, using the drag-and-drop method saves memory.

Another easy way to acquire an image is to import a file with a compatible file format. Because individual elements in bitmap images are not editable, importing bitmap files is a relatively straightforward process. However, importing vector files offers the distinct advantage of being able to edit the individual paths that make up the graphic. Depending on the complexity of the original graphic, as well as its native format, Fireworks may import the graphic as a single grouped object or as an ungrouped collection of individual editable objects. You can import vector objects into

Fireworks from many vector programs, including FreeHand, Adobe Illustrator, and CorelDRAW. Figure 1 shows the import file types available in the Import dialog box.

QUICKTIP
You can select Photoshop conversion options, such as layers and text, by opening the Preferences dialog box from the Edit menu, and then clicking the Import tab. For vector-based files, you can select a wide range of options in the Vector File Options dialog box that opens when you import the file.

For some files, when you open a file that was created in another program, you may be able to save the changes you've made to the file in the extant file format. For example, you can open a JPEG or GIF file, modify it, and use the Close or Save commands to save it as a JPEG or GIF. In that instance, you modify and save in the original file format. However, Fireworks recognizes non-editable modifications, such as adding new objects or Live Effects, and also prompts you to save the document as a .png file, which preserves the original file for a different use. For other files, such as some vector file formats that were created in other programs, the original

FIGURE 1
Import dialog box

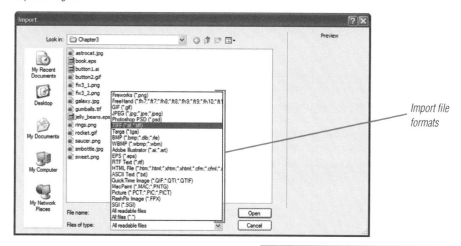

Import file formats

Understanding image resolution

For an image displayed on a computer screen—on the Web, attached to an e-mail, or inserted in a slide presentation—the unit of measurement is in PPI (pixels per inch). The standard resolution setting for Web images is 72 PPI, which is directly related to the display capability of computer monitors. The same picture that looks fabulous in a Web page often appears blurry when you enlarge it in a computer program because the same number of pixels is being spread over a larger number of inches. That picture also looks fuzzy when you print it because the on-screen resolution is too low for printing detailed tone transitions.

file is not affected regardless of the changes you make. In that case, the file that you open automatically is saved as a native Fireworks .png document when you click the Close, Save, or Save As commands on the File menu. To create a file in another format that you saved as a Fireworks .png document, you can select an export file format and export the file.

You can determine how Fireworks imports an Adobe Photoshop document by selecting different options on the Import tab of the Preferences dialog box shown in Figure 2. For a vector-based file, you can select options when you import the file in the Vector File Options dialog box, also shown in Figure 2. For example, in the File Conversion section of the

Vector File Options dialog box, you can determine whether to flatten layers or retain them. You can change settings in the Render as Images section to determine the number of individual objects Fireworks will import. In some cases, you might not need to edit the vector file, or you might simply prefer to import the file as a single bitmap image.

FIGURE 2
Import options

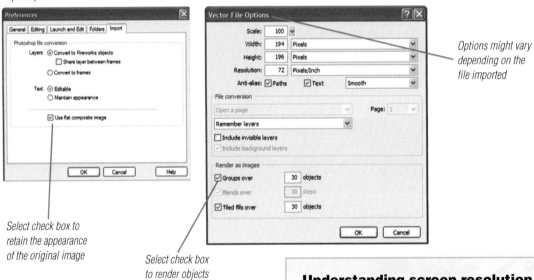

Options might vary depending on the file imported

Select check box to retain the appearance of the original image

Select check box to render objects as a bitmap

Understanding screen resolution

Computer monitors also have resolution settings that refer to the number of pixels contained across the horizontal and vertical axes—that is, how densely packed the pixels are on the screen. For example, a monitor set at a resolution of 1024×768 can display 1024 dots on each of 768 lines, totaling around 786,400 pixels. In contrast, a resolution of 800×600 displays less than half that amount of pixels. You can easily notice this when you change the resolution of your computer monitor: the lower the resolution, the larger the image appears, but it displays less detail than it does at a larger resolution.

FIGURE 3
Imported GIF

FIGURE 4
Imported Fireworks file

Import a .gif file

1. Open **fw3_1.png**, save it as **horizons.png**, then verify that the Info panel is open.

2. Change the name of Layer 1 on the Layers panel to **Spaceships**.

3. Click **File** on the menu bar, click **Import**, then navigate to the drive and folder where your Data Files are stored.

4. Click the **Files of type list arrow**, then click **All readable files** (if necessary) (Win).

   ⎸ TIP   You might need to scroll down the list
   ⎸ to find the file type.

5. Click **rocket.gif**, then click **Open**.

6. Position the **import pointer** ⌐ on the canvas at approximately 353 X/143 Y, then click the mouse to import the file.

   ⎸ TIP   If you can't position the mouse just
   ⎸ where you want it, enter the precise
   ⎸ coordinates in the X and Y text boxes
   ⎸ on the Property inspector after you click
   ⎸ the mouse.

7. Compare your image to Figure 3.

You imported a GIF file into a Fireworks document.

Import a Fireworks .png file

1. Click **File** on the menu bar, then click **Import**.

2. Double-click **saucer.png**.

3. Position the **import pointer** ⌐ on the canvas at approximately 65 X/290 Y, then click the mouse.

4. Compare your image to Figure 4, then save the file.

You imported a Fireworks file.

Import a vector file as editable paths

1. Click the **Background layer** in the Layers panel, click the **New/Duplicate Layer button** at the bottom of the Layers panel, then change the name of the new layer to **Book**.

2. Click **File** on the menu bar, click **Import**, then double-click **book.eps** to import it.

   The Vector File Options dialog box opens.

   TIP If the imported file was created in a program that is also designed for print media, such as Macromedia FreeHand or Adobe Photoshop, Fireworks converts the original color mode from print colors, such as CMYK, to RGB mode, which uses colors designed for the Web.

3. Compare your dialog box to Figure 5, then click **OK**.

4. Position the **import pointer** ⌐ in the upper-left corner of the canvas, click the mouse, then compare your image to Figure 6.

   The book appears on the canvas and the object appears on the Layers panel as a grouped object.

   You imported a vector file into a Fireworks document.

FIGURE 5
Vector File Options dialog box

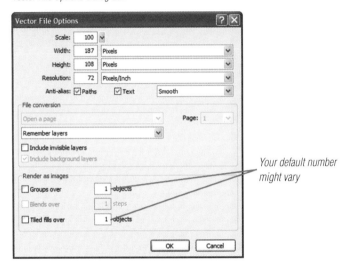

*Your default number
might vary*

FIGURE 6
Vector file imported as a group

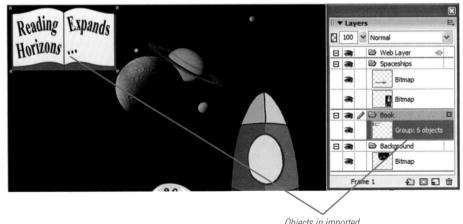

*Objects in imported
vector file are grouped*

FIGURE 7

Imported vector objects ungrouped

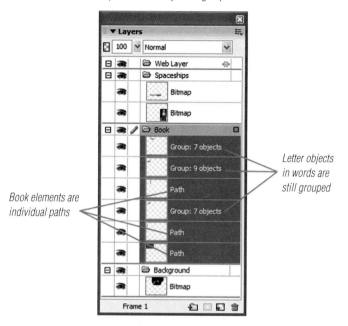

Book elements are
individual paths

Letter objects
in words are
still grouped

FIGURE 8

Modified object

Move word here

1. Verify that the books object is selected, click **Modify** on the menu bar, then click **Ungroup**.

   TIP You can also ungroup objects by pressing [Ctrl][Shift][G] (Win) or ⌘[Shift][G] (Mac).

2. Drag the bottom border of the Layers panel until all the layers are visible (if necessary), then compare your Layers panel to Figure 7.

   TIP You might need to collapse the Property inspector or drag the right border of the horizons.png Document window to the left to match Figure 7.

   Some individual paths are ungrouped, while other objects remain grouped (the individual letters). You could ungroup all the objects if you wanted to edit individually (for a total of 26 objects).

3. Click a blank part of the canvas to deselect the objects, click the **Group: 9 objects object** on the Layers panel to select the word **Horizons**, then drag the selected word to the location shown in Figure 8.

4. Click the **Book layer** on the Layers panel to select all the objects on the layer, click **Modify** on the menu bar, then click **Group**.

   The numerous book objects are regrouped into one object.

5. Save your work.

You ungrouped and modified an object, and then regrouped the objects.

WORK WITH BITMAP
SELECTION TOOLS

What You'll Do

In this lesson, you will use the marquee tools to select and change pixels in an image.

Understanding Pixel Selection Tools

Being able to select the precise pixels is the crucial first step to altering or editing parts of an image. Fireworks offers several ways to select and manipulate pixels in an image. This lesson covers some of those ways. When you select pixels on an image, Fireworks creates a flashing perimeter, known as a **marquee selection**, around the pixels. (This perimeter is also referred to as "marching ants" because of the way it looks.) Marquee selections are temporary areas of selected pixels that exist until you modify the pixels themselves, for example, by cutting, copying, or recoloring them.

You can save and recall a bitmap selection, but only one selection at a time. You cannot save bitmap selections in your document when you close it. In this lesson, you use the Marquee, Lasso, and Magic Wand tools to select and manipulate pixels in different ways. You can also use the selection tools in combination to select a complex area.

After you create a marquee selection, you can transfer it to another bitmap by clicking another bitmap object on the same or on a different layer. You can copy or cut a pixel selection into the layer of a document by using the Bitmap via Copy or Bitmap via Cut Insert command options on the Edit

Moving marquee selections

To move a marquee selection after you have created it, click any of the bitmap selection tools and drag the marquee on the canvas. To move a marquee selection while you are creating it, create an initial marquee, press and hold [Spacebar], move the selection to another area of the canvas, then release [Spacebar] and continue drawing the marquee.

menu. For example, if you select pixels and then click the Bitmap via Cut command, Fireworks cuts the selected pixels from the original bitmap and then pastes them as a new object on the active layer. Similarly, when you create a bitmap using the Bitmap via Copy command, Fireworks copies the selected pixels and pastes them as a new object on the active layer.

Using the Marquee Tools

Marquee tools select pixels on an image in a specific shape. The properties available for the marquee tools are shown in Figure 9.

You can press and hold [Shift] to constrain your rectangle or oval marquee to a square or circle. Use the Fixed Ratio style to constrain the height and width to a precise ratio and the Fixed Size style to set the marquee to an exact dimension.

Using the Transformation Tools

The transformation tool group consists of the Scale tool, Skew tool, and Distort tool. The Scale tool resizes an object, the Skew tool slants an object along the horizontal or vertical axes, and the Distort tool alters the size and proportion of an object and is useful for creating perspective in an object. Figure 10 shows skew and distort samples. When you select an object with any of the transformation tools, sizing handles surround the object. You can use these handles to transform the object. You can also use any transformation tool to rotate an object. The transformation tool pointer appears when you position the pointer over a sizing handle; the rotation pointer appears when you position the pointer in between the sizing handles or outside the object.

FIGURE 9
Properties for the marquee tools

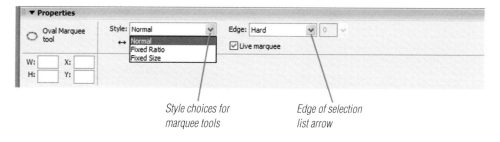

Style choices for marquee tools

Edge of selection list arrow

FIGURE 10
Skew and distort samples

Original object

Skewing slants object evenly

Distorting slants points independently

ect pixels using the arquee tool

1. Click the **Background layer** on the Layers panel, click the **New/Duplicate Layer button** , then change the name of the new layer to **Galaxy**.

2. Open galaxy.jpg.

3. Click the **Marquee tool** on the Tools panel, then verify that the Info panel is open.

4. Verify that **Normal** is the selected style in the Style list on the Property inspector and that **Anti-alias** is the Edge of selection setting.

5. Place the **pointer** ＋ on the canvas at approximately **40 X/6 Y**, then drag a rectangle that surrounds the galaxy, as shown in Figure 11.

6. Click **Edit** on the menu bar, click **Copy**, click **Edit** on the menu bar, then click **Paste**.

   The copied pixels are not noticeable because they are pasted on top of the original image on the canvas. The selection appears as the top object on the Layers panel.

7. Click the **Show/Hide Layer icon** next to the original bitmap on the Layers panel (the bottom one), then compare your image to Figure 12.

You set properties for the Marquee tool, created a rectangular marquee selection, and copied the selection.

FIGURE 11
Using the Marquee tool

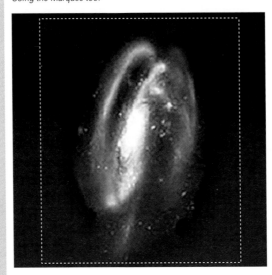

FIGURE 12
Rectangular marquee selection

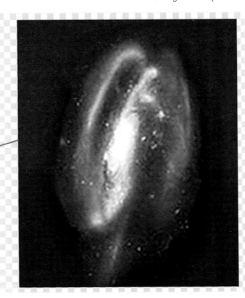

Anti-alias edge
appears sharp

FIGURE 13

Using the Oval Marquee tool

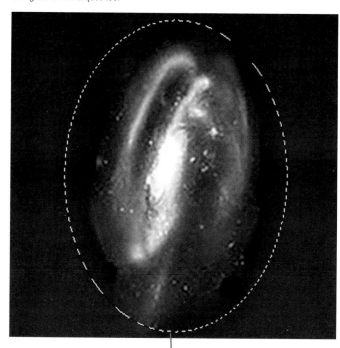

Create marquee by dragging
down and to the right while
pressing [Alt] (Win) or
[option] (Mac)

Select pixels using the Oval Marquee tool

1. Click the **Show/Hide icons** next to both galaxy bitmaps on the Layers panel to hide the rectangular selection and show the original image, respectively.

2. Press and hold the **Marquee tool** on the Tools panel, then click the **Oval Marquee tool**.

3. Verify that **Normal** is the selected style in the Style list on the Property inspector, click the **Edge of selection list arrow**, click **Feather**, double-click the **Amount of feather text box**, then type **20**.

4. Place the **pointer** ┼ in the middle of the canvas (180X/175Y), press and hold **[Alt]** (Win) or **[option]** (Mac), then drag down and to the right to create an oval marquee around the galaxy, as shown in Figure 13.

   Pressing and holding [Alt] (Win) or [option] (Mac) allows you to draw a marquee from the center point outward.

5. Drag the marquee or use the arrow keys to reposition the oval around the galaxy (if necessary).

   TIP You can reselect the marquee as many times as necessary. Notice that the marquee appears to be cropped when you release the mouse button if you extend it beyond the canvas.

   (continued)

6. Click **Edit** on the menu bar, point to **Insert**, then click **Bitmap Via Copy** to copy the selection.

7. Click the **Show/Hide Layer icon** 👁 next to the original bitmap on the Layers panel to hide it, then compare your image to Figure 14.

You set properties for the Oval Marquee tool, created an oval marquee selection, and then created a new bitmap from the original.

Transform a selection

1. Resize the galaxy.jpg Document window to make it smaller, then drag it to another part of the Fireworks window so that it, the horizons.png Document window, and the Info panel are all visible.

2. Verify that the oval bitmap is selected, click the **Pointer tool** ▶ on the Tools panel, then drag the selection from galaxy.jpg to the location in horizons.png shown in Figure 15.

3. Close galaxy.jpg without saving changes.

4. Maximize the horizons.png Document window, then click the **Scale tool** 🔲 on the Tools panel.

   Rotation handles appear around the selected objects.

   | TIP You can press and hold [Alt] (Win) or [option] (Mac) to scale an object from its center.

(continued)

FIGURE 14
Oval marquee selection

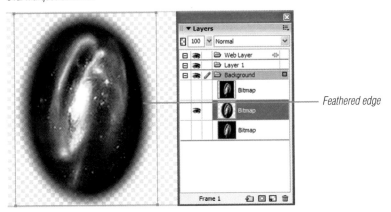

Feathered edge

FIGURE 15
Dropped selection

Importing, Selecting, and Modifying Graphics Chapter 3

FIGURE 16
Rotating a selection

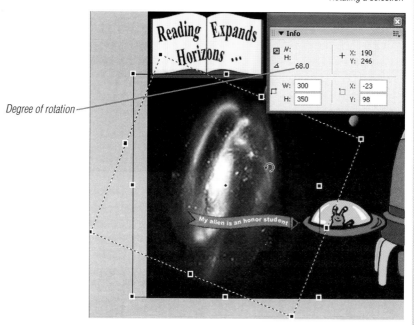

Degree of rotation

5. Place the **pointer** ⊹ outside the object until the rotation pointer ↻ appears, drag the selection counterclockwise 68 degrees, as shown in the Info panel, compare your image to Figure 16, then release the mouse button.

6. Click the **Opacity list arrow** on the Property inspector, drag the slider to **60**, then press **[Enter]** (Win) or **[return]** (Mac).

   | TIP If the Info panel covers the right side of the Property inspector, move or close it.

7. Click the **Pointer tool** ⬕ on the Tools panel, then drag the **Book object** and the **Saucer object** to the locations shown in Figure 17.

8. Save your work.

You dragged and dropped an object, rotated it, and changed its opacity.

FIGURE 17
Moved objects

Understanding resampling

If the bitmap selection you are copying has a print resolution that differs from the document into which you want to paste, a Resampling dialog box opens, asking if you want to resample the bitmap. Choose Resample if you want to preserve the selection's original dimensions, which will adjust the number of pixels as needed to maintain the bitmap's appearance. Choose Don't Resample to retain the number of original pixels, which may affect the size of the graphic when pasted.

LEARN ABOUT
SELECTION AREAS

What You'll Do

In this lesson, you will select pixels in an image using the lasso tools.

Using the Lasso Tools

As you have seen, the marquee tools select an area of pixels in a preset shape. Using the lasso tools, you can define an exact pixel selection with precision. The Lasso tool works well on images that appear to have curves, whereas the Polygon Lasso tool works well on images that have straight lines or asymmetrical outlines. With the Lasso tool, you create the marquee as you draw it on the canvas—its accuracy is linked to your tracing ability. The result is similar to the result obtained with tools such as the Pencil tool—what you draw is what you get, which might or might not be a good thing. Using the Polygon Lasso tool is similar to using the Pen tool—you create your marquee by clicking the mouse as you go along, although the final marquee does not contain points and is just like the other marquees you create.

Adding and subtracting pixels

To add pixels to an existing lasso selection, press and hold [Shift], then drag a new marquee. The pixels you select are added to the previously selected marquee. To subtract pixels from a marquee, press and hold [Alt] (Win) or [option] (Mac). Fireworks deletes the areas where the marquees overlap. To select just the intersection of marquees, create the first marquee, press and hold [Shift][Alt] (Win) or [Shift][option] (Mac), then create the second marquee. You can add or subtract pixels using other bitmap selection tools in much the same manner. Note that pressing [Shift] as you use the Polygon Lasso tool constrains the lines that you can draw to 45-degree angle increments.

Using Select Menu Commands

Using commands on the Select menu, you can adjust a pixel selection after you create it, as shown in Figure 18. You can edit the set of selected pixels, or add pixels to or subtract pixels from the selection marquee. The Select Inverse command selects all of the pixels except the ones enclosed by the marquee. Other commands, such as Expand Marquee or Contract Marquee, allow you to enter the number of pixels that add to or subtract from the selection's border. Creating a marquee can be a grueling process. Fortunately, after you are satisfied with a selection, you can use the Save Bitmap Selection and Restore Bitmap Selection commands to save it and recall it at any time during the current editing session or after the file has been saved, closed, and reopened.

FIGURE 18

Applying Select menu commands to a selection

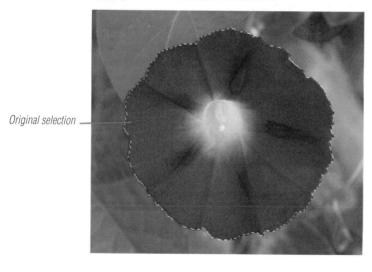

Original selection —

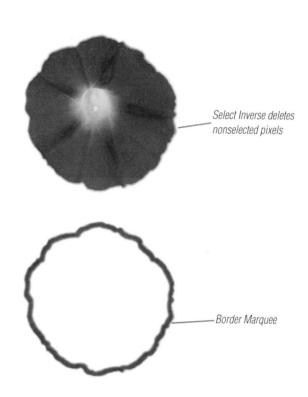

Select Inverse deletes
nonselected pixels

— Border Marquee

...ct pixels using the ...sso tool

1. Open astrocat.jpg.

2. Click the **Zoom tool** Q on the Tools panel, click the canvas until you can view the image in detail, then drag the borders of the Document window until the entire image is visible.

   You might need to adjust the magnification settings a number of times before you are satisfied.

   > TIP You can also increase magnification by clicking the Set magnification icon on the bottom of the Document window and then clicking a magnification setting from the Set magnification pop-up menu.

3. Click the **Lasso tool** ℗ on the Tools panel, click the **Edge of selection list arrow** on the Property inspector, click **Feather**, double-click the **Amount of feather text box**, then type **1**.

4. Drag the **pointer** 𝓼 along the perimeter of the cat, as shown in Figure 19, then notice the areas where the marquee is off the mark.

   Because the Lasso tool is sensitive to even the slightest deviations from the path you are drawing, the accuracy of your marquee will vary.

   > TIP You can change the pointer of most tools to a crosshair by pressing [Caps Lock], which can make it easier to see the pixels you want to select.

   (continued)

FIGURE 19
Creating a marquee with the Lasso tool

Drag pointer along
perimeter of image

Understanding magnification and the Zoom tool

You can increase the magnification of any area on the canvas. To change the magnification in preset increments, click the Zoom tool on the canvas or click a magnification setting in the Set magnification pop-up menu on the bottom of the Document window. To set a magnification between 6% and 6400%, use the Zoom tool to drag a zoom selection box on the canvas. The amount of magnification is based on the size of the zoom selection box. To zoom out of a selection, press and hold [Alt] (Win) or [option] (Mac), then click the canvas.

5. Click **Select** on the menu bar, then click **Deselect**.

   TIP   You can also remove a marquee by drawing another one, by clicking an area outside the selection with a marquee or lasso tool, or by pressing [Esc].

You selected pixels on an image using the Lasso tool.

Create a selection using the Polygon Lasso tool and save it

1. Press and hold the **Lasso tool** 🅿 on the Tools panel, then click the **Polygon Lasso tool** ⌣.

2. Create a selection by clicking the **pointer** ⌣ along the perimeter of the image, make sure you connect the start and end points, then compare your image to Figure 20.

   TIP   You can readjust your wrist or reposition the mouse on a flat surface in between clicks, which may ensure a more accurate selection.

3. Click **Select** on the menu bar, then click **Save Bitmap Selection**.

4. Type **Kitty** in the Name text box, then click **OK**.

You selected pixels on an image using the Polygon Lasso tool, and then saved the selection.

FIGURE 20
Marquee created with the Polygon Lasso tool

Marquee is
less erratic

...sform a selection

1. Click **Select** on the menu bar, click **Expand Marquee**, type **10** in the Expand by text box (if necessary), then click **OK**.

   The marquee expands 10 pixels in each direction.

2. Click **Select** on the menu bar, click **Contract Marquee**, type **20** in the Contract by text box, then click **OK**.

3. Click **Select** on the menu bar, click **Restore Bitmap Selection**, then click **OK** in the Restore Selection dialog box.

   The original marquee selection is restored.

4. Click **Select** on the menu bar, click **Smooth Marquee**, type **10** in the Sample radius pixels text box (if necessary), click **OK**, then compare your image to Figure 21.

   | TIP Fireworks removes pixels to smooth out the jagged points on the marquee.

5. Click **Select** on the menu bar, click **Restore Bitmap Selection**, then click **OK**.

   | TIP You can hide the marquee display by clicking the Hide Edges command on the View menu.

6. Click **Select** on the menu bar, click **Select Inverse**, then press **[Delete]**.

7. Click **Select** on the menu bar, click **Restore Bitmap Selection**, then click **OK**.

8. Click **Edit** on the menu bar, then click **Copy**.

9. Close astrocat.jpg without saving changes.

You applied different marquee commands to transform the selection, and then restored the original marquee.

FIGURE 21
Result of Smooth Marquee command

Smoothing
removes pixels

FIGURE 22

Results of numeric transform

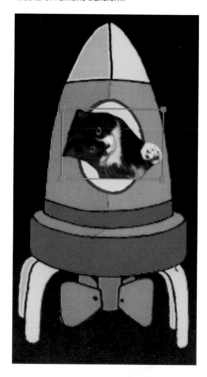

FIGURE 23

Repositioned and rotated selection

Position cat image
in window frame

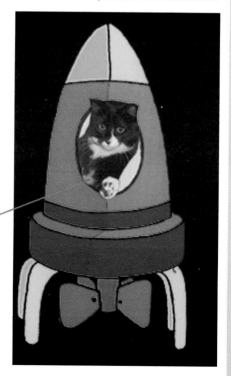

1. Click the **Pointer tool** on the Tools panel, then click the **large rocket object** on the canvas.

2. Click **Edit** on the menu bar, then click **Paste**.

3. Click **Modify** on the menu bar, point to **Transform**, then click **Numeric Transform**.

   The Numeric Transform dialog box opens, where you can scale an object by a percentage, resize it by pixels, or rotate an object.

4. Verify that **Scale** is selected in the drop-down list and that the **Scale attributes and Constrain proportions check boxes** are selected.

   The padlock indicates that the object will be resized proportionately.

5. Double-click the **width percentage text box**, type **50**, then click **OK**.

6. Drag the **cat image** on top of the rocket window, then compare your image to Figure 22.

7. Click the **Scale tool** on the Tools panel, position the **rotation pointer** outside the object, then drag the pointer clockwise to **–73** degrees, as indicated on the Info panel.

8. Click the **Pointer tool** on the Tools panel, then drag the image to the location shown in Figure 23.

9. Save your work.

You transformed the copied selection.

SELECT AREAS BASED
ON COLOR

What You'll Do

 In this lesson, you will add select areas of color using the Magic Wand tool, merge layers, and then flatten the image.

Using the Magic Wand Tool

The marquee and lasso tools select pixels by enclosing them. The Magic Wand tool allows you to select similarly colored areas of a bitmap image. The Magic Wand tool includes edge and tolerance settings. **Tolerance** refers to the range of colors the tool will select. The higher the setting, the larger the selection range. The Magic Wand tool works well on areas of strongly defined color, such as photographic images.

QUICKTIP

Depending on your graphic, you might find it more efficient to add pixels to a Magic Wand selection by pressing and holding [Shift], rather than increasing the tolerance setting and reclicking the bitmap.

The tolerance setting also affects the pixels selected when you click the Select Similar command on the Select menu. The Magic Wand tool selects pixels of contiguous color tone, not contiguous pixels on the image. When you use the Select Similar command, any matching pixels on the image are selected. Figure 24 shows four selections. The photo on the left shows the pixels selected with a low tolerance setting and those selected at that setting using the Select Similar command. The photo on the right demonstrates the same principle at a higher tolerance setting.

Merging and Flattening Objects and Layers

After you start creating, copying, or importing vector and bitmap objects in a document, your Layers panel can quickly fill up and appear unruly. Although creating and collapsing layers can help manage the large number of objects, you can also flatten or merge the objects you create into a single image, just as grouping objects assembles them into a single arrangement. Flattening and merging objects and layers helps to manage objects, layers, and file size. However, you can no longer edit individual objects after you flatten or merge them.

QUICKTIP

It's a good idea to save an unflattened version of your document as a backup.

The Merge Down command on the Modify menu merges selected objects with the bitmap object that lies beneath the lowest selected object. The Flatten Selection command on the Modify menu flattens two or more objects, even if they are on different layers (the top object moves to the bottom-most object), converting them to bitmap objects. If you want to move all your objects to a single layer and remove all other layers, you can use the Flatten Layers command.

FIGURE 24

Sample Magic Wand and Select Similar selections

 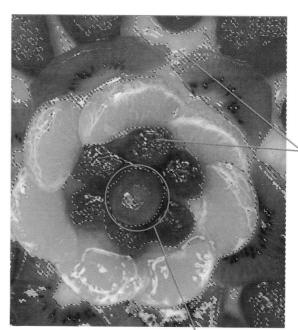

Select Similar command selects more green pixels

Select Similar command selects pixels in more colors

Tolerance 16 selects some green grape pixels

Tolerance 64 selects nearly all of grape

Select and copy pixels using the Magic Wand tool

1. Click the **bitmap object** (with the planets) on the Background layer to select it.

2. Click the **Magic Wand tool** on the Tools panel, double-click the **Tolerance text box** on the Property inspector, type **64**, click the **Edge of selection text box**, then click **Anti-alias** (if necessary).

3. Click the center of the small green moon, click **Edit** on the menu bar, point to **Insert**, then click **Bitmap Via Copy** to copy the selection.

   Although you cannot see the copy on the canvas (because it is directly on top of the original), notice that a new layer is created on the Layers panel.

4. Click **Select** on the menu bar, click **Deselect**, click the **Pointer tool** on the Tools panel, click the **copied bitmap** on the canvas, then drag it to the location shown in Figure 25.

5. Click the **Add Filters button** on the Property inspector, point to **Adjust Color**, then click **Hue/Saturation**.

6. Click the **Colorize check box** to select it, enter the values shown in Figure 26, then click **OK**.

   The colors change in the copied selection.

You selected pixels using the Magic Wand tool, and then copied, moved, and changed the color of the selection.

FIGURE 25
Pixels selected and moved with the Magic Wand tool

Move copied
selection here

FIGURE 26
Hue/Saturation dialog box

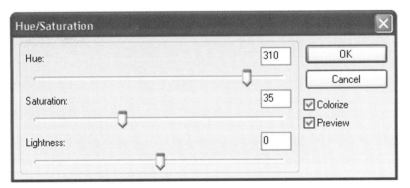

FIGURE 27
Selected pixels

All yellow pixels
are selected

FIGURE 28
Modified bitmap selections

Reading Expands
Horizons ...

My alien is an honor student

Pixels modified
after being copied

Pixels modified after
being selected

FIGURE 29
Flattened layers

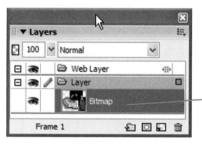

Bitmap and vector
objects flattened
onto one layer

Select and alter pixels

1. Click the **rocketship bitmap object**, click the **Magic Wand tool** on the Tools panel, then click the right yellow half of the nose cone.

2. Click **Select** on the menu bar, click **Select Similar**, then compare your image to Figure 27.

3. Click **Filters** on the menu bar, point to **Blur**, then click **Zoom Blur**.

4. Double-click the **Amount text box**, type **50**, double-click the **Quality text box**, type **20** (if necessary), then click **OK**.

5. Click **Select** on the menu bar, click **Deselect**, then compare your image to Figure 28.

You added similar pixels to a selection, and applied a filter to it.

Merge and flatten objects and layers

1. Click the **Pointer tool** on the Tools panel, then click the purple planet object.

2. Click **Modify** on the menu bar, then click **Merge Down** to merge this layer with the layer below it.

3. Click **Modify** on the menu bar, then click **Flatten Layers**.

4. Click the **Layer layer**, click **Modify** on the menu bar, click **Flatten Selection**, compare your Layers panel to Figure 29, save and close your work, then exit Fireworks.

You merged and flattened objects and layers.

Import files.

1. Open fw3_2.png, then save it as **sweet_essence.png**. (*Hint*: Because the canvas is narrow, readjust the size of the Document window if desired.)
2. Verify that the Info panel is open.
3. Change the name of Layer 1 to **Small Bottle**.
4. Import smbottle.jpg, placing the import cursor on the upper-left corner of the canvas.
5. Center the small bottle on the blue bottle so that it appears to be floating inside it.
6. Import sweet.png, placing the import cursor on the upper-left corner of the canvas.
7. Move the text to the bottom of the canvas.
8. Save your work.

Edit an imported vector object.

1. Create a new layer and change the name to **Jellies**.
2. Import jelly_beans.eps, accepting the default import settings, and placing the import cursor on the upper-left corner of the canvas.
3. Regroup the objects, then resize them so they fit across the top of the canvas.
4. Save your work.

Use the marquee tools.

1. Hide the Background layer, then select the text bitmap object.
2. Select the Marquee tool, verify that the Style is Normal and the Edge is Anti-alias, then draw a rectangular marquee around the text object.

3. Copy the selection using the Bitmap Via Copy command. (*Hint*: Use the Insert command on the Edit menu.)
4. Hide the original text bitmap on the Layers panel, then note the selected area.
5. Delete the copied rectangular marquee selection.
6. Save your work.

Transform a selection.

1. Show the original text bitmap, then select the Oval Marquee tool.
2. Set the Edge to Feather 10 pixels on the Property inspector, then draw an oval marquee around the text object.
3. Select the inverse of the selection and then delete it.
4. Deselect all objects, select the Scale tool, select the oval bitmap object, then rotate the oval bitmap object −90 degrees (clockwise). (*Hint*: View the rotation angle on the Info panel.)
5. Center the text bitmap selection on top of the small blue bottle.
6. Select the Background layer on the Layers panel.
7. Save your work.

Use the lasso tools.

1. Open rings.png, then select the Lasso tool.
2. Set the Edge to Feather 1 pixel on the Property inspector, adjust the magnification setting as desired, then create a marquee around the center ring.
3. Deselect the marquee.

4. Select the Polygon Lasso tool, then create a marquee around the two adjoining green rings to the left of the orange ring.
5. Save the bitmap selection.
6. Save your work.

Transform a selection and a copied selection.

1. Expand the marquee 5 pixels.
2. Contract the marquee 15 pixels.
3. Smooth the marquee 10 pixels.
4. Restore the bitmap selection.
5. Select the inverse of the bitmap selection, then deselect it.
6. Restore the bitmap selection.
7. Copy and paste the object to the sweet_essence.png document.
8. Close rings.png without saving changes.
9. Position the green rings selection so it appears to be floating near the bottom of the bottle on the left.
10. Save your work.

Use the Magic Wand tool.

1. Open gumballs.tif, then select the Magic Wand tool.
2. Adjust the Tolerance to 32 and the Edge to Feather 1 pixel.
3. Click the middle of the orange gumball, then click Select Similar.
4. Add pixels as necessary to the selection. (*Hint*: Press and hold [Shift].)

5. Drag and the drop the selection in the first bottle in the sweet_essence.png document. (*Hint*: If prompted to sample the selection, click Resample.)

6. Repeat for the yellow, white, and pink gumballs. (*Hint*: Work with each gumball separately.)

7. Close gumballs.tif without saving changes.

Select and alter pixels.

1. Using Figure 30 as a guide, resize and change the layer position of the gumballs.

2. Select the white gumball object, then apply a Hue/Saturation effect to it with the following settings: Colorize check box selected, Hue: 260, Saturation: 40, and Lightness: 5.

3. Save your work.

Merge objects and flatten layers.

1. Click the Jellies layer on the Layers panel, then merge down the layer. (*Hint*: Use the Modify menu.)

2. Click the Small Bottle layer on the Layers panel, then flatten the layers.

3. Select all the objects, then flatten the selection.

4. Save your work, then compare your image to Figure 30.

FIGURE 30
Completed Skills Review

You and your friends are going to partici-pate in a charity auction by creating a one-of-a-kind jacket. You are going to col-lect hundreds of different buttons and sew, staple, and glue them in solid cover-age over a jean jacket. The auction has a Web site, so you will use your Fireworks skills to create the background for a Web page announcing this item.

1. Obtain images of buttons and/or jean jackets in different file formats that will convey something unique about your jacket. You can obtain images from your computer, from the Internet, from a digital camera, or from scanned media. You can use images from the Web that are free for both personal and commercial use (check the copyright information for any such file before down-loading it).

2. Create a new document and save it as **mybuttons.png**.

3. Create a background image using any of the images you've obtained or create one using vector tools and applying a fill, stroke, style, or effect to it. You can also adjust its transparency. (*Hint*: The background in the sample is a rectangle filled with the Impressionist-Green pattern.)

4. Import the following files and the files you obtained in Step 1 into your document or open and select them using the bitmap selection tools.
   - button1.ai
   - button2.gif

5. Create visual elements using the images in your document, changing their size, color, and other properties as needed. (*Hint*: Various buttons have been skewed or distorted.)

6. Flatten the layers and selections in your document, if desired.

7. Save your work, then examine the sample shown in Figure 31.

FIGURE 31
Sample Completed Project Builder 1

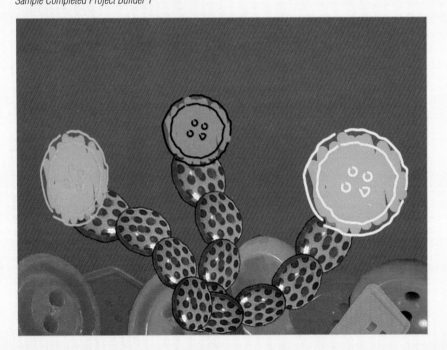

You're driving a moving truck across the country with a friend, and to occupy the time when you're not driving, you will use your new digital camera to take photographs. To memorialize this road trip, you will create a Web page dedicated to your adventure.

1. Obtain images that will fit your theme. You can obtain images from your computer, from the Internet, from a digital camera, or from scanned media. You can use images from the Web that are free for both personal and commercial use (check the copyright information for any such file before downloading it).
2. Create a new document and save it as **roadtrip.png**.
3. Import the files into your document or open and select them using the bitmap selection tools.
4. Create an interesting arrangement of your images, changing their size, color, and other properties as needed. (*Hint*: The lights of the long building in the example were selected using the Select Inverse command.)
5. Flatten the layers and selections in your document as necessary.
6. Save your work, then examine the sample shown in Figure 32.

FIGURE 32
Sample Completed Project Builder 2

Before you can build a visual element of a Web page, you need the visuals. As a designer, you'll want to be able to access as many images as possible to create a meaningful visual experience. Because dynamic Web sites are updated frequently to reflect current trends, this page might be different from Figure 33 when you open it online.

1. Connect to the Internet and go to *www.course.com*. Navigate to the page for this book, click the Student Online Companion, then click the link for this unit.
2. Open a document in a word processor, or open a new Fireworks document, then save the file as **mountainclimb**. (*Hint*: Use the Text tool in Fireworks to answer the questions.)
3. Explore the site and answer the following questions:
   - Identify different techniques that could have been used to isolate photographs.
   - Is a cropping technique evident? If so, identify.
   - How do the images affect the site design?
   - How are photographic images and illustrations used in the site?

- Who is the target audience for this site, and how does the design reinforce that goal?
4. Save your work.

FIGURE 33
Design Project

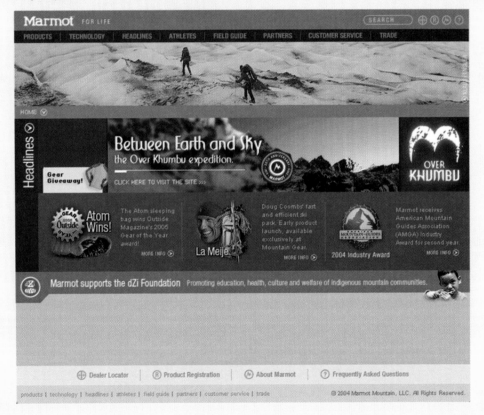

Students from the entomology department at a local college are preparing an educational Web site for the reluctant public. The group, Give a Bug a Break, wants to show how beneficial insects are to the ecosystem and our lives. Your group is in charge of developing a sample template the group can show to potential sponsors.

1. Obtain images of insects, and choose an insect to feature in the document. You can obtain images from your computer, from the Internet, from a digital camera, or from scanned media. You can use images from the Web that are free for both personal and commercial use (check the copyright information for any such file before downloading it).

2. Create a new document and save it as **mybug.png**.

3. Import the files into your document or open and select them using the bitmap selection tools.

4. Create an interesting arrangement of your images, changing their size, color, and other properties as needed. (*Hint*: The praying mantis has a feathered edge on an oval marquee and is placed on an oval vector object with inner bevel and emboss effects.)

FIGURE 34
Sample Completed Portfolio Project

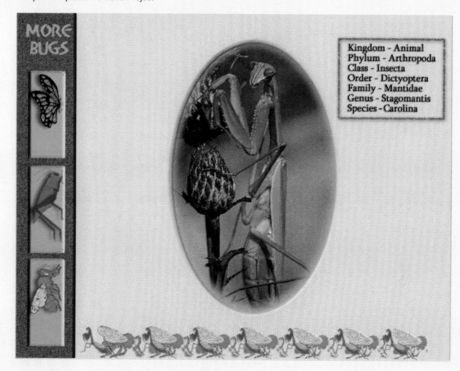

5. Flatten layers and selections in your document as desired.

6. Save your work, then examine the sample shown in Figure 34.

MODIFYING PIXELS AND
MANIPULATING IMAGES

M A C R O M E D I A   F I R E W O R K S   8

1. Alter pixels on a bitmap.

2. Work with masks.

3. Understand color.

4. Sample and store color.

5. Use the Creative commands to change images.

6. Use the Red Eye Removal tool.

7. Apply a blend mode.

Altering Pixels

As you work with bitmap images in Fireworks, you often need to edit them so that they have the impact you want them to have. The look and feel of your design dictates what you may need to do to the pixels on a bitmap graphic; for example, you might want to lighten, darken, blur, smudge, erase, replace pixels, or mask parts of an image. Fireworks has several bitmap tools designed specifically for editing an image pixel by pixel, if necessary.

Being able to mask an image offers many possibilities. Using a **mask**, you can modify the shape and transparency, including gradients, of an underlying image. You can use either a vector object or bitmap image as the masking object.

Learning about color, specifically additive and subtractive colors, aids in adjusting color in Fireworks. You can sample colors in a bitmap using the Eyedropper tool. You can pick out an exact pixel to use to match colors throughout your document. You can also use the Replace Color tool to select pixels of a specific color and replace them with another color.

Flash photography can create an annoying and unnatural red glow that dominates a subject's eyes. The Red Eye Removal tool is very effective at painting over the red.

You can also paint color into an image by applying a blending mode to an image. Fireworks also includes built-in Creative commands on the Commands menu that enhance your ability to modify an image, from adding objects such as arrowheads, to manipulating pixels in new ways using commands such as Twist and Fade.

Tools You'll Use

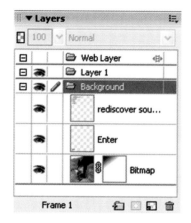

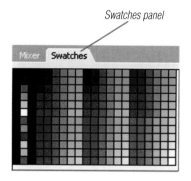

Swatches panel

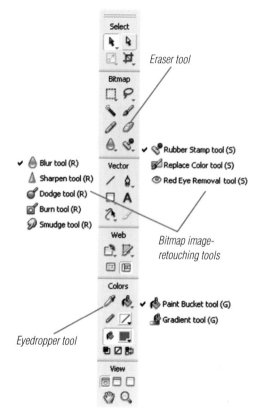

Eraser tool

Bitmap image-
retouching tools

✓ 🖊 Rubber Stamp tool (S)
📷 Replace Color tool (S)
👁 Red Eye Removal tool (S)

✓ 💧 Blur tool (R)
△ Sharpen tool (R)
🖌 Dodge tool (R)
🖌 Burn tool (R)
👆 Smudge tool (R)

✓ 🪣 Paint Bucket tool (G)
🖌 Gradient tool (G)

Eyedropper tool

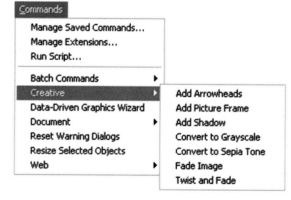

ALTER PIXELS ON
A BITMAP

What You'll Do

In this lesson, you will use various bitmap tools to lighten, darken, rubber stamp, erase, blur, and replace pixels in your document.

Understanding the Image-Retouching Tools

The bitmap image-retouching tools in Fireworks consist of the Blur, Smudge, Sharpen, Dodge, Burn, Rubber Stamp, Replace Color, and Red Eye Removal tools. They are referred to as retouching tools because the tools change the appearance of the bitmap pixels with which they come in contact.

The Blur tool and the Sharpen tool change the focus of the pixels you touch in opposite ways. The overall effect is similar to commands on the Filters menu or in the Filters section of the Property inspector. However, with those commands, you apply the filter to objects. The Blur and Sharpen tools allow you to have precise control over which pixels in a bitmap are affected and to what extent. You can set the intensity with which you blur or sharpen each area of an image, as shown in Figure 1.

Another set of companion tools are the Dodge and Burn tools, which lighten or darken areas of an image, respectively. The range setting that is available on the Property inspector when you use these tools has three options that allow you to target specific color areas: Shadows has an impact on the dark regions; Highlights has an impact on the lighter regions; and Midtones has an impact on the shades in between the two. The exposure setting works much like the exposure setting on a camera: it determines how much light is applied to the selected area.

> QUICKTIP
> You can switch between the Dodge and Burn tools by pressing and holding [Alt] (Win) or [option] (Mac) as you drag the pointer.

Using the Smudge tool has much the same effect as blending colors on an artist's canvas. The colors are blended in whatever direction the pointer is moving. In addition to adjusting the tip size, shape, edge, and pressure of the Smudge tool, you can select two other options to enhance the effect. You can select a smudge color from the color pop-up window that initiates each new smudge, and you can select the Use Entire Document check box to smudge using colors from every object on every layer. Figure 1 shows sample applications of the Blur tool and Smudge tool.

QUICKTIP

The Blur, Sharpen, Dodge, Burn, and Smudge tools are all part of the same bitmap image tool group on the Tools panel, which you can select by pressing [R]. You can select the Rubber Stamp, Replace Color, and Red Eye Removal tools by pressing [S].

Using the Rubber Stamp Tool and the Eraser Tool

The Rubber Stamp tool and the Eraser tool also work with pixels in opposite ways, as shown in Figure 2. The Rubber Stamp tool allows you to replicate pixels from one area on the bitmap and stamp them onto another. You can use the edge setting to blend the area selected by the tool and the

FIGURE 1
Blur tool and Smudge tool examples

Blur tool

Smudge tool

FIGURE 2
Eraser tool and Rubber Stamp tool examples

Eraser tool

Rubber Stamp tool

image area together. Unlike the other image-retouching tools that you simply drag on the canvas, using the Rubber Stamp tool is a two-step process. First, you select the area you want to replicate, and then you stamp the destination area with the selected pixels.

The Eraser tool erases pixels on the selected image and reveals the pixels of an underlying image based on the properties you set in the Property inspector. For example, you can adjust the brush size and shape, edge softness, and opacity of the eraser. You can think of the Eraser tool as changing the opacity of the erased pixels to zero or whatever opacity setting you choose, which has the net effect of making them transparent, but not physically separating them from the image. For example, if you bisect an image by erasing pixels across the breadth of the image and then move the object, it moves as a whole, just with a transparent line in the middle.

Using the Replace Color Tool
The Replace Color tool allows you to select a color you want to replace from your document and then replace it with another color that you choose in the same manner. You can determine exactly how much color you want to replace by adjusting the tolerance and strength settings on the Property inspector. Similar to the tolerance setting for the Magic Wand tool, you can choose the range of pixels you want to include. You set the darkness of the application using

the strength setting. Figure 3 shows properties and an example of the Replace Color tool.

You can select the color to change in a few ways. When you select the Swatch option as the From image, you can select a color from the color pop-up window or click the Eyedropper pointer on a specific color in the image. That way, only the pixels matching what you select will be replaced. If you select the Image option, every pixel in the image will be painted with the To color.

QUICKTIP
If your graphic contains similarly colored pixels in close proximity to the pixels you want to replace, you can adjust the tolerance setting and brush tip size to affect just the pixels you want.

Using the Image Editing Panel
The Image Editing panel contains a collection of the tools you use most frequently when editing a bitmap image. You can conveniently access bitmap retouching and selection tools, as well as transformation, filters, and view options.

FIGURE 3
Replace Color tool example

Replace Color tool

FIGURE 4
Properties for the Burn tool

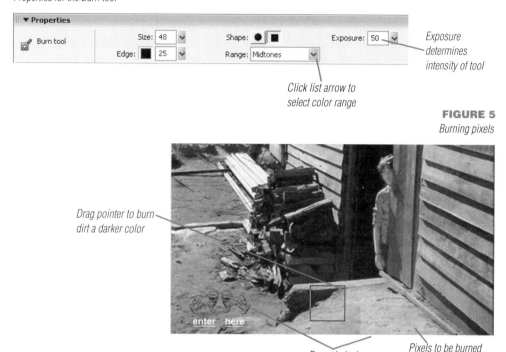

FIGURE 5
Burning pixels

*Drag pointer to burn
dirt a darker color*

enter   here

Burned pixels   *Pixels to be burned*

*Exposure
determines
intensity of tool*

*Click list arrow to
select color range*

Use the Burn tool to darken pixels

1. Open fw4_1.png, then save it as **se_asia.png**.

2. Press and hold the **Blur tool** 🖊️ on the Tools panel, then click the **Burn tool** 🔥.

3. Enter the properties shown in Figure 4.

4. Position the pointer on the ground by the plants, then drag the pointer to burn all of the ground, as shown in Figure 5.

   The pixels of the dirt appear darker.

   > TIP As long as you press and hold the mouse button, the Dodge and Burn tools will not continue to lighten or darken pixels, regardless of how many times you sweep over the same area with the pointer. If you release the mouse button and then press it again, sweeping over the area again will lighten or darken the area with the selected exposure setting.

5. Save your work.

You darkened the pixels in the image using the Burn tool.

Understand histograms and levels

A basic photograph contains 256 discrete brightness levels, the values of which range from absolute black (0) to absolute white (255). A **histogram** graphically displays the brightness levels contained in an image by graphing them in a vertical line format. When changing the tonal values in an image, viewing a histogram can help you make better decisions about what to adjust.

To view and adjust a histogram, open the Levels panel from the Adjust Color command on the Filters menu or in the Filters section of the Property inspector. The darkest values are on the left and the brightest values are on the right. The histogram displays how the pixels are distributed throughout the image, in shadow areas, highlight areas, and midtone areas.

Use the Dodge tool to lighten pixels

1. Click the **Zoom tool** 🔍 on the Tools panel, then click the **wood pile** as many times as necessary to view it in detail.

2. Press and hold the **Burn tool** 🖌 on the Tools panel, then click the **Dodge tool** 🖌.

3. Enter the properties and position the pointer in the location shown in Figure 6.

4. Carefully drag the pointer to dodge the face of the woodpile, taking care to stay just on the woodpile.

5. Compare your image to Figure 7.

You lightened pixels using the Dodge tool.

FIGURE 6
Positioning the Dodge tool

Dodge pixels
in this area

Click list arrow to
select Highlights

FIGURE 7
Results of the Dodge tool

Dodged pixels

FIGURE 8
Properties for the Rubber Stamp tool

Place pointer over
area to be sampled

JPEG (Document)

▼ Properties

Rubber Stamp tool | Size: 15 | ☑ Source aligned | 100 | N
Edge: ● 70 | ☐ Use entire document

Click Source aligned check box
to stamp with the same area

FIGURE 9
Results of stamping

Crosshair remains
over sampled area

Stamped pixels
cover pixels of the
red wrapper

Use the Rubber Stamp tool

1. Click the **Zoom tool** 🔍 on the Tools panel, then click the **red wrapper** on the ground until you can see it in detail.

   TIP To return to 100% magnification at any time, press [Ctrl][1] (Win) or ⌘[1] (Mac).

2. Click the **Rubber Stamp tool** 🖋 on the Tools panel.

3. Enter the properties and position the pointer in the location shown in Figure 8.

   TIP To repeatedly stamp with the initially selected area, select the Source aligned check box.

4. Press and hold **[Alt]** (Win) or **[option]** (Mac), then click the mouse button to select pixels.

   The crosshair remains over the selected area.

5. Position the pointer over the red wrapper, then click the mouse button to stamp over the red pixels, as shown in Figure 9.

   The red pixels are covered by the selected area.

   TIP You can stamp the area as many times as necessary until the red pixels have been covered.

6. Save your work.

You replicated the pixels in one area and stamped them onto another.

Use the Eraser tool to remove pixels

1. Drag the Document window scroll bars so that the Enter and Here objects are centered in the Document window.

    TIP Adjust the magnification of the canvas as needed.

2. Click the **Pointer tool** on the Tools panel, then click the **Enter layer** on the Layers panel to select it.

3. Click the **Eraser tool** on the Tools panel, then enter the properties shown in Figure 10.

4. Drag the pointer over the **right foo-dog** and **here text** to erase them.

    The pixels of the dog and text are erased, revealing the pixels of the underlying ground.

5. Compare your image to Figure 11.

You erased pixels on the Enter object using the Eraser tool.

Use the Blur tool

1. Click the **Pointer tool** on the Tools panel, then click the **Bitmap layer** on the Layers panel to select it.

2. Zoom out so that you can see the crops in the background.

3. Press and hold the **Dodge tool** on the Tools panel, click the **Blur tool**, then enter the properties shown in Figure 12.

4. Drag the pointer over the crops, then compare your image to Figure 13.

You blurred pixels in the image.

FIGURE 10
Properties for the Eraser tool

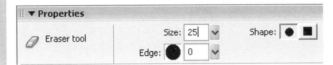

FIGURE 12
Properties for the Blur tool

Click list arrow to set amount of blurring

FIGURE 11
Results of the Eraser tool

Erased pixels

FIGURE 13
Results of blurring

Blurred area

FIGURE 14

Selecting the From option

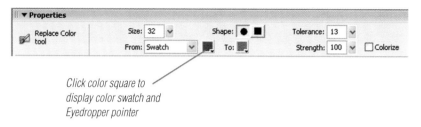

*Click color square to
display color swatch and
Eyedropper pointer*

FIGURE 15

Properties for the Replace Color tool

FIGURE 16

Results of Replace Color tool

Replaced pixels

Use the Replace Color tool to replace pixels

1. Click the **Enter object** on the Layers panel.

2. Click the **Set magnification pop-up menu**
   100% ▾ on the bottom of the Document
   window, click **150%**, then scroll to see the
   Enter text and foo-dog (if necessary).

3. Press and hold the **Rubber Stamp tool**
   on the Tools panel, then click the **Replace
   Color tool** .

4. Verify that **Swatch** is selected as the **From**
   option on the Property inspector, compare your
   Property inspector to Figure 14, press and hold
   the **From Color box** , position the **eyedropper pointer** over the middle of the foo-dog,
   then click the **mouse button**.

   The Swatch option allows you to choose the
   color that will be replaced from a color pop-up
   window or from the image. The Image option
   replaces image pixels with the To color every-
   where you paint with the Replace Color tool.

   ┃ TIP   Your default settings might vary.

5. Click the **To Color box** , type **#00FFCC** in
   the hexadecimal text box, then press **[Enter]**
   (Win) or **[return]** (Mac).

6. Enter the remaining properties shown in
   Figure 15.

7. Drag the pointer over the foo-dog, double-
   click the **Zoom tool** on the Tools panel,
   then compare your image to Figure 16.

   The light pixels in the foo-dog are replaced
   with the darker jade ones.

8. Save your work.

You replaced the color of the foo-dog image.

WORK WITH
MASKS

What You'll Do

 In this lesson, you will create bitmap and vector masks, and disable, enable, and apply a mask.

Understanding Masks

In the real world, a mask can hide any object, or control what areas it does reveal, but your masking flexibility is limited by the materials at your disposal. Because Fireworks is both a vector and a bitmap application, you have more creative masking options. By applying different masking techniques and adjusting properties, you can make your masks quite artistic. Fireworks offers several methods for applying a mask, and you might want to experiment with techniques and combinations before settling on the right one for your purposes. One efficient use of a mask is to cover the parts of an image you do not want to appear while preserving the bitmap as a whole.

One of the many advantages of using masks in Fireworks is that you make all your changes on the mask, not on the source image. That way, you can modify the mask as you want—the source image is undisturbed. Fireworks masks are always editable, all the time. Regardless of the technique you use to create a mask, you can edit, replace, disable, apply, or delete any mask you create. When you add a mask to an object, a **mask thumbnail** appears next to the object thumbnail on the Layers panel. When the mask is selected, it is surrounded by a yellow box. You can select just the mask or just the object, or both, depending on your editing needs.

Working with Bitmap and Vector Masks

You can use a bitmap or a vector object as either the **mask object** or the object being masked. For example, you might use a **bitmap mask** to create a mist or fog effect, setting the transparency of the mask object to determine the visibility and appearance of the object(s) beneath it. You can also use the outline of a bitmap object to mask the objects beneath it.

To use the outline of a bitmap object as the mask object, select the objects, point to Mask on the Modify menu, click Group as Mask, select the mask thumbnail, then select Alpha Channel as the Mask to option on the Property inspector. The alpha channel is the opaque area of the object.

When you use a vector object as the mask object, a different set of masking opportunities presents itself. The **vector mask** is the shape through which the underlying object is viewed, and you can include the fill and stroke of the vector object. You use the shape of the vector object to cut or crop the underlying image, just as a metal form can be used to cut a shape in concrete or cookie dough. The underlying object can be a bitmap or vector object. You can also paste an image inside a vector object, such as text. Figure 17 shows sample bitmap and vector masks and their properties on the Property inspector.

Deleting a Mask

You can delete a mask using commands from the Layers panel or by using the Mask command on the Modify menu. Fireworks gives you three options when you choose to delete a mask. You can apply the mask, which eliminates the editability of the mask by creating a solitary bitmap that has the mask incorporated in it. You can discard the mask to remove the mask and any changes you've made to it. Finally, you can cancel the delete operation and return to the state of the mask before you clicked the Delete Mask command. When you disable a mask, you can view or modify the pixels in the unmasked full image.

QUICKTIP
You can convert a vector mask to a bitmap mask by flattening it.

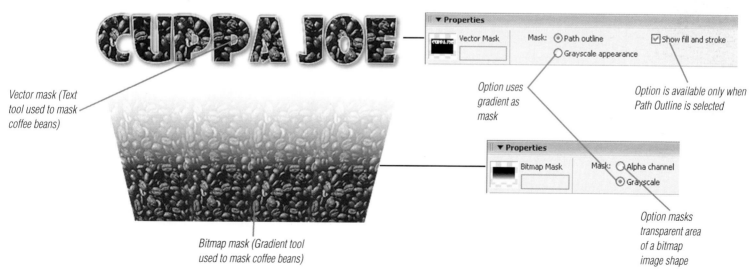

FIGURE 17
Sample vector and bitmap masks

Vector mask (Text tool used to mask coffee beans)

▼ Properties
Vector Mask   Mask: ⦿ Path outline   ☑ Show fill and stroke
                     ◯ Grayscale appearance

Option uses gradient as mask

Option is available only when Path Outline is selected

▼ Properties
Bitmap Mask   Mask: ◯ Alpha channel
                     ⦿ Grayscale

Bitmap mask (Gradient tool used to mask coffee beans)

Option masks transparent area of a bitmap image shape

Create a bitmap mask

1. Click the **Bitmap object** on the Layers panel (if necessary), then click the **Add Mask button** ⊡ on the bottom of the Layers panel.

2. Press and hold the **Paint Bucket tool** 🪣 on the Tools panel, then click the **Gradient tool** 🪣.

3. Click the **Fill Color box** 🪣▇ on the Property inspector, click the **Preset list arrow**, click **Black, White**, then click a blank part of the Fireworks window.

4. Using Figure 18 as a guide, drag the **pointer** 🪣 in the location shown.

   TIP You can redraw a gradient as many times as necessary.

5. Compare your image to Figure 19.

6. Save your work, then close se_asia.png.

You created and applied a bitmap mask.

FIGURE 18
Applying a bitmap mask

Begin dragging here

Stop dragging here

FIGURE 19
Applied mask

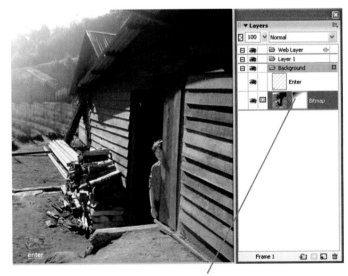

Selected mask has green border

FIGURE 20
Results of Paste Inside command

Stroke is retained

Create a vector mask using the Paste Inside command

1. Open fw4_2.png, then save it as **tea.png**.

   | TIP Notice that the text has a stroke applied to it.

2. Click the **Pointer tool** 🔧 on the Tools panel, click the **Bitmap object** to select it, click **Edit** on the menu bar, then click **Cut**.

   | TIP You can also press [Ctrl][X] (Win) or ⌘[X] (Mac) to cut an object.

3. Click the **enjoy gourmet text object** to select it, click **Edit** on the menu bar, then click **Paste Inside**.

   The leaves bitmap appears inside the text, which retains the stroke. The two objects are also now grouped as one on the Layers panel.

   | TIP You can also press [Ctrl][Shift][V] (Win) or ⌘[Shift][V] (Mac) to paste inside.

4. Compare your image to Figure 20.

5. Save your work.

You created a vector mask using the Paste Inside command.

Using other mask commands

You can quickly add a mask using reveal and hide commands. To apply a bitmap mask to an entire object, point to Mask on the Modify menu, and then click Reveal All to apply a transparent mask, or click Hide All to apply an opaque mask. Similarly, you can apply a mask to selected pixels, such as a marquee selection: point to Mask on the Modify menu and then click Reveal Selection or Hide Selection.

Create a vector mask using the Paste as Mask command

1. Verify that the Bitmap object and its mask are selected, click **Modify** on the menu bar, click **Ungroup**, then click a blank area outside the canvas to deselect both objects.

   The text and bitmap objects reappear unmasked.

2. Click the **enjoy gourmet text object** to select it, click **Edit** on the menu bar, then click **Cut**.

3. Click the **Bitmap object** to select it.

4. Click **Edit** on the menu bar, then click **Paste as Mask**.

   The text masks the bitmap and loses the stroke, as shown in Figure 21.

   > TIP You can also access the Paste as Mask command by pointing to the Mask command on the Modify menu.

5. Click the **Add filters button** ➕ in the Filters section on the Property inspector, point to **Shadow and Glow**, click **Drop Shadow**, drag the **Softness slider** to **5**, then press **[Enter]** (Win) or **[return]** (Mac).

6. Compare your image to Figure 22.

You created a vector mask using the Paste as Mask command. You also used a Drop Shadow filter to add impact to your image.

FIGURE 21
Results of Paste as Mask command

Stroke no longer appears on text

FIGURE 22
Drop Shadow filter added Mask

Drop shadow filter adds depth

FIGURE 23

Disabled mask

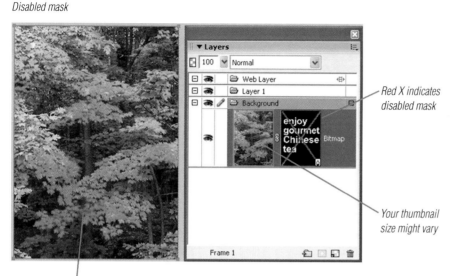

Red X indicates
disabled mask

*Your thumbnail
size might vary*

*Bitmap object
appears without text*

FIGURE 24

Applied mask

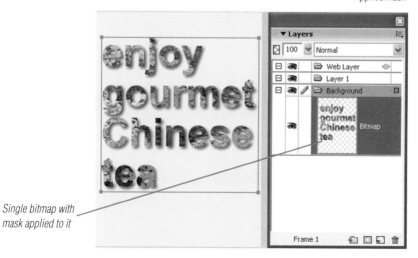

*Single bitmap with
mask applied to it*

Disable, enable, and apply a mask

1. Verify that the Bitmap object and its mask are selected, click **Modify** on the menu bar, point to **Mask**, then click **Disable Mask**.

   The image is no longer masked and a red X appears over the mask thumbnail on the Layers panel.

   TIP You can disable a mask as long as either the mask or the object is selected.

2. Compare your image to Figure 23.

   TIP Depending on the thumbnail size selected for the Layers panel, the red X might not be noticeable.

3. Click the **mask thumbnail** to select it, which also enables the mask.

   The mask thumbnail is surrounded by a green border.

4. Click **Modify** on the menu bar, point to **Mask**, then click **Delete Mask**.

5. Click **Apply** when the Apply mask to bitmap before removing? prompt appears.

   The object on the Layers panel appears as a single bitmap thumbnail without a mask.

6. Compare your image to Figure 24.

7. Save your work, then close tea.png.

You disabled, enabled, and applied a mask to an object. You also converted an object and its mask into a single bitmap object.

UNDERSTAND
COLOR

What You'll Do

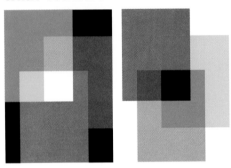

 In this lesson, you learn key concepts of color and RGB channels, so that you better understand how to manipulate color in Fireworks.

The relationship between light and color is crucial to understanding how to manipulate color in Fireworks. Being able to view the amount of color in specific color channels can help you to remove a color cast from a photo or correct a color. Working with individual color channels allows you to adjust the color balance until you are satisfied with the results.

When we talk about color, we also—by implication—talk about light. For those living in this solar system, the sun is the primary source of light. The light that reaches the Earth from the sun and other stars is known as the **electromagnetic spectrum**, which includes the full range of frequencies, such as gamma rays, X-rays, microwave, and radio waves. As human beings, our eyes have rather limited photosensitive receptor cells. The visible light that we can perceive is known as **white light**. For us, visible light is a narrow slice of the electromagnetic spectrum bounded by long infrared wavelengths at one end and by short ultraviolet wavelengths at the other.

White light can be bent to separate the colors that form it. For example, when you shine a light through a prism, it separates white light into its component colors. The most common experience we have seeing separated white light is when we see a rainbow. Combined, raindrops act like prisms, bending, or refracting, the light into the familiar color arc of the rainbow: red, orange, yellow, green, blue, indigo, and violet. Each color has a specific wavelength. Red, which has a longer wavelength, is always on the outside of the arc; violet, which has the shortest wavelength, is always on the inside of the arc.

Understanding RGB Color and Channels

RGB is the default color model used for computer monitors, television screens, and any other medium that emits the light itself. Red, green, and blue are the additive primary colors of light. In Fireworks, you adjust these colors in their individual channels.

Additive colors combine to produce other colors, as shown in Figure 25. The range of RGB colors is 0 to 255, which represents all possible levels of red, green, or blue. Adding 100% of all three colors, 255 red, 255 green, and 255 blue, produces white. A value of 0 red, 0 green, and 0 blue, which is the absence of light, produces black. Note that additive primary colors—red, green, and blue—differ from the primary colors we learned about in basic art class—red, blue, and yellow.

Understanding CMYK Color

In addition to RGB, the other main color model is **CMYK** (Cyan, Magenta, Yellow, Black) color. CMYK are secondary colors used primarily for print media in what is known as four-color process printing. The difference between the two models lies in how color is produced from the light source. RGB is based on emitted, or projected, light. CMYK is based on reflected and absorbed light. You can think of CMYK as mixing pigment, whereas RGB mixes light. When the sun shines white light on a surface, some of the light spectrum is absorbed by the surface and the rest of the light is reflected to your eye. The color we perceive in printed materials is based on subtractive colors of light.

Subtractive colors create color by subtracting cyan, magenta, yellow, and black from white light, as shown in Figure 26. For example, when you combine CMYK colors in equal amounts, you produce black; the absence of color is white. The percentages between them form the color spectrum.

FIGURE 25
Additive primary colors

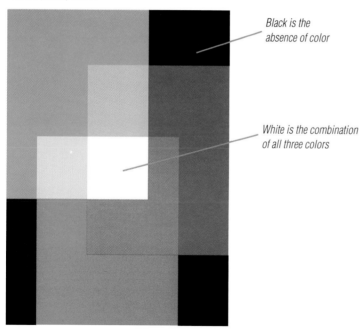

Black is the absence of color

White is the combination of all three colors

FIGURE 26
Subtractive secondary colors

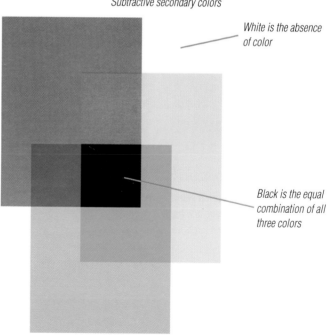

White is the absence of color

Black is the equal combination of all three colors

SAMPLE AND STORE COLOR

What You'll Do

In this lesson, you will select a pixel color from a bitmap image and apply it to a vector object, and then add the color to the Swatches panel.

Using the Eyedropper Tool

Being able to match the colors in your document exactly is very useful. Like its glass and rubber counterpart, the Eyedropper tool can pick up, or **sample**, a drop of color, which in Web graphics is a pixel. The Eyedropper tool can sample a single pixel, the average of a 3x3 pixel area, or the average of a 5x5 pixel area. You can use the Eyedropper tool to sample color in any object or image in your document, and designate it as the current stroke, fill, or text color.

You can also sample color when you open the text, fill, or stroke color pop-up windows and move the eyedropper pointer over a pixel in an image. Although the eyedropper pointer looks similar to the Eyedropper tool pointer, the color you sample is always just one pixel. You can change text color using Eyedropper tool settings by selecting the text object, and then selecting the Eyedropper tool. You can change fill or stroke color by selecting the Eyedropper tool and then clicking the fill or stroke icon, but not the color box, next to the Fill Color or Stroke Color tools on the Tools panel. Figure 27 shows the difference between sampling a color using the Eyedropper tool and a color pop-up window.

DesignTIP **Understanding how color works on the Web**
The colors in your image correspond to the colors in a color palette—in other words, only the colors defined in the color palette appear in your graphic. However, not all the colors in your images or the colors that you choose from a color pop-up window will appear the way you expect them to when displayed on the Web.

Adding Sampled Colors to the Swatches Panel

The Swatches panel contains colors from the active Fireworks color palette. After you sample a color using the Eyedropper tool, you can add it to the Swatches panel so that you can access it at any time. You can also edit and delete swatches in the Swatches panel. Because the Swatches panel is not document-specific, after you add a color swatch, you can use it in all your documents.

The prevailing assumption is that computer monitors can display 256 colors; however, the vast majority of monitors can display many more, up to approximately 16,777,000 colors. Depending on your browser and computer platform, the appearance of a color can vary considerably. You can ensure that your colors will display correctly and consistently without dithering by selecting Web-safe colors. There are 216 Web-safe colors. You can apply the Web 216 color palette to ensure that your colors will be approximately the same on Windows, Macintosh, and UNIX platforms. You can also apply a WebSnap Adaptive palette, which converts colors to a close equivalent on the Web 216 palette.

FIGURE 27

Sampling a color using the Eyedropper tool and color pop-up window

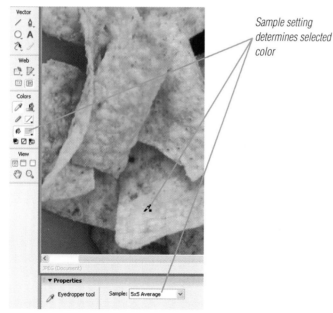

Sample setting determines selected color

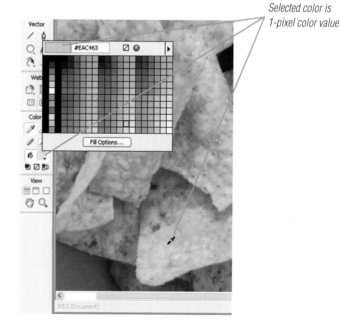

Selected color is 1-pixel color value

Sample a color using the Eyedropper tool

1. Open se_asia.png from the location where you are saving Data Files for this book, then verify that the Info panel is displayed.

   TIP You can use the Open Recent command on the File menu to see a short list of recently opened files.

2. Click the **Text tool** A on the Tools panel, then enter the properties shown in Figure 28.

3. Click the upper-left corner of the canvas at approximately **20 X/52 Y**, then type the following words, each on a separate line: **rediscover south east asia**.

   TIP You can easily insert special characters into a text block by opening the Special Characters panel from the Window menu, and then clicking the character you want to insert.

4. Click the **Eyedropper tool** on the Tools panel, click the **Sample list arrow** on the Property inspector, then click **5x5 Average**.

5. Move the **pointer** over the shirtsleeve, then click the canvas at approximately **290 X/346 Y**, as shown in Figure 29.

   The text Fill Color box on the Tools panel changes to the shade of red representing the average of all of the shades of red displayed in the 5x5 pixel area.

   TIP To select a Web-safe color, press and hold [Shift].

   (continued)

FIGURE 28
Properties for the Text tool

FIGURE 29
Sampling a color

Click sleeve here

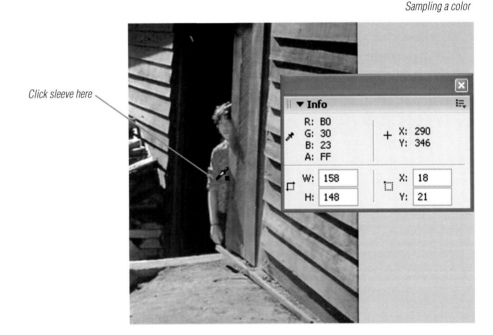

FIGURE 30
Sampled color applied to text

*Text color changes
to sampled color*

6. Click the **Pointer tool** on the Tools panel, click the **Add Filters button** on the Property inspector, point to **Shadow and Glow**, then click **Glow**.

7. Click the **Halo offset width list arrow**, drag the slider to **1**, click the **Color box**, type **#FFCCFF** in the hexadecimal text box, press **[Enter]** (Win) or **[return]** (Mac), then click a blank area outside the canvas.

8. Click **Select** on the menu bar, click **Deselect**, then compare your image to Figure 30.

You sampled a color and applied it to text. You also used a Glow filter to add impact to your text.

Add a swatch to the Swatches panel

1. Click **Window** on the menu bar, then click **Swatches** to display the Swatches panel (if necessary).

   TIP You can also open the Swatches panel by pressing [Ctrl][F9] (Win) or ⌘ [F9] (Mac).

2. Position the **pointer** in the blank bottom portion of the panel, then click the **mouse** to add the swatch.

   The red swatch is added to the bottom of the Swatches panel.

   TIP To delete a swatch, press and hold [Ctrl] (Win) or ⌘ (Mac), position the pointer over the swatch, then click the mouse.

3. Compare your Swatches panel to Figure 31.

4. Save your work, then close se_asia.png.

You added the sampled swatch to the Swatches panel.

FIGURE 31
Swatch added to the Swatches panel

*Your swatches
might vary*

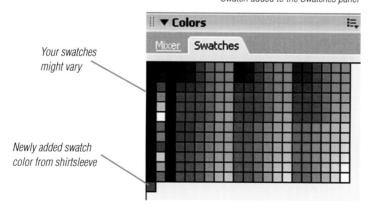

*Newly added swatch
color from shirtsleeve*

USE THE CREATIVE
COMMANDS TO CHANGE IMAGES

What You'll Do

In this lesson, you will apply the Add Picture Frame and Twist and Fade Creative commands.

Using the Creative Commands

Fireworks contains built-in programs designed by third parties that work seamlessly in the application. For example, you might have already experimented with Alien Skin filters. The Creative commands add even more variety to your Fireworks projects. Sample applications of two of the Creative commands are shown in Figure 32.

The Add Arrowheads command allows you to add an arrowhead to any open path you've drawn. For example, you can draw a line with the Line tool or plot a path with the Pen tool, and then apply any of 17 different shapes to the start or end of the arrow.

The Add Picture Frame command combines document information with fill and effect settings from the Property inspector. You can select a pattern for the picture frame from any of the patterns available on the Property inspector as a fill or texture.

QUICKTIP

You can also create a picture frame by dragging the Frame Auto Shape from the Auto Shapes panel to the canvas, and then using the control points to select a pattern and adjust size.

Using the Twist and Fade command

The Twist and Fade command taxes your computer's memory and processing resources considerably. The more objects and steps you add, the greater the demand. You might find it useful to close other open programs or restart your computer before you experiment with this feature. For additional information and updates to Twist and Fade, visit the creators' Web site: *www.phireworx.com*.

The Shadow command adds a perspective shadow to any vector object. You can adjust the shadow using control points, opacity, and filters. You can convert the colors of any object in your document to grayscale or sepia. The Convert to Grayscale and Convert to Sepia commands only affect the selected objects so that you can have color and mono-chromatic images in the same document.

The Fade Image command applies one of eight available bitmap masks to your selected object or objects. Each mask is already designed to fade your selected object in a different distance and direction. Styles choices include fade-ins from differ-ent sides in rectangular or elliptical shapes. You can apply the command to any selected object(s) in your document.

The Twist and Fade command is an easy way to radically change an object. This com-mand duplicates the selected object(s), and then resizes, spaces, rotates, and changes the opacity of the duplicates. The results, as shown in the sample in Figure 32, can be remarkable.

QUICKTIP

To make it appear that the objects fade out as they are duplicated and twisted, click Options in the Twist and Fade dialog box, then click the fade opacity option.

FIGURE 32
Sample Creative commands

Add Picture Frame command

Twist and Fade command

Apply the Twist and Fade command

1. Open tea.png.

2. Import leaves.png, then position the leaves in the location shown in Figure 33.

3. Click **Commands** on the menu bar, point to **Creative**, then click **Twist and Fade**.

   The Twist and Fade dialog box opens. You can preview the effects before you apply them.

4. Drag the sliders as close as possible to the locations shown in Figure 34, then click **apply**.

   The leaves appear to be falling and twisting.

5. Compare your image to Figure 35.

You applied the Twist and Fade Creative command to an object.

FIGURE 33
Positioning leaves on the canvas

Move leaves here

FIGURE 34
Twist and Fade dialog box

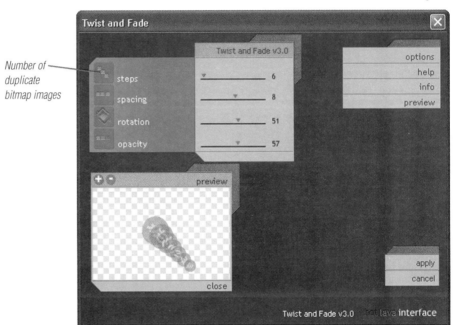

Number of duplicate bitmap images

FIGURE 35
Results of the Twist and Fade command

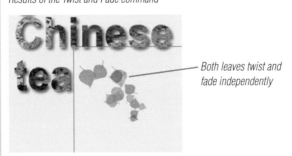

Both leaves twist and fade independently

FIGURE 36
Results of the Add Picture Frame command

Leaves pattern in picture frame

1. Click **Commands** on the menu bar, point to **Creative**, then click **Add Picture Frame**.

   The Add Picture Frame dialog box opens.

2. Click the **Select a pattern list arrow**, scroll down the list, click **Leaves**, double-click the **Frame Size text box**, then type **12**.

3. Click **OK**, then compare your image to Figure 36.

   The Add Picture Frame command automatically applies the frame to the entire document, regardless of the object selected when you applied the command. A new locked layer, Frame, is added to the Layers panel.

4. Save your work, then close tea.png.

You added a picture frame and chose its size and pattern.

USE THE RED
EYE REMOVAL TOOL

What You'll Do

▶ *In this lesson, you will use the Red Eye Removal tool to remove the red glow in a subject's eyes.*

Understanding the Red Eye Removal Tool

The appearance of glowing red eyes in some photographs is caused by your camera's flash. Because a camera flash occurs faster than our pupils can contract in response, the flash can travel through the opening of the eye and reflect off the red surface of the retina, causing this annoying result. Luckily, Fireworks provides a quick way to remove it.

DesignTIP Removing the glow in animals' eyes

Many animals, especially nocturnal animals such as cats, have a reflective membrane directly beneath their retinas. As a result, in addition to the red glow created by the human retina, animal eyes can appear green or white in a photograph. The Red Eye Removal tool removes only red or orange pixels; therefore, it is not effective on green or white glow. To remove the green or white glow from the eyes of your animal subjects, activate the Brush tool, set the stroke color to black, change the blending mode to Darken, then adjust the opacity until the results look natural. Start with an opacity of 75%, then go up or down as needed. Always click the pupil with glowing pixels; if you drag the brush, you will oversaturate the pixels. The pixels turn shades of gray and black, which simulates natural eye color.

The Red Eye Removal tool functions similarly to a brush tool; you can adjust its size, strength, and tolerance properties to suit the image. The tolerance setting for the Red Eye Removal tool is geared specifically for reds and oranges. It selects a range of hues from 0 (only red) to 100 (all hues that contain any red). The Strength setting determines the depth of grays. Figure 37 shows properties for the Red Eye Removal tool, which is located beneath the Rubber Stamp tool group on the Tools panel.

Properties for the Red Eye Removal tool

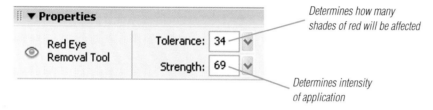

Determines how many shades of red will be affected

Determines intensity of application

Sample red eye removal

Use the Red Eye Removal tool

1. Open fw4_3.png, then save it as **sculpted_stucco.png**.

2. Click the **Zoom tool** 🔍 on the Tools panel, then click the canvas until the man's eyes fill the window.

3. Press and hold the **Replace Color tool** 🖌 on the Tools panel, then click the **Red Eye Removal tool** 👁.

   TIP You can also open the Image Editing panel to access the Red Eye Removal tool and other common image editing tools, filters, and commands.

4. Drag the **Tolerance slider** to **58** on the Properties panel, drag the **Strength slider** to **75**, then press **[Enter]** (Win) or **[return]** (Mac).

5. Drag the pointer around the left eye, as shown in Figure 39, then repeat for the right eye.

   The red pixels in the eye glow are removed.

   TIP You can redrag the Red Eye Removal tool as often as necessary.

   (continued)

FIGURE 39
Drawing red eye removal marquee

Red Eye
Removal tool

Draw marquee
around eye

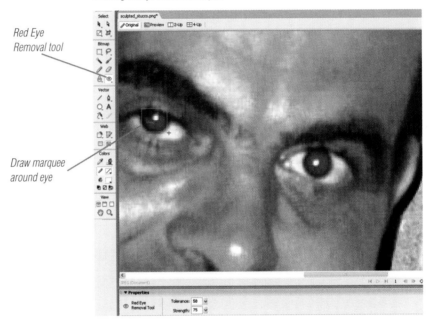

Modifying Pixels and Manipulating Images   Chapter 4

FIGURE 40

Completed red eye removal

6. Press and hold **[Ctrl]** (Win) or ⌘ (Mac), then press **0**.

   The document fits on the screen.

7. Compare your image to Figure 40, then save your work.

You removed the red eye in an image.

DesignTIP   **Reducing Red Eye During Photography**

One of the easiest ways to avoid red eye in your subjects is to use a camera with a specific feature for reducing this occurrence. Many newer digital cameras have a pre-light feature for this purpose. The flash emits a short burst of flashes, known as pre-light, before the main flash goes off. The rapid light flashes cause the subject's pupil to contract, which reduces the area through which the flash can travel and reflect off the retina.

If your camera does not have a feature for reducing red eye, try to increase the ambient light in the location and instruct your subjects to look at the camera but not look for the flash.

APPLY A BLEND MODE

What You'll Do

In this lesson, you will apply a blend mode, change the order of objects on the Layers panel, and compare the difference.

Understanding Blend Modes

A **blend mode** creates new color—and visual effects—using the color from two or more bitmap or vector objects. Fireworks offers over three dozen blend modes. Each operates on the same basic principle: a base color is mixed with a blend color, which produces a result color. The base color is in the selected object; the blend color is the next visible object beneath the base color object. A sample blend mode is shown in Figure 41.

You can access the blend mode list any time an object is selected on the Layers panel and a tool is active that supports blend modes. Some tools, such as the Brush, Rubber Stamp, Scale, Skew, Distort, Pointer, Pencil, and Text tools, have blend mode available on the Property inspector.

Many blend modes combine, multiply, or select the base and blend colors to produce the result color. Some blend modes are described in the following list:

- Darken—Selects the darker color of base or blend colors
- Screen—Multiplies the inverse (opposite) of the blend color by the base color, which lightens many areas
- Overlay—Multiplies (darkens) or screens (lightens) colors and replaces base color with mix
- Soft Light and Hard Light—If the blend color is lighter or darker than 50% gray, respectively, lightens or darkens the image accordingly
- Hue—Combines the hue of the base color with the saturation and luminosity of the blend color

- Difference—Subtracts the color from either the base or blend color that is least bright from the brighter color
- Tint—Adds gray to the base color

Each object can have its own blend mode, but grouped objects retain only the blend mode that is applied to it.

QUICKTIP
Adjusting the opacity of an object can also dramatically affect the effect of a blend mode.

FIGURE 41
Sample blend mode

Original images

Next visible object is blend color

Top object is base color

Selected blend mode

Apply blend modes

1. Click the **Pointer tool** on the Tools panel, then click the **Sahara sunset object** on the Layers panel.

2. Click the **Blend mode list arrow** on the Property inspector, then click **Soft Dodge**.

   The result colors are slightly psychedelic, as shown in Figure 42.

3. Click the **KB object**, then drag it to the top of the Layers panel.

   TIP The blend modes of other objects in the layer beneath the base object do not affect future blends.

4. Click the **Blend mode list arrow** on the Property inspector, then click **Soft Dodge**.

   The result colors have a deep orange color cast and the sand dunes dominate the image, as shown in Figure 43.

5. Drag the **Sahara sunset object** on top of the KB object.

(continued)

FIGURE 42
Soft Dodge blend mode

Result colors

Click list arrow to select blend mode

FIGURE 43
Results of blend mode on reversed objects

FIGURE 44
Adjusted opacity with blend mode

Opacity

6. Click the **Opacity list arrow** on the Property inspector, then drag the slider to **75**.

   The result colors are slightly less dramatic, as shown in Figure 44.

7. Deselect the Sahara sunset object.

8. Save your work, then close sculpted_stucco.png.

You applied a blend mode, compared the same blend mode applied to objects in a different order, and adjusted the opacity of an object.

Darken and lighten pixels.

1. Open fw4_4.png, then save it as **goats.png**.
2. Verify that the Info panel is open.
3. Select the Burn tool and set the following properties: Brush tip size: 70, Edge: 100, Square brush tip, Range: Highlights, and Exposure: 35.
4. Verify that the Habitat layer is selected, darken the pixels of the top rock ledge in one motion, from the trees to just before the standing goat at the top of the canvas.
5. Select the standing goat to the upper-right of the picture, select the Dodge tool, and then set the following properties: Brush tip size: 20, Edge: 100, Round brush tip, Range: Midtones, and Exposure: 50.
6. Lighten the pixels of the goat at the top of the canvas.
7. Save your work.

Replicate and stamp pixels.

1. Select the Rubber Stamp tool and set the following properties: Size: 100, Edge: 78, and Source aligned selected.
2. Make sure the Habitat object is selected, then select pixels in the rock face between the large walking goat and the baby goats on the left side of the canvas.
3. Stamp the pixels over the large goat to the left so that it no longer appears. (*Hint*: You can drag the pointer or click repeatedly.)
4. Save your work.

Erase and blur pixels.

1. Select the Eraser tool and set the following properties: Size: 45, Edge: 100, Round eraser, and Opacity: 60%.
2. Select the Goat_in_wild object, then erase the blue sky to the left of the goat at the top of the canvas. (*Hint*: Use Figure 45 as a guide.)

3. Select the Habitat object, select the Blur tool, and set the following properties: Size: 48, Edge: 28, Round brush tip, and Intensity: 30.
4. Blur the trees at the top of the canvas.
5. Save your work.

FIGURE 45
Completed Skills Review (1)

Replace color.

1. Select the Replace Color tool and set the following properties: Size: 50, Shape: Round brush tip, Tolerance: 100, and Strength: 200.
2. Set the Change color to the white clouds behind the blurred trees and the To color to #003399.
3. Replace the colors in the region where you blurred the trees.
4. Save your work.

Create a bitmap mask.

1. Add a mask to the Habitat layer using the Add Mask button on the Layers panel.
2. Select the Gradient tool and a Linear gradient that is White, Black.

3. Place the pointer slightly below the ledge where the baby goats are standing, then drag the pointer to the bottom of the canvas.
4. Save your work.

Understand color.

1. Use the Text tool or open a document in your favorite word-processing program, then save it as **color**.
2. Describe the part of the electromagnetic spectrum that is visible to the human eye.
3. Explain what happens when white light is separated into its component colors.
4. Explain the difference between RGB and CMYK color modes.
5. Write your name at the top of the file, then save and close it.

Create vector masks.

1. Open fw4_5.png, then save it as **zoo2u.png**.
2. Create a mask that pastes the giraffeskin bitmap inside the text. (*Hint*: Cut the bitmap.)
3. Ungroup the object and mask.
4. Create a mask that pastes the text as a mask. (*Hint*: Cut the text.)
5. Select the Show fill and Stroke check box on the Property inspector (if necessary).
6. Save your work.

Disable, enable, and apply a mask.

1. Disable the mask.
2. Enable the mask.
3. Delete the mask and apply changes.
4. Save your work.

Sample and store color.

1. Make sure the goats.png document is active, then show and select the text object.
2. Select the Eyedropper tool, then sample the baby goat with a 5x5 average at approximately 378 X/235 Y.
3. Display the Swatches panel and add the swatch to the panel.
4. Compare your image to Figure 45.
5. Save your work, then close goats.png.

Use Creative commands.

1. Copy the giraffeskin bitmap object, then numerically transform it to 25%.
2. Move and center the copied bitmap object below the original.
3. Apply a twist and fade command and set the following properties: steps: 8, spacing: 14, rotation: 154, and opacity: 75.
4. Apply a picture frame Creative command and set the following properties: pattern: Cloth-Blue and Frame Size: 10.

5. Compare your image to Figure 46.
6. Save your work, then close zoo2u.png.

Remove red eye.

1. Open fw4_6.png, then save it as **bearhug.png**.
2. Select the Red Eye Removal tool and set the following properties: Tolerance: 93 and Strength: 68. (*Hint*: Zoom in as necessary.)
3. Remove the red eye glow.
4. Save your work.

FIGURE 46
Completed Skills Review (2)

Apply blending modes.

1. Zoom out so you can see the entire image, then show the gummies layer on the Layers panel.
2. Set the Blend mode to Fuzzy Light.
3. Drag the bearhug layer above the gummies layer, then set the Blend mode to Fuzzy Light.
4. Notice the difference between the same blend mode applied to a different object.
5. Set the Blend mode to Tint.
6. Compare your image to Figure 47.
7. Save your work, then close bearhug.png.

FIGURE 47
Completed Skills Review (3)

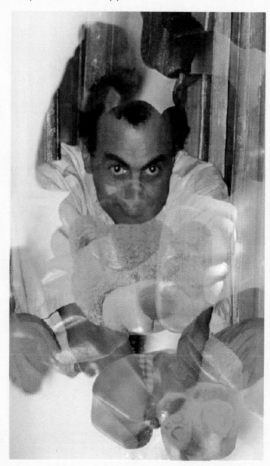

To boost morale, your company is going to hold a treasure hunt. Your division was assigned the lowest morale rating, so management has decided you should coordinate the event. Your first step is to announce the treasure hunt in an e-mail message.

1. Obtain images that pertain to a treasure hunt and use the one provided. You can obtain images from your computer, from the Internet, from a digital camera, or from scanned media. You can use images from the Web that are free for both personal and commercial use (check the copyright information for any such files before downloading them).

2. Create a new document and save it as **treasure_hunt.png**.

3. Import ship.jpg, then resize it as necessary to fit in your document.

4. Use the images you've obtained to create at least one vector or bitmap mask. (*Hint*: The sailing ship in the sample is a bitmap mask of the ship and a map with the Alpha Channel option selected.)

5. Apply at least one Creative command to two objects. (*Hint*: The happy faces were created and twisted using Creative commands.)

6. Create other visual elements using the images you've downloaded, changing their size, color, and other properties as needed.

7. Save your work, then examine the sample shown in Figure 48.

FIGURE 48
Sample Completed Project Builder 1

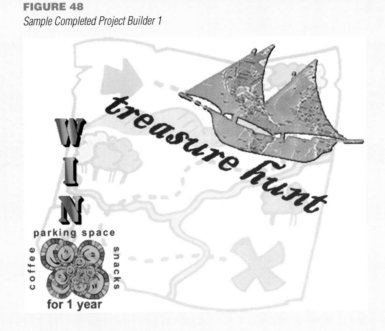

A local organic food coop is going to feature a produce item each month. They
want to include the item in both in-store
posters and on their Web page. You're
going to develop the intro splash screen,
featuring at least two uses of the fruit or
veggie. You can choose the produce item
of your choice.

1. Obtain images that will fit your theme. You
   can obtain images from your computer,
   from the Internet, from a digital camera, or
   from scanned media. You can use images
   from the Web that are free for both personal
   and commercial use (check the copyright
   information for any such files before downloading them).
2. Create a new document and save it as
   myproduce.png.
3. Import at least two files into your document
   or open and select them using the bitmap
   selection tools.
4. Apply bitmap or vector masks to at least two
   of the images. (*Hint*: The two coconut
   images in the sample each have bitmap
   masks applied to them.)
5. Apply a vector mask to text. (*Hint*: The text
   has another coconut image pasted inside it.)
6. Use the bitmap retouching tools or sample
   the colors in the document, as necessary.
   (*Hint*: Various coconuts have been erased or
   rubber stamped.)

7. Apply one of the Creative commands to the
   object of your choice. (*Hint*: The image
   has an Add Picture Frame command
   applied to it.)

FIGURE 49
Sample Completed Project Builder 2

8. Save your work, then examine the sample
   shown in Figure 49.

Finding the right images for your project is one of the first steps in creating a good design. Using those images in your design often requires that you change them so that they best convey your intent or message. Because dynamic Web sites are updated frequently to reflect current trends, this page might be different from Figure 50 when you open it online.

1. Connect to the Internet and go to *www.course.com*. Navigate to the page for this book, click the Student Online Companion, then click the link for this unit.
2. Open a document in a word processor, or open a new Fireworks document, then save the file as **shorebank**. (*Hint*: You can use the Text tool in Fireworks to answer the questions.)
3. Explore the site and answer the following questions:
   ■ Identify the possible order of the images above and below the navigation bar on the Layers panel.
   ■ Is a masking technique evident? If so, identify.
   ■ Which images could have been erased, rubber stamped, or sampled?
   ■ Who is the target audience for this site, and how does the design reinforce that goal?
   ■ How are photographic images and illustrations used in the site?
   ■ What changes would you make to this site?
4. Save your work.

FIGURE 50
Design Project

Your group can assign elements of the project to individual members, or work collectively to create the finished product.

Your class on international trading requires your group to create a faux import company and design its Web page. Your group must decide on the country or region, and the wares you'll sell.

1. Obtain images of the country you've chosen or the products you'll sell. You can obtain images from your computer, from the Internet, from a digital camera, or from scanned media. You can use images from the Web that are free for both personal and commercial use (check the copyright information for any such files before downloading them).

2. Create a new document and save it as **imports.png**.

3. Import the files into your document or open and select them using the bitmap selection tools.

4. Apply a vector or bitmap mask to at least one image. (*Hint*: The lake and building image has a bitmap mask applied to it.)

5. Use the bitmap retouching tools, as necessary. (*Hint*: The trees have been rubber stamped, the building at the left has been blurred, and parts of the images have been erased.)

6. Sample the colors in the document, as necessary. (*Hint*: The title text was sampled using the color of the boat and has an Eye Candy 4000 LE Motion Trail effect applied to it.)

7. Apply at least one Creative command to your document. (*Hint*: The lake and building image has been converted to a sepia tone.)

8. Apply at least one blend mode to the document. (*Hint*: The text has a Luminosity blend mode applied to it, with the color layer beneath it.)

9. Save your work, then examine the sample shown in Figure 51.

FIGURE 51
Sample Completed Portfolio Project

5 WORKING WITH
INTERACTIVITY

1. Create slices and hotspots.

2. Create links.

3. Create rollovers.

4. Create buttons.

Understanding Web Functionality

One important goal of any Web site is to engage the viewer. Interactivity is one way to accomplish this. Your Web site can change appearance or perform specific tasks based on input from the user. For example, you can set up a graphic to display additional information when a user rolls the mouse over it, or you can design a button that sends the user to another page on your site when the user clicks it. Anyone who has surfed the Web has taken advantage of interactivity. Fireworks makes it easy to add these features to your own site.

You can split your document into manageable or functional pieces by defining individual slices in your document. Once defined, for example, you can optimize each slice separately based on the type of

artwork it contains and how important the image quality is to the exported file. You can also add interactivity that causes something to happen in response to a mouse action. For example, when the mouse pointer moves over a slice, the text can change color, or a drop-down menu or image can appear anywhere on the screen. Fireworks offers several ways to add behaviors to a slice, depending on the complexity of the behavior or on your work preference. Best of all, you don't need to learn a programming language.

You can use hotspots to link users to Web pages within your Web site or anywhere on the Web. You can apply behaviors to hotspots or use hotspots to enable behaviors.

You can also easily create buttons in your document that aid your visitors in navigating your Web site.

Tools You'll Use

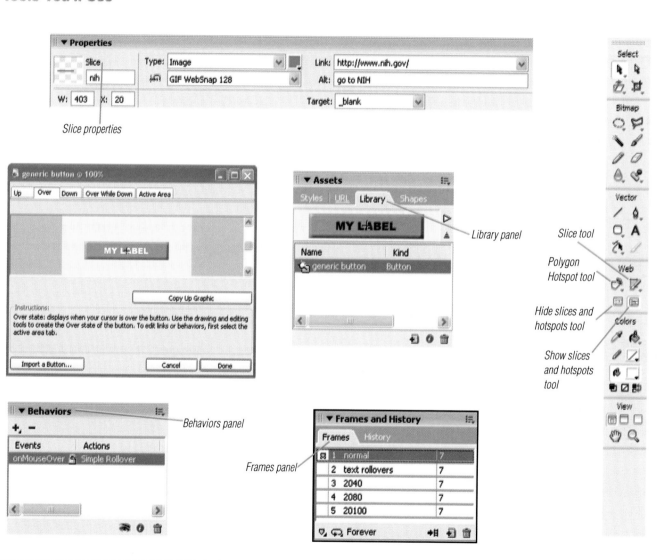

Slice properties

Library panel

Slice tool

Polygon Hotspot tool

Hide slices and hotspots tool

Show slices and hotspots tool

Behaviors panel

Frames panel

CREATE SLICES
AND HOTSPOTS

What You'll Do

 In this lesson, you will add slices and hotspots to a document.

Understanding Interactivity

On a conceptual level, **interactivity** involves a dialog or an exchange between the user and the Web site. Interactivity can be as simple as a button changing appearance when the user clicks it, or as complex as an animation that is launched each time a user clicks a graphic. Interactivity allows visitors to your Web site to affect its content—input from the user via the mouse or the keyboard can cause something to happen on-screen.

Understanding Slices and Hotspots

You use slices and hotspots to add interactivity to your Web document. Think of a **slice** as containing the image (and any interactivity you've assigned) beneath it. Each slice exports as a separate image file, which offers distinct advantages. You can add individual functionality to each slice, which will help visitors navigate your site and will give the site its unique look and feel. You can also easily update the information associated with individual slices,

especially information that changes frequently, such as a featured product or person. Finally, you can export each slice in the file format that best matches its use on your Web page. For example, you may want to export photographs as JPEGs, or line art as GIFs. To create a slice, you can use the Rectangular Slice tool or the Polygon Slice tool on the Tools panel and then draw the slice shape you want, or you can select an object and use the Slice command from the Insert command on the Edit menu.

A **hotspot** is an area in your document to which you can assign a Web address, known as a **uniform resource locator (URL)**, or other type of navigational interactivity, such as an e-mail message pop-up window. Hotspots initiate specific actions, such as linking to a new Web page, after being triggered by a mouse action. A hotspot can also initiate a behavior in a browser, such as a swap image pop-up menu. You can create a hotspot of just about any shape, using the Rectangle Hotspot tool, Circle Hotspot tool, or

Polygon Hotspot tool on the Tools panel. You can also create a single hotspot from multiple images. You can apply many of the same options, such as inserting URL links, to both slices and hotspots. The options on the Property inspector change slightly, depending on whether you select a slice or a hotspot. An **image map** is a graphic that has one or more hotspots associated with it. For example, assume you have one large graphic, such as a map, and you want users to be able to click on a region of the map for specific information. You can create hotspots over each region, assign a different URL to each hotspot, and then export the graphic containing the hotspots as an HTML file that includes image map data.

QUICKTIP

Before you can use a slice or hotspot tool, first click the Show slices and hotspots button on the Tools panel or click the Show/Hide icon on the Web Layer of the Layers panel.

What precisely is in a slice or a hotspot? Until you export them, they don't actually "contain" anything. During export, Fireworks uses slices and hotspots to write HTML code. The code instructs your Web browser to execute certain commands, such as changing a button color, swapping an image, or linking to a URL.

When slicing, you should try to create neatly spaced slices that emulate a grid pattern, and remember to try to leave no

region unsliced. Slicing allows you to optimize and export the areas in your document in pieces. To export efficiently, the pieces should fit together well. If you leave gaps in between slices, Fireworks will export additional files, which can increase the number of downloadable files. For optimal functioning, slices should be contiguous (adjacent to each other); if they do overlap, Fireworks applies the attributes assigned to the top slice. The sample document shown in Figure 1 depicts a document partially sliced, with slices and hotspots turned off and on in a document.

FIGURE 1
Slices and hotspots in a document

Document as it appears in a Web browser

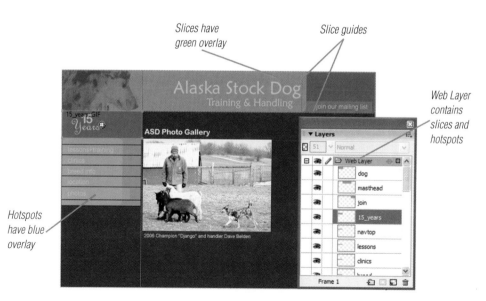

Slices have green overlay

Slice guides

Web Layer contains slices and hotspots

Hotspots have blue overlay

Understanding the Web Layer on the Layers Panel

Because slices and hotspots are Web objects, Fireworks stores them on the **Web Layer** of the Layers panel. The Web Layer is always the top layer on the Layers panel and you cannot delete it. However, you can create, name, hide, show, and delete objects on the Web Layer just as you do with other objects on the Layers panel.

The names of the slices on the Web Layer determine the name of the image file when you export the slice. Slice names cannot have spaces, uppercase letters, forward slashes, and high ASCII characters. High

ASCII characters extend the basic ASCII set. They include characters and letters from foreign languages and drawing symbols for characters 128 to 156. You can change the default naming convention for all slices by selecting options in the Document Specific tab of the HTML Setup dialog box, available on the File menu. You should refer to Help for additional information before you make changes.

Customizing Slice Overlay and Guide Colors

By default, Fireworks uses a light blue overlay for hotspots, a lime green overlay for slices, and red slice guide lines. Depending on the colors in your document, you might want to change these colors so you can distinguish them more readily (the overlays won't be visible to the user). You can change the hotspot or slice overlay color by selecting a slice or hotspot, and

then clicking the Color box on the Property inspector to open the color pop-up window. You can edit guides by opening the Guides dialog box from the Guides command on the View menu to change slice guide color or to hide or show the slice guides. You can change the color of an individual slice or a group of slices, which can help you organize them in your document. Note that slice and guide colors are document-specific. Figure 2 shows how to change slice overlay and guide colors.

FIGURE 2
Slice overlay and guide colors

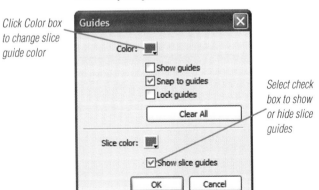

Click Color box to change slice guide color

Select check box to show or hide slice guides

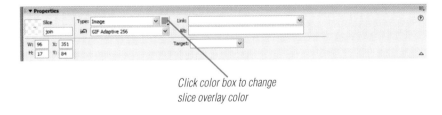

Click color box to change slice overlay color

Create a slice from an object

1. Open fw5_1.png, then save it as **offworld.png**.

2. Click **View** on the menu bar, then verify that **Slice Guides** and **Slice Overlay** are selected.

3. Verify that the **Show slices and hotspots button** ⊞ is selected on the Tools panel.

   Slices and hotspots already inserted in the document are visible.

   TIP Objects on the Web Layer appear grayed out until the Show slices and hotspots button is active.

4. Click the **Pointer tool** ▸ on the Tools panel (if necessary), then click the **head object** on the canvas to select it.

5. Click **Edit** on the menu bar, point to **Insert**, click **Rectangular Slice**, then compare your image to Figure 3.

   A slice covers the head and a new Slice object appears at the top of the Web Layer on the Layers panel.

   TIP You can also insert a rectangular slice by pressing and holding [Alt][Shift][U] (Win) or [option][Shift][U] (Mac).

6. Name the new Slice object at the top of the Web Layer **head**.

   The slice name automatically changes in the Edit the object name text box on the Property inspector.

   TIP You can also rename a slice on the Property inspector.

You inserted a slice on top of an object.

FIGURE 3
Newly added slice

Slice covers image

Fireworks autonames slice on Property inspector

Slice is assigned a default name in the Layers panel

Use the Slice tool to create a slice

1. Click the **CONTACT US text** on the red navigation bar to select it.

2. Click **Edit** on the menu bar, point to **Insert**, click **Rectangular Slice**, then compare your image to Figure 4.

    The slice covers the text only, leaving the rectangular area around the text unsliced.

3. Press **[Backspace]** (Win) or **[delete]** (Mac) to delete the slice.

4. Click the **Slice tool** 🖉 on the Tools panel, then draw a slice over the CONTACT US rectangle and text, as shown in Figure 5.

    | TIP   Zoom in on the object as necessary.

5. Change the name of the Slice object to **contactus** in the **Edit the object name text box** on the Property inspector, then press **[Enter]** (Win) or **[return]** (Mac).

    The slice name automatically changes on the Web Layer on the Layers panel.

You created a slice using the Slice tool.

FIGURE 4
Slice inserted over text

Slice covers text

FIGURE 5
Drawing a slice with the Slice tool

Draw slice over text and rectangle

FIGURE 6

Selected slice and areas to be sliced

Slice guide

Remaining areas
to be sliced

Slice covers
entire area

FIGURE 7

Results of resizing slice

Drag slice to be
even with existing
slice guides

Edit a slice

1. Click the **Pointer tool** on the Tools
   panel, then click the **Off This World title text**
   to select the slice, as shown in Figure 6.

   The slice guidelines created by the text slice
   are visible. You will extend the slice to cover
   the remaining blue area above the words Off
   This World.

2. Click **View** on the menu bar, point to **Guides**,
   then verify that **Snap to Grid** is not selected.

3. Drag the **left sizing handles** to the left side
   of the canvas.

   Resizing a slice or polygon is similar to
   resizing any object on the canvas.

   | TIP You can drag the slice guides of any
   | slice to change its size or position.

4. Drag the **other sizing handles** until the slice
   covers the entire blue area, then compare
   your image to Figure 7.

   | TIP Slices should align with other slices.

You edited a slice to cover an area.

Create a hotspot with the Circle Hotspot tool

1. Click the **Show/Hide Layer icon** next to the planetback slice object on the Web Layer to hide it.

2. Click the **Pointer tool** on the Tools panel (if necessary), then click the **planet object** on the canvas to select it.

3. Press and hold the **Rectangle Hotspot tool** on the Tools panel, then click the **Circle Hotspot tool**.

4. Draw a circular hotspot around the WHO'S PLAYING text, as shown in Figure 8.

   | TIP   Use the arrow keys to align the hotspot.

5. Change the name of the Hotspot object to **who**.

You created a circular hotspot.

FIGURE 8
Results of the Circle Hotspot tool

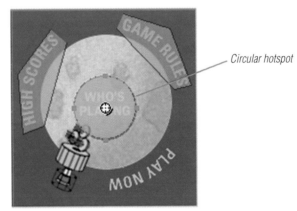

Circular hotspot

FIGURE 9
Using the Polygon Hotspot tool

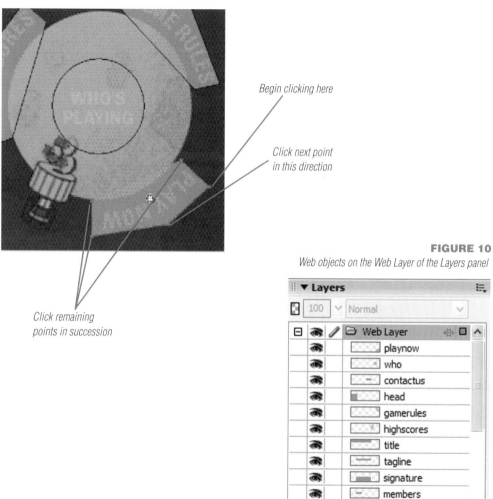

Begin clicking here

Click next point
in this direction

Click remaining
points in succession

FIGURE 10
Web objects on the Web Layer of the Layers panel

Use the Polygon Hotspot tool

1. Press and hold the **Circle Hotspot tool** 🔘 on the Tools panel, then click the **Polygon Hotspot tool** 🔷 .

   TIP You can use the Polygon Slice tool to create a polygon slice in the same manner.

2. Click the canvas in the locations and direction shown in Figure 9 to create a polygon hotspot.

   A polygon hotspot covers the text, but does not touch the other hotspots so that the links will be distinct.

3. Change the name of the hotspot to **playnow**.

4. Click the **Show/Hide Layer icon** ▢ next to the planetback slice object on the Web Layer to show it.

5. Compare your Web Layer on the Layers panel to Figure 10.

6. Save your work, then close offworld.png.

You created a polygon hotspot.

CREATE
LINKS

What You'll Do

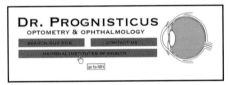

 In this lesson, you will add relative, absolute, and e-mail links to slices, add alternate text to the links, and preview the links in Fireworks and in a Web browser.

Assigning a URL to a Slice or Hotspot

After you create a Web object, you can assign a URL to it and link it to a Web page. For example, you can select a hotspot in the document and enter a URL and other options in the Property inspector. You can insert a URL in the Link text box, or select a URL from a previously entered address or a selected URL library. When a user clicks the link in a Web browser, the browser navigates to that Web page. If you enter **alternate text** in the Alt text box on the Property inspector, it appears when you position the mouse pointer over a slice or hotspot. Alternate text resembles a tool tip in Fireworks—the text that appears when you hold the mouse over a tool on the Tools panel. Note, however, that alternate text behaves differently (or not at all) depending on your browser and computer platform. In some Web browsers, this text might appear as the linked URL is loading in the browser. Alternate text also appears if

graphics are not turned on in a Web browser and can be crucial for visually impaired Web surfers. For example, if the user has a screen reader to interpret pages, the reader reads the alternate text out loud. Without the alternate text, the screen reader has nothing to read and the user does not know that the link exists.

You can determine how the linked Web page will be displayed in the browser by selecting an option in the Target text box. For example, the Web page can open in a separate window or replace the current Web page. Target options are shown in Figure 11 and described in detail in the following list:

- **_blank** opens the link in a new browser window (unnamed).
- **_parent** opens the link in the parent frameset (the Web page that joins the frame pages together) of the current frame.
- **_self** replaces the link in either the current frame or browser window.
- **_top** opens the link in the full browser window, replacing all frames.

QUICKTIP

If you do not specifically select a target option, a URL link opens in the current browser window.

You can assign different types of URLs as links. An **absolute URL** is fixed and is the full and exact address of a Web page. Use absolute URLs when linking to a Web page outside of your Web site. A **relative URL** is a link based on its location as it relates to the current page in the Web site's folder. You can use a relative URL to link to a page within your Web site. You can also create a **mailto URL** to open an e-mail address window.

Accessing URLs
You might want to add the same URL to several slices or hotspots in different documents, such as a Home button. Fireworks stores each URL you enter in the Current URL list in the URL panel and displays it on the Property inspector. You can use the URL panel to store often-used URLs, or delete and edit URLs. After you open a document that contains a URL list, you can access these addresses for every document you open during the *current* editing session. If you add a URL to a library, you can access it at any time and in any document. You can add individual URLs to the main URLs.htm library, create your own **libraries** (such as related groups of URLs), and import URLs from a Netscape Navigator Bookmarks file or from an Internet Explorer Favorites file.

Understanding Preview Options
When you add interactivity such as a URL link to a slice, you can preview the mouse action in a preview view on the Document window, although the Preview view is the most efficient view. The Preview views display the document as it would appear in a Web browser, using the current optimization settings. To actually link to the URL and view alternate text, you need to preview your document in a Web browser. Fireworks allows you to preview a document in up to two different browsers. Depending on the computer and the browser, your Web document might appear and function differently. It's a good idea to preview your Web page using different settings on different systems.

QUICKTIP

To set a Web browser for preview in Fireworks, click the applicable primary or secondary browser option from the Preview in Browser command on the File menu, select the folder where your browser software is located, click the executable (.exe) filename (Win) or the application (Mac), then click Open (Win) or Choose (Mac).

FIGURE 11
Link properties on the Property inspector

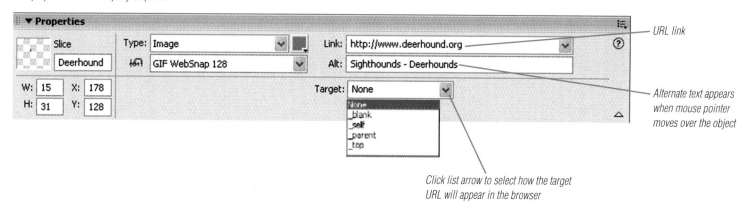

URL link

Alternate text appears when mouse pointer moves over the object

Click list arrow to select how the target URL will appear in the browser

Assign relative and absolute links to slices

1. Open fw5_2.png, then save it as **eyedoc.png**.

2. Click the **Show slices and hotspots button** on the Tools panel (if necessary).

3. Click the **Pointer tool** on the Tools panel, then click the **SEARCH OUR SITE slice** to select it.

4. Click the **Link text box** on the Property inspector, type **searchpage.htm**, then press **[Enter]** (Win) or **[return]** (Mac).

   TIP When published, the HTML file referenced by a relative link is in the same folder as the current HTML file.

5. Click the **Alt text box**, type **search our site**, press **[Enter]** (Win) or **[return]** (Mac), then compare your Property inspector to Figure 12.

6. Click the **NATIONAL INSTITUTES OF HEALTH slice** to select it.

7. Click the **Link text box** on the Property inspector, type **http://www.nih.gov/**, then press **[Enter]** (Win) or **[return]** (Mac).

   TIP After you add a link, you can assign it to another slice or hotspot by selecting a Web object, clicking the Link list arrow, and then clicking the link you want.

8. Click the **Alt text box**, type **go to NIH**, then press **[Enter]** (Win) or **[return]** (Mac).

9. Click the **Target list arrow**, then click **_blank**.

   The URL opens in a new browser window.

You assigned links to slices and set alternate text and a target.

FIGURE 12
Entering alternate text

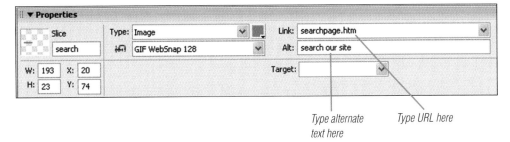

Type alternate text here

Type URL here

FIGURE 13
Preview in Fireworks

*Pointer indicates
interactivity*

Preview links in Fireworks and in a browser

1. Click the **Preview button** 🔲 Preview on the Document window.

   The current slice appears without a white translucent slice over it.

2. Click the **Hide slices and hotspots button** 🔲 on the Tools panel.

3. Move the mouse pointer over the SEARCH OUR SITE object, then compare your image to Figure 13.

   TIP Alternate text is not visible when you preview in Fireworks.

4. Click **File** on the menu bar, point to **Preview in Browser**, then click the first browser in the list to open the primary browser.

   TIP You can press [F12] (Win) or [option][F12] (Mac) to open the primary browser. Press [Ctrl][F12] (Win) or ⌘ [F12] (Mac) to open the secondary browser.

   (continued)

5. Move the mouse pointer over the **SEARCH OUR SITE** and **NATIONAL INSTITUTES OF HEALTH objects**, then compare your image to Figure 14.

The alternate text is visible when the mouse pointer moves over the objects.

| TIP   Depending on your browser, alternate text might not be visible.

6. Click the **NATIONAL INSTITUTES OF HEALTH object**.

If you are online, the browser opens the home page of the National Institutes of Health in a new browser window.

7. Close your browser windows.

You previewed the document in Fireworks and in your primary browser.

FIGURE 14
Previewing in a Web browser

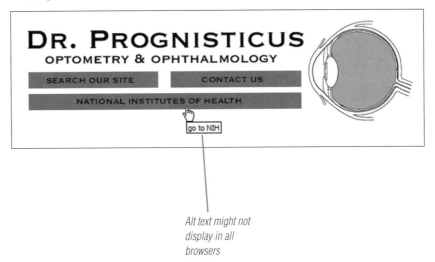

Alt text might not display in all browsers

FIGURE 15
E-mail message window opening from your browser

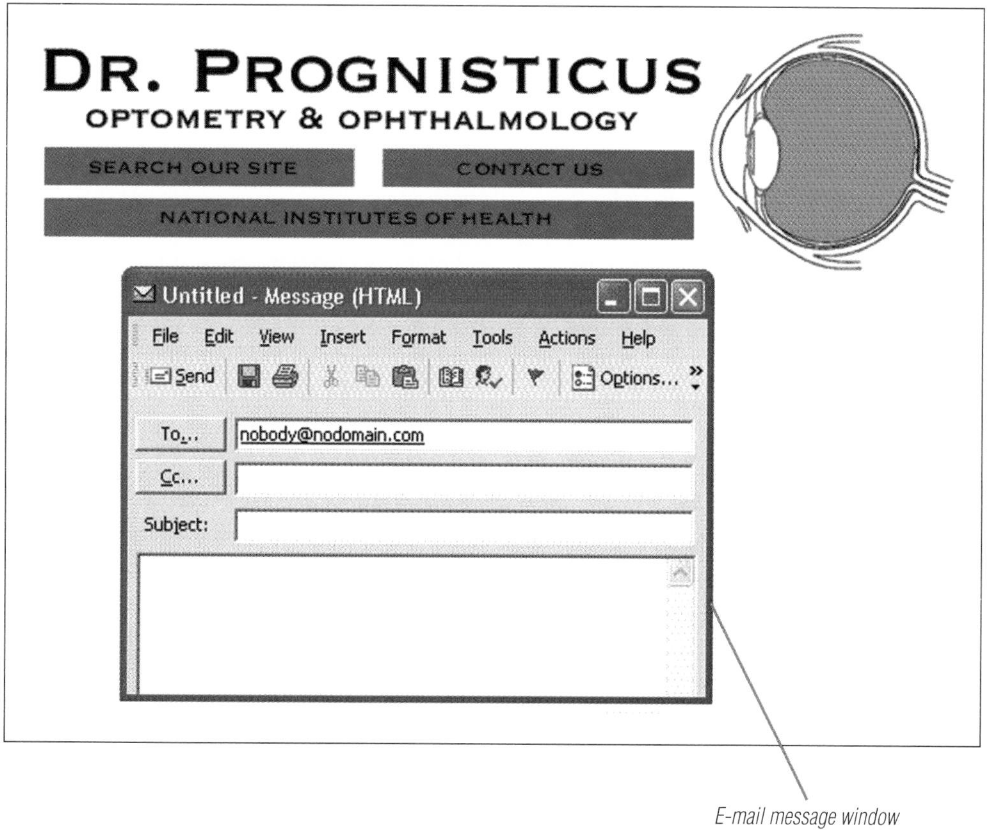

E-mail message window

1. Click the **Original button** ✎ Original on the Document window.

2. Click the **Show slices and hotspots button** 🖼 on the Tools panel.

3. Click the **contact slice** on the Layers panel to select it.

4. Click the **Link text box** on the Property inspector, type **mailto:nobody@nodomain.com**, then press **[Enter]** (Win) or **[return]** (Mac).

5. Click the **Alt text box**, type **contact us**, then press **[Enter]** (Win) or **[return]** (Mac).

6. Preview your image in your browser, move the mouse pointer over the **CONTACT US** link, then click the object.

   A new Untitled e-mail message window opens addressed to nobody@nodomain.com.

7. Compare your image to Figure 15, close the e-mail window without saving, then close your browser.

   | TIP   If prompted to save changes, click No.

8. Save your work, then close eyedoc.png.

You assigned an e-mail message window link to a slice.

CREATE
ROLLOVERS

▶ *In this lesson, you will create rollovers for different slice objects.*

Understanding Rollovers

In a basic Web page, graphics often change appearance in response to a mouse action—more specifically, one graphic is often swapped for another graphic when you click it or roll over it with the mouse. In Fireworks, a rollover contains a behavior. A **rollover** is a graphic element in a Web page that changes appearance when you trigger it with the mouse. The trigger can be a roll or a click and the result can occur anywhere on the Web page. A **disjoint rollover** is a rollover that swaps an image in a different part of the screen than where you triggered it. To create a rollover, you need to coordinate a few items: first, you need to create at least two images and at least one new frame, then create a slice over the image to be swapped. Finally, add an action that results in a change in appearance.

Working with Behaviors

You create a rollover action by adding a behavior to a slice, button, or hotspot. A **behavior** is a preset piece of JavaScript code that consists of an **event trigger** (such as a mouse click on an object) that causes an **action** (such as text changing color or a photograph appearing). **JavaScript** is a Web-scripting language that interacts with HTML code to create interactive content. You can think of behaviors as the means by which Fireworks encapsulates JavaScript so you can easily add them to Web objects.

Fireworks provides different ways to add a behavior: you can add a behavior from the Behaviors panel, drag and drop a behavior onto a slice, or write your own JavaScript. The Behaviors panel contains five main behavior groups, ranging from a simple rollover to a pop-up menu and navigation bar, as shown in Figure 16. Dragging and dropping from a slice or hotspot onto another slice is the fastest way to add a behavior. When you add a behavior to a slice or a hotspot, a **behavior handle** appears at the center of the object. You can drag a behavior handle and drop a rollover behavior onto the same slice or onto a different slice. A blue behavior line extends from the behavior handle to the top left of the affected slice, indicating that you've applied a behavior to it. You can use the drag-and-drop behavior to attach a behavior to one or more slices, and to easily swap an image in a rollover.

Usually, you create two images for a rollover: one for the event trigger (the *before* version), and another copy of the object as the action (the *after* version).

QUICK**TIP**

For swap image behaviors, you can fully expand the Behaviors panel horizontally to view additional slice details.

Using the Frames Panel

The Frames panel contains the frames for your document. Fireworks uses **frames** to house various rollover and button state images and to play animation (which you'll learn about in the next chapter). By default, each document has one frame, Frame 1, which contains the images that appear when a user first opens the Web page. To function, a rollover requires at least one additional frame. For example, in a simple rollover, the original image appears in Frame 1, and the "after" image appears in Frame 2. After you create a

behavior, you can modify or move the images in your document without affecting the behavior. You can edit the objects that lie beneath a slice or hotspot by hiding the slice or hotspot before you edit the object. Figure 17 shows the progression of a simple rollover.

QUICK**TIP**

You can also edit an object while slices and hotspots are displayed by clicking and holding the Pointer tool on the Tools panel and then clicking the Select Behind tool.

FIGURE 16
Behaviors panel

FIGURE 17
Progression of a simple rollover

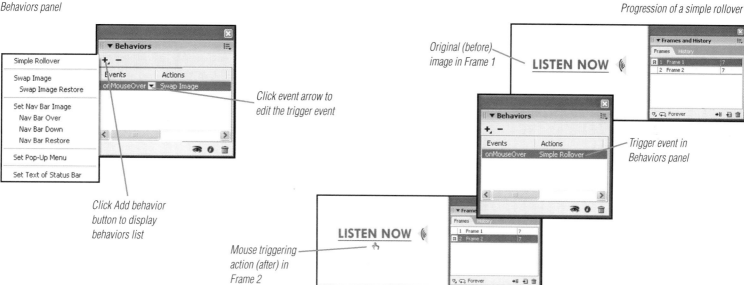

Click event arrow to edit the trigger event

Click Add behavior button to display behaviors list

Original (before) image in Frame 1

Trigger event in Behaviors panel

Mouse triggering action (after) in Frame 2

Add a swap image behavior to a slice

1. Open fw5_3.png, then save it as **eyetest.png**.

2. Click **Window** on the menu bar, click **Frames**, click **Window** on the menu bar, then click **Behaviors**.

   The Frames and History panel opens, showing four frames with the first frame, normal, selected, and the Behaviors panel opens.

3. Click the **Preview button** 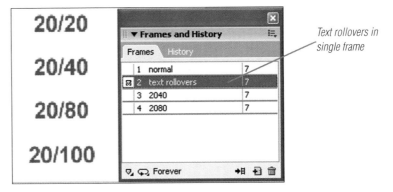 on the Document window, then move the mouse pointer over the **20/20**, **20/40**, and **20/80** text objects, noticing how the text color changes as the mouse rolls over each number pair.

   The 20/100 text object does not have a behavior assigned and does not change.

4. Click the **text rollovers frame** (Frame 2) on the Frames panel, then compare your image to Figure 18.

   Each of the text objects has been copied in red to Frame 2. If you were working in a new document, you would need to add a frame at this step. You will use the text rollovers frame as the target for your rollover.

5. Click the **Original button** 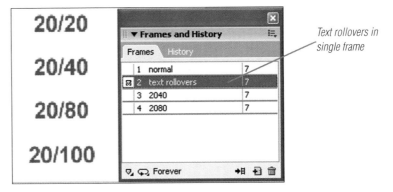 on the Document window, click the **normal frame** on the Frames panel, then click the **Show slices and hotspots button** on the Tools panel.

   The document has slices already inserted in it.

   (continued)

FIGURE 18
Text rollovers frame

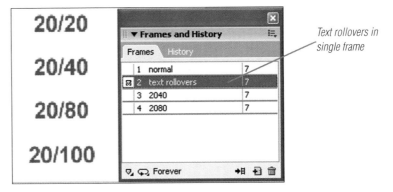

Text rollovers in single frame

FIGURE 19
Text rollovers frame

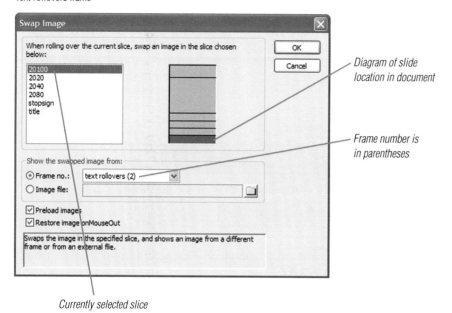

Diagram of slide
location in document

Frame number is
in parentheses

Currently selected slice

6. Click the **20100 slice** on the Web Layer on the Layers panel to select it, then click the **Add behavior button** ➕ on the Behaviors panel.

7. Click **Swap Image** from the behaviors list, then compare your dialog box to Figure 19.

    The Swap Image dialog box opens, showing a list and diagram of existing slices.

8. Verify that **20100** is the currently selected slice and that **text rollovers (2)** appears as the Frame No., click **OK**, then compare your image to Figure 20.

    The Swap Image behavior appears in the Behaviors panel, and a blue behavior line appears from the Behavior handle to the edge of the slice. The image will swap from Frame 2, text rollovers.

9. Click the **Preview button** 🖼Preview on the Document window, then click the **Hide slices and hotspots button** ▦ on the Tools panel.

10. Roll the mouse pointer over the **20/100 text object**, noticing that it changes color, just like the other text objects.

You applied a Swap Image rollover behavior to a slice.

FIGURE 20
Swap Image behavior applied to slice

Blue behavior
line indicates
swap image
behavior is
connected to
the same slice

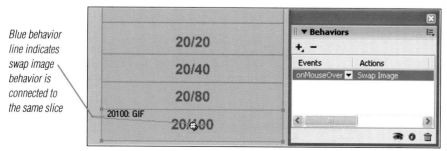

Create and duplicate a frame

1. Click the **Original button** ✎ Original on the Document window.

2. Click the **2080 frame** (Frame 4) on the Frames panel, then click the **New/Duplicate Frame button** ⊞ on the bottom of the Frames panel.

   A new blank frame, Frame 5, appears as the bottom frame. It would require several steps to copy the stop sign into the blank frame and prepare it for the rollover; duplicating and editing an existing frame is often an easier alternative.

3. Click the **Delete Frame button** 🗑 on the bottom of the Frames panel to delete Frame 5.

4. Click the **2080 frame** on the Frames panel (if necessary), then drag it on top of the **New/Duplicate Frame button** ⊞ on the bottom of the Frames panel, as shown in Figure 21.

   A copy of the 2080 frame appears in Frame 5.

   | TIP You can also duplicate a frame by clicking the Options menu button and then clicking Duplicate Frame.

5. Double-click **2080** in Frame 5, type **20100**, then press **[Enter]** (Win) or **[return]** (Mac).

You duplicated an existing frame in the Frames panel and renamed it.

FIGURE 21
Duplicating a frame in the Frames panel

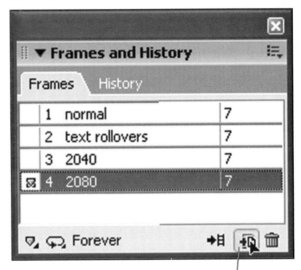

Drag selected frame on top of New/Duplicate Frame button to duplicate it

FIGURE 22

Multiple rollovers from a single slice

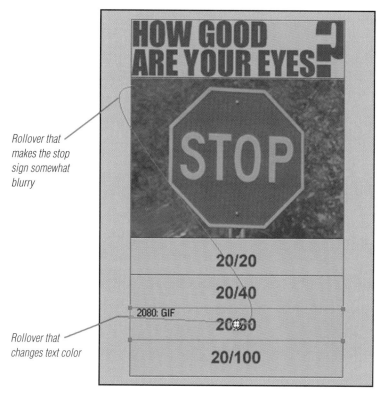

Rollover that
makes the stop
sign somewhat
blurry

Rollover that
changes text color

2080: GIF

HOW GOOD
ARE YOUR EYES?

STOP

20/20

20/40

20/60

20/100

Add a disjoint rollover to a slice

1. Click the **20100 frame** on the Frames panel (if necessary), then click the **stop sign image** on the canvas to select it.

   TIP Be sure to select slices and frames as specified in these steps.

2. Double-click the **Gaussian Blur filter** in the Filters section on the Property inspector, drag the **Blur radius slider** to **6.6**, then click **OK**.

   The stop sign image is very blurry.

3. Click the **Show slices and hotspots button** 🖿 on the Tools panel, click the **normal frame** (Frame 1) on the Frames panel, then click the **stopsign slice** on the canvas.

   TIP The three behavior lines are visible for the rollovers that connect the visual acuity text to the stop sign.

4. Click the **2080 slice** on the canvas, then compare your image to Figure 22.

   Two behavior lines are visible: the rollover behavior connected to the text (red) and the rollover behavior that connects the text to the stop sign (blurry).

5. Click the **20100 slice** on the canvas.

   The behavior line for the existing text rollover is visible.

   (continued)

6. Position the **pointer** 🖑 over the **behavior handle**, then drag a behavior line to the top-left corner of the stop sign image, as shown in Figure 23.

The behavior line connects the slice to the image and the Swap Image dialog box opens.

7. Click the **Swap image from list arrow**, click **20100 (5)**, then click **OK**.

A new behavior line connecting the 20100 slice to the stop sign appears on the canvas. When the mouse rolls over the 20/100 text object, the stop sign image will swap with the image in Frame 5, 20100 (5), and appear very blurry.

You added a disjoint rollover to a slice.

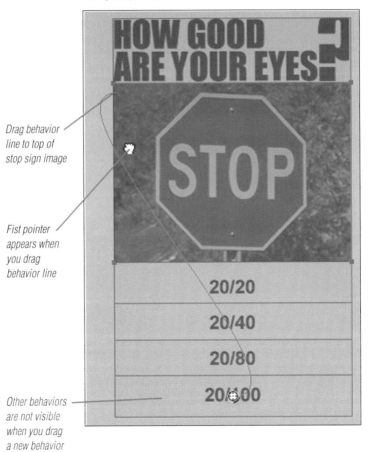

FIGURE 23
Adding a disjoint rollover

Drag behavior line to top of stop sign image

Fist pointer appears when you drag behavior line

Other behaviors are not visible when you drag a new behavior line

FIGURE 24
Previewing rollovers

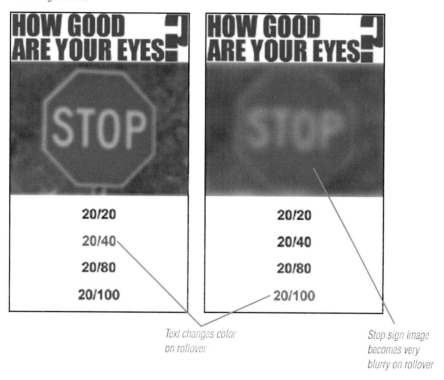

*Text changes color
on rollover*

*Stop sign image
becomes very
blurry on rollover*

1. Click the **Preview button** Preview on the Document window, then click the **Hide slices and hotspots button** on the Tools panel.

2. Roll the mouse over each of the visual acuity measurements starting with 20/20, 20/40, and so on, as shown in Figure 24, noticing the changes in the text and the stop sign image.

   When the mouse rolls over each text object, the text color changes to red and the stop sign becomes increasingly blurry.

3. Save your work, then close eyetest.png.

You previewed and tested the rollovers in Fireworks.

CREATE
BUTTONS

What You'll Do

In this lesson, you will convert an object to a symbol and use it to create buttons.

Understanding Symbols and Instances

As you work with Web graphics, you'll find that you want to reuse graphical elements in your documents. The easiest way to reuse a specific object is to convert it to a **symbol**. Fireworks supports three types of symbols: graphic, animation, and button. Graphic symbols can be a combination of objects. Animation symbols have different properties, such as frame count, distance, direction, and scale, each with a slightly different depiction of the image. Button symbols contain up to four frames that correspond to the button's appearance based on a mouse action.

Fireworks stores symbols in the **Library panel**. Symbols are document-specific, although you can drag a symbol from one document to another. As soon as you convert an object on the canvas to a symbol or drag, import, or copy a symbol from the Library panel onto the canvas, it is known as an **instance**. You can think of an instance as being a shortcut to its symbol—any edit you make to the symbol affects each instance in

the document, which makes global modifications to a symbol extremely efficient. You also reduce file size considerably by using symbols instead of duplicating graphics in your document. Using the Symbol Properties dialog box, you can name a symbol and choose the type of symbol you need.

QUICKTIP

If you reuse a graphic element in a document, it's advisable to convert that object to a symbol and modify properties of its instances as needed.

Understanding Buttons and Button States

Adding buttons to your Web page can serve a dual purpose. Functionally, they provide your users with a well-configured way to navigate around the site. Visually, buttons can be a design element that distinguishes your site from others. Fireworks lets you create a button from nearly any graphic or text. As you've no doubt noticed in your own Web surfing, a button changes appearance based on the mouse action you've performed. A button can have up to four **states** associated with it, although most contain two, Up (or normal) and Over. For example, modifying a button in the Over state causes the button's appearance to change when you roll the mouse over it. Figure 25 shows common button states.

QUICKTIP

When you drag an instance of a button symbol to the canvas, the instance automatically has a slice added to it.

You can assign button states using the Button Editor. The available button states are described in the following list.

Up—Default state, not affected by mouse movement.

Over—State when mouse passes over button.

Down—State when user clicks button.

Over While Down—State when mouse passes over button after user clicks it (in Down state).

Active Area—The active area of the button is defined by a slice object linked to the button. Use the Property inspector to define the URL and other link properties when the button instance is selected on the canvas.

Using the Library Panel

You can create, duplicate, edit, and import symbols in your document using the Library panel. When you create a new document,

the Library panel is empty. As you create symbols, Fireworks adds them to the Library panel. The Library panel is divided into a preview area and a list of symbols. You can sort symbols by name, type, and date and toggle their sort order. Each symbol type has a unique icon in the Library panel, but the instances of every symbol on the canvas share a common small arrow icon, indicating that the object is a symbol instance. Figure 26 shows a sample Library panel.

QUICKTIP

You can duplicate a symbol in the Library panel by dragging it on top of the New symbol button on the bottom of the Library panel.

FIGURE 25
Button Editor and sample button states

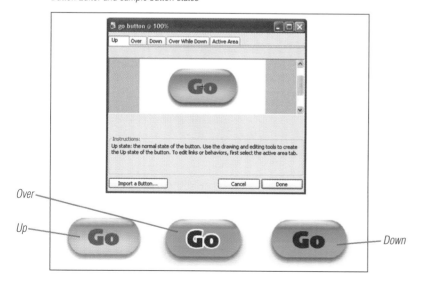

FIGURE 26
Symbols in the Library panel

Symbol preview

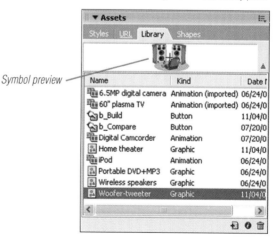

Create a button symbol

1. Open fw5_4.png, save it as **petpalace.png**, then verify that the Hide slices and hotspots button is selected.

2. Click **Window** on the menu bar, then click **Library**.

   | TIP You can also open the Library panel by pressing [F11] (Win) or [option][F11] (Mac).

3. Click the **Pointer tool** 🔍 on the Tools panel (if necessary), press and hold **[Shift]**, click the **red rectangle**, click the **MY LABEL text** on the canvas, then release **[Shift]**.

4. Click **Modify** on the menu bar, point to **Symbol**, then click **Convert to Symbol**.

   The Symbol Properties dialog box opens.

   | TIP You can also convert an object to a symbol by pressing [F8].

5. Type **generic button** in the Name text box, click the **Button option**, compare your screen to Figure 27, then click **OK**.

   A new button symbol, generic button, appears in the Library panel, and an arrow icon appears on the instance on the canvas.

   | TIP You can also assign a target to a button symbol.

6. Compare your image to Figure 28.

You converted two objects to a single button symbol.

FIGURE 27
Symbol Properties dialog box

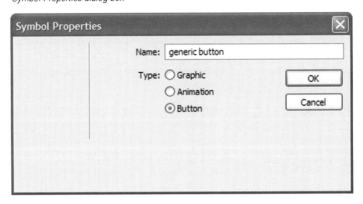

FIGURE 28
Button added to Library panel

Arrow icon indicates object is an instance

New button symbol

FIGURE 29

Copying the Up graphic in the Button Editor

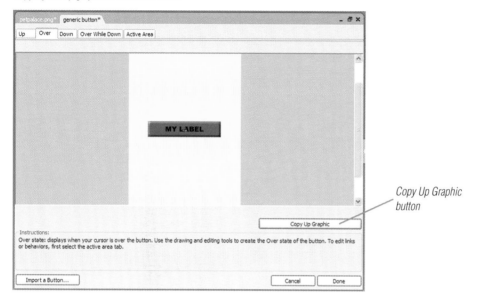

Copy Up Graphic
button

FIGURE 30

Previewing the button in the Over state

Button in
Over state

Add a rollover state to a button

1. Double-click the **generic button instance** on the canvas.

   The Button Editor opens, with the title of the currently selected symbol in the title bar.

2. Click the **Over tab**, click the **Copy Up Graphic button** to copy the objects from the Up tab, then compare your Button Editor to Figure 29.

3. Click the **rectangle object**, then double-click **Inner Bevel filter** in the Filters section on the Property inspector.

4. Click the **Button preset list arrow**, click **Highlighted**, then click **a blank part** of the Fireworks window.

5. Click the **MY LABEL text object**, click the **Color box** ▪ on the Property inspector, click the **first white color swatch**, then click **Done** on the Button Editor.

   TIP   You may need to move the Property inspector to see the Done button.

6. Click the **Preview button** 🖼Preview on the Document window.

7. Roll the mouse pointer over the generic button to view it in the Over state, then compare your image to Figure 30.

   The rectangle appears lighter and the text turns white.

You added a rollover state to a button.

Duplicate button instances

1. Click the **Original button**  on the Document window.

2. Verify that the generic button symbol is selected on the canvas.

3. Press and hold **[Alt]** (Win) or **[option]** (Mac), then drag a duplicate instance of the button instance directly below the original instance, as shown in Figure 31.

4. Click **Edit** on the menu bar, then click **Repeat Duplicate** to duplicate and place another instance on the canvas.

   Three duplicate button instances are aligned on the canvas.

   | TIP You can also repeat the last action by pressing [Ctrl][Y] (Win) or ⌘ [Y] (Mac).

You created two duplicates of a button instance.

Customize and preview instances

1. Click the **top instance** to select it, select the text in the **Button name text box** on the left side of the Property inspector, type **dogs**, then press **[Enter]** (Win) or **[return]** (Mac).

   The button symbol on the Layers panel is renamed "dogs."

2. Select the text in the **Text box** on the Property inspector, type **DOGS**, press **[Enter]** (Win) or **[return]** (Mac), then compare your Property inspector to Figure 32.

   The text on the dogs button instance is renamed "DOGS."

(continued)

FIGURE 31
Duplicated button instance

Drag instance
below original

FIGURE 32
Renamed symbol and edited text on the Property inspector

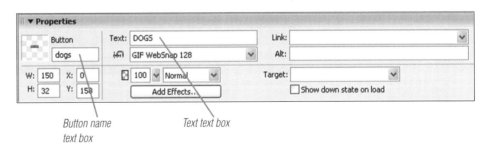

Button name
text box

Text text box

FIGURE 33
Edited symbol and text

Edited symbol
and text

FIGURE 34
Previewing new buttons

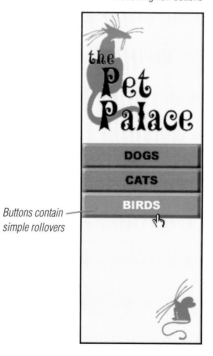

Buttons contain
simple rollovers

3. Repeat Steps 1 and 2 for the middle instance, changing the name of the button to **cats** and the text to **CATS**, as shown in Figure 33.

4. Repeat Steps 1 and 2 for the bottom instance, changing the name of the button to **birds** and the text to **BIRDS**.

5. Click the **Show slices and hotspots button** ▦ on the Tools panel, then notice that the buttons have slices added to them.

6. Click the **Hide slices and hotspots button** ▦ on the Tools panel, then click the **Preview button** ▦ Preview on the Document window.

7. Test the buttons, then compare your image to Figure 34.

   TIP You would complete the document by adding a slice to the mouse area and adding links for the buttons.

8. Save your work, then close petpalace.png.

You edited the text for buttons and
previewed them.

Add slices to a document.

1. Open fw5_5.png, then save it as **zoo.png**.
2. Show slices and hotspots.
3. Select the Giraffe image and insert a slice over it.
4. Name the slice **giraffepic**.
5. Select the Slice tool, then draw a slice over the Feedback text.
6. Name the slice **feedback**.
7. Save your work.

Add hotspots to a document.

1. Select the Circle Hotspot tool, then draw a hotspot over the giraffe's face.
2. Name the hotspot **facepic**.
3. Select the Polygon Hotspot tool, then draw a hotspot that outlines the Zoo text and exclamation mark.
4. Name the hotspot **zoo**.
5. Compare your image to Figure 35.
6. Save your work, then close zoo.png.

FIGURE 35
Completed Skills Review (1)

Create links in a document.

1. Open fw5_6.png, then save it as **tax4u.png**.
2. Show slices and hotspots.
3. Select the visit slice and enter the following relative link: **visitorpage.htm**.
4. Enter the following Alt text: **Visit Us**.
5. Select the irs slice and enter the following absolute link: **http://www.irs.gov/**.
6. Enter the following Alt text: **Internal Revenue Service**.
7. Select the contact slice and enter the following e-mail link: **mailto:nobody@nodomain.com**.
8. Enter the following Alt text: **Contact Us**.
9. Hide slices and hotspots.
10. Preview the document in Fireworks and in a browser.
11. Compare your image to Figure 36.
12. Save your work, then close tax4u.png.

FIGURE 36
Completed Skills Review (2)

Add a swap image behavior to a slice.

1. Open fw5_7.png, then save it as
   toyparade.png.
2. Show slices and hotspots.
3. Select the dolls slice on the canvas.
4. Open the Behaviors panel.
5. Add a Swap Image behavior to the slice and
   select the buttons over (2) frame.
6. Hide slices and hotspots.
7. Preview the rollover in Fireworks.
8. Save your work.

Create a duplicate frame.

1. Return to Original view, then show slices
   and hotspots.
2. Open the Frames panel, then select the
   books over frame.
3. Add a new frame, then delete it.
4. Duplicate the books over frame.
5. Change the name of the duplicated frame to
   dolls over.
6. Select the Text tool with the following properties: Font: Arial Narrow, Font Size: 11,
   Color: White, and Bold.
7. Change the text on the canvas to
   COLLECTIBLE DOLLS & ACTION FIGURES.
   (*Hint*: Open the Text Editor if you cannot see
   the text easily.)
8. Save your work.

Add a disjoint rollover to a slice.

1. Select the dolls slice on the canvas. (*Hint*:
   You should still have the dolls over frame
   selected.)

2. Drag the Behavior handle to the left side of the
   dark blue rectangle where the text appears.
3. Select dolls over (6) as the Swap image
   from frame.

FIGURE 37
Completed Skills Review (3)

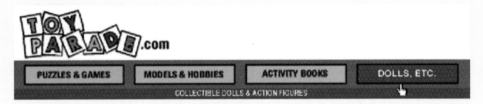

4. Hide slices and hotspots.
5. Preview the rollover in Fireworks, then compare your image to Figure 37.
6. Save your work, then close toyparade.png.

Convert objects to a button symbol.

1. Open fw5_8.png, then save it as **visitrome.png**.
2. Open the Library panel.
3. Select the green rectangle and the NAVIGATION text.
4. Convert the objects to a button symbol.
5. Change the name of the symbol to **navigation button**.

Create button states.

1. Open the Button Editor from the Symbol Properties dialog box.
2. Select the Over tab, then copy the Up graphic.
3. Change the color of the rectangle to #999900.
4. Change the text color to black (#00000).
5. Close the Button Editor, then preview the button in Fireworks.
6. Save your work.

Duplicate button instances.

1. Return to Original view.
2. Select the navigation button on the canvas (if necessary).
3. Duplicate the navigation button on the canvas two times.
4. Save your work.

Customize and preview button symbols.

1. Change the name of the left button instance on the Property inspector to **airfares**.
2. Change the text on the button instance to **AIRFARES**.

3. Change the middle button name to **hotels** and the text to **HOTELS**.
4. Change the right button name to **sights** and the text to **SIGHTS**.

FIGURE 38
Completed Skills Review (4)

5. Preview the buttons in Fireworks, then compare your image to Figure 38.
6. Save your work, then close visitrome.png.

The people in your apartment building have decided to hold a massive yard sale and donate the proceeds to your local animal shelter. You've volunteered to add to the mass confusion by designing a Web site for the clothing section so that folks can catalog what they're bringing. You've seen these people, understand their fashion sense, and pretty much know what to expect to spring from their closets.

1. Obtain images that will reinforce your theme. You can obtain images from your computer, from the Internet, from a digital camera, or from scanned media. You can use images from the Web that are free for both personal and commercial use (check the copyright information for any such file before downloading it).

2. Create a new document and save it as **geekchic.png**.

3. Import the following file and the files you obtained in Step 1 into your document or open and select them using the bitmap selection tools.
   ■ picture.jpg

4. Create a title, tagline, and at least five objects for accessory- and clothing-related sections. (*Hint:* To keep with the geekchic visual style, try to avoid straight-line text.)

5. Draw hotspots over each of the accessory and clothing links and add appropriate absolute, relative, and e-mail links and alternate text.

6. Rename Web Layer objects and Layer objects.

7. Save your work, then examine the sample shown in Figure 39.

FIGURE 39
Sample Completed Project Builder 1

You recently won a free art class about masks and mask making. After studying the universal fascination with masks, the class made their own masks. You have crafted what you'd hoped would be an elegant Venetian mask, but you've decided to express your mask appreciation using your Fireworks skills instead. An owner of a mask gallery has asked you to create a Web page for the gallery.

1. Obtain images of masks that will fit your theme. You can obtain images from your computer, from the Internet, from a digital camera, or from scanned media. You can use images from the Web that are free for both personal and commercial use (check the copyright information for any such file before downloading it).

2. Create a new document and save it as **maskgallery.png**.

3. Copy or import the files into your document or open and select them using the bitmap selection tools.

4. Create at least six additional objects or buttons as desired, then draw slices or hotspots over them as needed.

5. Apply multiple behaviors, including disjoint rollovers, to at least six slices, hotspots, or buttons. Add frames as necessary. (*Hint*: The objects at the bottom have a swap image applied to them.)

6. Add a relative, absolute, and e-mail link and alternate text to at least three slices. (*Hint*: The mask buttons and navigation buttons at the bottom have links and alternate text applied to them.)

7. Rename Web Layer objects and Layer objects and add slices as necessary.

8. Preview the document, save your work, then examine the sample shown in Figure 40.

FIGURE 40
Sample Completed Project Builder 2

In general, creativity can be about bending or even breaking the rules. When it comes to interactivity in a Web site, however, you ultimately need to keep your users in mind. The discussion of form versus function in Web page design can be a lively one. Because dynamic Web sites are updated frequently to reflect current trends, this page might be different from Figure 41 if you open it online.

1. Connect to the Internet and go to *www.course.com*. Navigate to the page for this book, click the Student Online Companion, then click the link for this chapter.
2. Open a document in a word processor, or open a new Fireworks document, then save the file as **interactive**. (*Hint*: You can also use the Text tool in Fireworks to answer the questions.)
3. Explore several sites, then, when you find one or two that interest you, answer the following:
   - Discuss your ideas on real-world interactivity using the following examples. Include how motivation and expectation affect interactivity:
     - Opening the wrapper of your favorite candy bar.
     - Walking on an icy sidewalk.
     - Filling out a job or school application or completing a tax form.
   - Who is the target audience for this site, and how does the design reinforce that goal?
   - Describe the interactivity in this site.
   - Identify buttons and rollovers.
   - Identify hotspots and links.
   - Is the site form- or function-oriented? Explain.
   - How would you change the interactivity in this site?
4. Save your work.

FIGURE 41
Design Project

Your group can assign elements of the project to individual members, or work collectively to create the finished product.

Your group is going to design an informative Web page that promotes learning through technology. Your group will choose the technology you want to promote and how to best convey your message.

1. Obtain images of the technology you've chosen. You can obtain images from your computer, from the Internet, from a digital camera, or from scanned media. You can use images from the Web that are free for both personal and commercial use (check the copyright information for any such file before downloading it).

2. Create a new document and save it as **mytech.png**.

3. Copy or import the files into your document or open and select them using the bitmap selection tools.

4. Create at least four objects or buttons as desired, then draw slices or hotspots over them as needed. (*Hint*: The circles have hotspots drawn on them.)

5. Apply multiple behaviors, including at least two disjoint rollovers, to the majority of your objects. Add frames as necessary. (*Hint*: The circles have an Over state that changes the color of the button and a disjoint rollover behavior applied to them that displays explanatory text. The text slices have a swap image that changes the position of the text.)

6. Rename Web Layer objects and Layer objects and add slices as necessary.

7. Preview the document, save your work, then examine the sample shown in Figure 42.

FIGURE 42
Sample Completed Portfolio Project

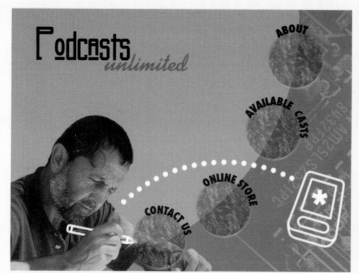

6

CREATING
ANIMATION

1. Prepare and plan animation.

2. Create basic animation.

3. Create frame animation.

4. Add tweening to animation.

5. Optimize, save, and export files.

chapter 6 CREATING ANIMATION

Planning

Developing and following a plan when you create an animation or a Web page ensures that your outcome will match your vision. Otherwise, you could spend a lot of time redoing pieces of your animation, or could discover that it does not function properly in a browser or look at all the way you had intended. However, even with the best tools at your fingertips, the most important aspect of successful animation is you, the designer.

Understanding Animation on the Web

Animation has become one of the most distinguishing and notorious features of the Web. Although pop-up windows and messages may command your attention simply because they're in the way of what you really want to be looking at, animation has the power to entice you. The most sophisticated online animation shares a common feature with its 90-year-old ancestor—it tells a story or shows change, however brief.

Fireworks features make it easy to add a lot of on-screen activity, so it might be tempting to animate everything you can. However, from a design perspective, you must keep your viewers in mind. Your visitors may very well leave a site that is over-the-top in moving images and blinking signs just as quickly as they would a static site.

Creating basic animation in Fireworks is as easy as creating a symbol and then completing a dialog box. Depending on what you want to animate, you can change frames one by one, or you can create more extensive animation by selecting two or more instances of the same symbol, modifying one, and directing Fireworks to create the frames that show the transition between them.

Ultimately, you'll want to use your graphics or animation on the Web or perhaps in another application. The optimization and export features in Fireworks ensure that your graphics or animation are in the best format for the medium you've chosen, and fine-tuned for use.

Tools You'll Use

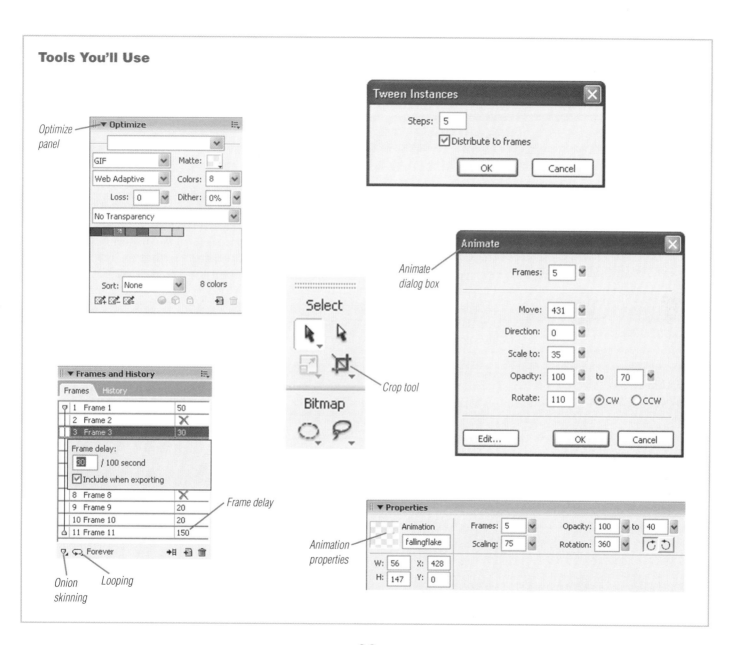

Optimize panel

Tween Instances

Animate dialog box

Crop tool

Frame delay

Animation properties

Onion skinning

Looping

PREPARE AND PLAN
ANIMATION

What You'll Do

Frame 1
heaping plate

Frame 6
rising steam
rolling meatball

Frame 15
small plate
rest. id

▶ *In this lesson, you will learn about planning. You will also learn how creating a storyboard before you create your Web site elements can lead to the best design for your site.*

Planning—Keyboard—Action!

Following a plan, such as a script, before speaking in front of a class or directing a $100M film is generally considered an asset that improves the final product. Although not considered particularly high-tech or exciting, planning is the critical piece that can determine the success of your animations and Web sites. When you integrate multimedia concepts into a Web page that includes interactive behaviors and animations, it's important to identify how these elements act together. You need to outline the structure of the Web page, such as its look and feel, as well as its content.

Understanding Storyboards

One of the most effective planning techniques is to create a storyboard.

DesignTIP **Storyboarding: from stick figure to action verb**

Storyboards originated in the early days of animation filming. With only a text script to guide them, animation directors could not adequately explain or depict dialog, camera angles, or camera effects. With a storyboard, each scene was sketched out, captioned, and, thus, made much easier to shoot. Animators made small, rough storyboards, which they posted by their drawing tables. These small sketches were known as *thumbnails*. Today, storyboarding is essential to any complex animation or computer game proposal.

Storyboard styles can be quick sketches, four-color art pieces, or even 3D models, known as animatics. Storyboard panels, individual studies, and even a single cel panel from an animation all figure prominently in the collectibles market. For example, a cel and background from the 1934 Disney cartoon, *Orphan's Benefit*, starring Donald Duck, sold for $286,000 (limited edition reprints are $1,500). If your interests are more historically inclined, you could pick up Del Sarto's *Head of St. Joseph*, a fragmentary chalk study for a painting, for $11,395,008 (2005 auction price).

A **storyboard** is a visual script you use to show action. It consists of a series of panels that plot the key scenes and illustrate the flow of the animation. For some animations, it can resemble a comic strip. Usually, each panel in a storyboard correlates to a keyframe in the animation. Learning to storyboard can be the first translation of the images in your head into the language of animation. Figure 1 shows a sample storyboard. Figure 2 shows the animation based on that storyboard.

For some people, having a visual guide inspires their creativity and their animation. Others might not consider it useful—especially for very short animation sequences. One of the benefits of creating a storyboard for any length animation is that you can clearly see the beginning, middle, and end of the sequence, which

can help you organize your ideas. After you create a baseline storyboard, you can use it as a springboard for more ideas and enhancements.

First, you should visualize the overall concept and decide how it can work in Fireworks. Then, construct the graphics for static images and animation, direct the movement of the animation, create the user interface, and present your product. You should begin by answering the following questions, adding any others that will further clarify your goals:

- What is the purpose of the animation or behavior? To introduce your logo? Solicit a mouse event? Just look cool?
- Where will this animation or interactive behavior appear?
- Who is the audience? Sale shoppers? Golfers? Online gamers?

- What resources do you have to work with? What is the source for your artwork? Who's paying for it?
- How many ideas do you need to express and how can you best convey them?
- Does your Web page have entertainment value, such as drama, humor, or shock?
- Who will review the storyboard? Clients? Friends?
- How will you receive and respond to feedback?

QUICKTIP

A quick way to determine if you need to remove or redo a scene on your storyboard is if you cannot determine what is going on in the scene without reading the storyboard panel's caption.

FIGURE 1
Sample storyboard for restaurant animation

FIGURE 2
Completed animation

Frame 1
heaping plate

Frame 6
rising steam
rolling meatball

Frame 15
small plate
rest. id

CREATE BASIC ANIMATION

What You'll Do

 In this lesson, you will insert instances of a symbol in the frames of a document, create an animation symbol, and store it in the Library panel.

Understanding Animation in Fireworks

Animation conveys action, and an action of some kind is often one of the goals of a Web site. Fireworks has several tools to use to add animation to your document. **Animation** is created by rapidly playing a series of still images in a sequence, which creates the illusion of movement.

You can use several techniques in Fireworks to animate objects. One easy way to create animation is to create an **animation symbol**. You can create an animation symbol out of any object or instance on the canvas. Large Fireworks documents can include many symbols and their instances. Animation symbols are an efficient way to manage animation, and you can create instances of animation symbols in any document. Fireworks stores symbol information, such as color and shape, when you create the symbol. After that, you are free to create and modify instances of the symbol.

Design TIP   Understanding animation and persistence of vision

Translating light into sight involves a fancy, albeit instantaneous exchange between your eyes and your brain. Depending on the brightness of an image, you can retain its impression for approximately $1/30^{th}$ of a second. Our capacity to retain an image even as a new image is "burned" on top of it is known as *persistence of vision*. It creates the illusion of movement. Because your eyes and brain cannot keep up with each new image, you're tricked into seeing smooth motion. Movies play at 24 frames per second, so our eyes never see that a film is dark approximately half the time. You can examine the concept of persistence of vision by watching a silent movie, which runs only 16 frames per second, and has noticeable flickering.

You can create an animation symbol by converting an object to a symbol and then selecting the Animation option in the Symbol Properties dialog box. You also create an animation symbol when you animate an object directly, using the Animation Selection command under the Animation command on the Modify menu. When you animate a selection, Fireworks automatically converts the object to an animation symbol and opens the Animate dialog box, shown in Figure 3. You can select the number of frames for the animation, how far the animation will move and in which direction, how much it will change in size or opacity, how much the symbol will rotate, and in which direction.

Click the Don't Show again check box to avoid seeing the prompt to add frames each time you animate a selection. To reset warnings, click Commands on the menu bar, then click Reset Warning Dialogs.

You can adjust the animation trail in your document by dragging the **motion path**; each dot on the path corresponds to a frame in the animation. To extend the animation, drag the green or red **animation handles**. To move the animation (and the object), drag a blue animation handle. To move to a particular frame, you can click a handle on the motion path.

QUICKTIP

Unlike Macromedia Flash or Director, Fireworks does not use keyframes or support sound files in animation.

After you create a symbol, you can change the attributes of the graphic on which it is based, such as color or size, and affect each instance of the symbol in your document. If you change the attributes of individual instances, you can add to the illusion of sophisticated animation, such as numerous multicolored lights blinking on and off. Using instances also helps you keep a manageable file size because you're simply using several instances of a single symbol.

FIGURE 3
Animate dialog box properties for sample animation

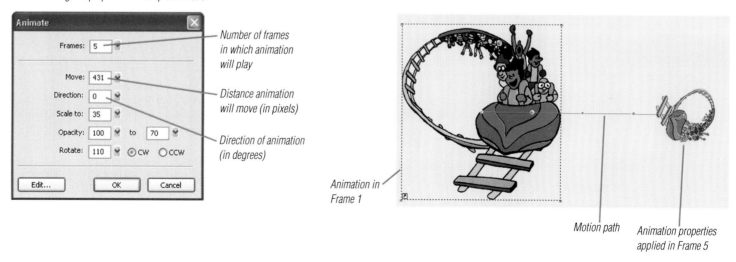

Number of frames in which animation will play

Distance animation will move (in pixels)

Direction of animation (in degrees)

Animation in Frame 1

Motion path

Animation properties applied in Frame 5

To edit the animation settings of an existing animation, select the animation instance on the canvas, and then change properties on the Property inspector.

Sharing Layers Across Frames

If you want nonanimated objects on a layer to appear in every frame, be sure to set the layer to share across frames. Otherwise, when you play an animation, the static images will only be visible in the first frame. If you share a layer across frames, each frame will include all the objects on that layer. You can edit an object in a layer that is shared across all frames at any time; Fireworks automatically updates the changes in every frame, which helps reduce file size.

QUICKTIP

To share a layer across frames, select a layer, then select the Share This Layer option on the Options menu in the Layers panel. To disable frame sharing, deselect Share This Layer, then choose how you want Fireworks to copy the object.

Previewing Animation

You can preview animation in the Original and Preview views by using the **frame controls** on the bottom of the Document window, as shown in Figure 4. You can play the animation as a whole or review it frame by frame. Note that previewing an animation in Original view might not convey an accurate rendering of how your animation will play on a Web page. You must first select an Export file format in the Optimize panel before you can accurately view and assess how your animation will play.

FIGURE 4
Playing an animation using frame controls

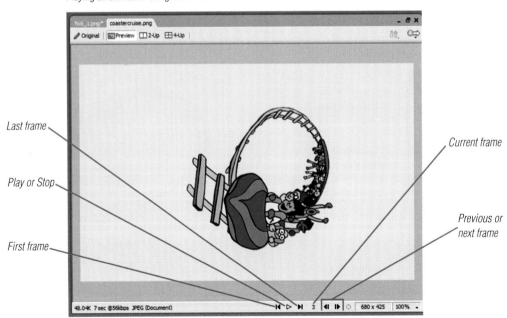

Last frame

Play or Stop

First frame

Current frame

Previous or next frame

Create and modify instances

1. Open fw6_1.png, then save it as **winterwonder.png**.

2. Open the Library and Frames panels.

   The document already contains instances of the snowflake symbol.

3. Click the **New/Duplicate Layer button** on the Layers panel, then change the name of the new layer to **Falling**.

4. Drag an instance of the **snowflake graphic symbol** from the Library panel to the top-right corner of the canvas.

5. Click **Modify** on the menu bar, point to **Transform**, click **Numeric Transform**, double-click the **Width percentage text box**, type **50**, then click **OK**.

6. On the Property inspector, type **428** in the X text box, type **0** in the Y text box, then press **[Enter]** (Win) or **[return]** (Mac).

7. Compare your image to Figure 5, then save your work.

   The scale settings are applied only to the selected instance.

You added an instance to a document and modified it.

Create an animation symbol

1. Click **Modify** on the menu bar, point to **Animation**, then click **Animate Selection**.

   The Animate dialog box opens.

   > TIP You can also press [Alt][Shift][F8] (Win) or [option][Shift][F8] (Mac) to open the Animate dialog box. (Mac users may also need to press and hold [Fn]).

   (continued)

FIGURE 5
Rescaled instance

Instance positioned
and scaled

2. Enter the values shown in Figure 6, click **OK** to close the dialog box, then click **OK** when prompted to automatically add new frames.

   A motion path is attached to the new animation symbol on the canvas, a new animation symbol is added to the Library, and the snowflake instance on the Layers panel becomes an animation symbol.

3. Compare your image to Figure 7.

4. Change the name of the animation symbol on the Property inspector to **fallingflake**.

You created an animation symbol and set animation properties.

Modify an animation

1. Drag the **red animation handle** to the bottom of the canvas, as shown in Figure 8.

   TIP Press and hold [Shift] to constrain the motion path to a straight line.

2. Click the **Play button** ▷ on the bottom of the Document window, then click the **Stop button** ■ after the animation has played a couple of times.

   The snowflake appears to fall, get smaller, and fade out, but none of the other images is visible except when the animation plays in Frame 1.

3. Click the **First frame button** ◁| on the Document window to return to Frame 1 (if necessary), then click the **fallingflake animation symbol** to select it.

   (continued)

FIGURE 6
Animate dialog box

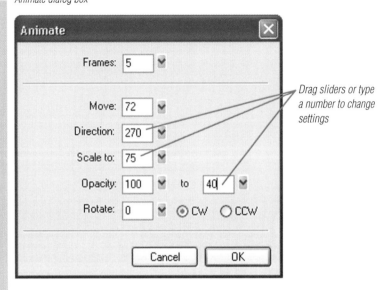

Drag sliders or type a number to change settings

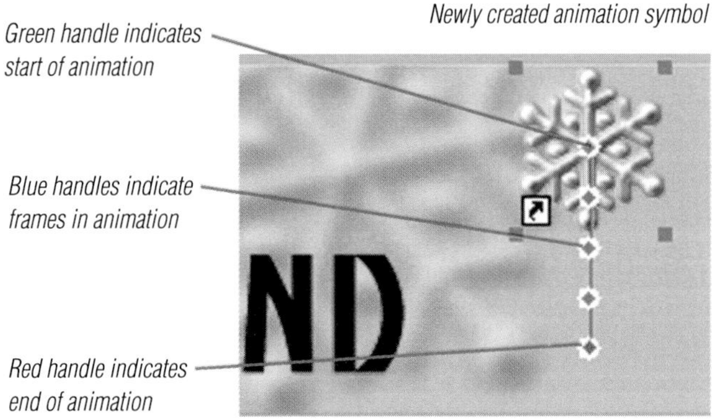

FIGURE 8
Modified motion path

Drag red handle to bottom of canvas

FIGURE 7
Newly created animation symbol

Green handle indicates start of animation

Blue handles indicate frames in animation

Red handle indicates end of animation

FIGURE 9

Layer shared across frames

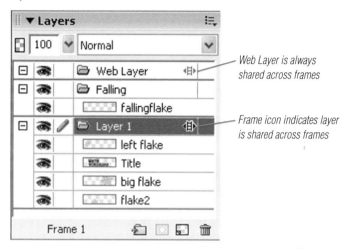

Web Layer is always
shared across frames

Frame icon indicates layer
is shared across frames

4. Double-click the **Rotation text box** on the
   Property inspector, type **360**, then press
   [Enter] (Win) or **[return]** (Mac).

   The snowflake will rotate during the animation.

5. Click **Layer 1** on the Layers panel to select
   all of its objects.

6. Click the **Options menu button** ≣, on
   the Layers panel, click **Share This Layer**,
   click **OK** in the warning dialog box that opens,
   then compare your Layers panel to Figure 9.

   All the images will be visible when the
   animation plays.

*You modified an animation and shared layers
across frames.*

Preview an animation

1. Click the **Play button** ▷ on the bottom
   of the Document window, then click the **Stop
   button** ■ after the animation has played
   a couple of times.

   The snowflake rotates and tumbles and the
   other images are visible in each frame.

2. Click the **Preview button** ▣ Preview on the
   Document window, then repeat Step 1.

   The animation plays at a slower pace.

3. Click the **Previous frame button** ◀❙ or
   the **Next frame button** ❙▶ until you reach
   Frame 3.

4. Compare your image to Figure 10.

5. Save your work, then close
   winterwonder.png.

*You previewed an animation in Original view and
in Preview view.*

FIGURE 10

Previewing animation

Static images from
Frame 1 appear in
each frame

Snowflake as it
appears in Frame 3

CREATE FRAME
ANIMATION

What You'll Do

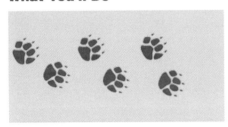

 In this lesson, you will create frame-by-frame animation, set the frame delay for different frames, and view several frames of the animation at once.

Understanding Frame-by-Frame Animation

You've seen how easy it is to animate an instance and modify its properties. You can also copy objects into different frames and then modify the objects in each frame, a process known as **frame-by-frame animation**. When you create an animation symbol, Fireworks automatically copies the image to the selected number of frames. Frame-by-frame animation requires that you create individual frames for your animation manually.

Frame-by-frame animation lets you change the physical attributes of the objects in each frame, such as color and effects. Because you control the changes in each frame, you can create effects such as text blinking from one color to another, or create gradual shape changes or distortions. However, you must make the changes in every frame you create, which is not an easy task. On the other hand, you do realize a certain historical authenticity with traditional animators, who had to draw each frame of their animations by hand.

Managing Animation with the Frames Panel

You use the Frames panel to manage the frames in your animation. You can rename frames (by default, they are numbered sequentially), and add, delete, move, copy, or exclude frames as needed. You can also set the number of times your animation will play in the browser and set its direction: forward or reverse. You can add, copy, delete, and rename frames on the Frames panel just as you do the layers on the Layers panel.

In addition to previewing your animation one frame at a time, you can also view several or all of the frames simultaneously. **Onion skinning** allows you to view one or more additional frames while in the current frame. The term refers to the superthin sheets of transparent paper used in traditional animation as overlays to view an animation series. By seeing where and how the preceding and succeeding frames interact with the image in the current frame, you can precisely align your animation. The Onion Skinning pop-up menu offers several frame choices for viewing frames, or you can create a custom range of frames to view. When onion skinning is turned on, the frames that precede and succeed the current frame are displayed in a lower opacity. Figure 11 shows sample onion skinning.

QUICKTIP

You can edit the objects that appear in the multiple frames when onion skinning is turned on. Click the Onion Skinning button on the bottom of the Frames panel, then click Multi-Frame Editing.

Understanding Frame Delay

You can fine-tune your animation by adjusting the display time or **frame delay** for each frame. Frame delay is measured in hundredths of a second—the default frame delay is 7/100 of a second. Even a small change can affect your animation dramatically: the lower the number, the faster the frame animation will play. If the frame delay is too short, the image will appear indistinct; if it is too long, the image will appear jerky or erratic. The frame delay is displayed in the right column of the Frames panel. You can adjust the delay for one or more frames at any time by pressing

and holding [Shift] as you click the frames whose frame delay you want to change. In addition to setting the frame delay, you can select the frames that will be included when you export the animation. When you deselect a frame, a large red X appears in place of the frame delay setting on the Frames panel, as shown in Figure 12.

QUICKTIP

To exclude an animation frame from the exported file, double-click the frame delay column, then deselect the Include when Exporting check box.

FIGURE 11
Sample onion skinning

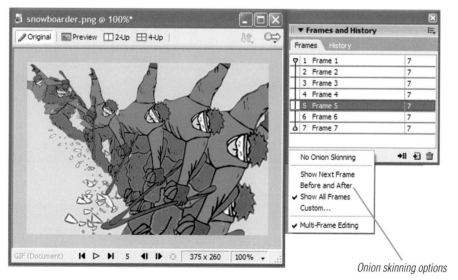

Onion skinning options

FIGURE 12
Sample frame delay

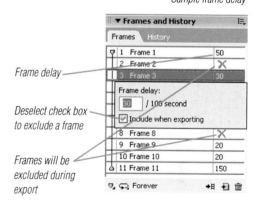

Frame delay

Deselect check box to exclude a frame

Frames will be excluded during export

Create frame-by-frame animation

1. Open fw6_2.png, save it as **bearpaw.png**, then notice the instances visible in the document as you click **Frame 2** and then **Frame 3** on the Frames panel.

   The document has an instance of the left paw and right paw graphic symbols placed in Frames 2 and 3.

2. Drag **Frame 3** on top of the **New/Duplicate Frame button**  on the bottom of the Frames panel to create a duplicate frame, Frame 4.

3. Drag an instance of the **left paw graphic symbol** from the Library panel above and in front of the right paw instance, as shown in Figure 13.

4. Repeat Step 2 to create a duplicate frame of Frame 4, then repeat Step 3 to drag an instance of the **right paw graphic symbol** from the Library panel below and in front of the new left paw instance.

5. Create two more frames, alternating between the left paw and right paw symbol, until your canvas resembles Figure 14.

6. Drag **Frame 7** on top of the **New/Duplicate Frame button** on the Frames panel, then drag an instance of the **grizzlies graphic symbol** from the Library panel to the center of the canvas.

(continued)

FIGURE 13
Instance added to duplicate frame

Position instance here

FIGURE 14
Instances positioned on the canvas

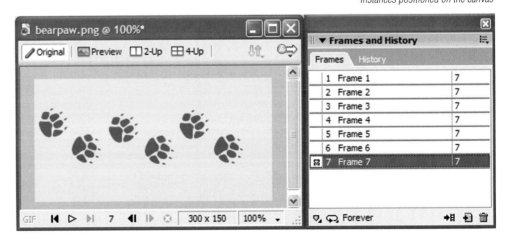

7. Drag **Frame 8** on top of the **New/Duplicate Frame button** on the Frames panel, click the **Filters button** in the Filters section on the Property inspector, point to **Shadow and Glow**, then click **Glow**.

8. Click the **Color box**, click the first magenta color swatch in the first column, press **[Enter]** (Win) or **[return]** (Mac), then compare your image to Figure 15.

You added instances to individual frames to create animation, and modified one of the instances you added.

FIGURE 15
Glow effect added to instance

Effect added to instance in Frame 9

Creating animation by distributing objects to frames and importing files

You can distribute objects to frames by selecting them and then clicking the Distribute to Frames button on the bottom of the Frames panel, or by clicking the Distribute to Frames command on the Frames panel Options menu. Fireworks automatically adds a frame for each object. You can use this method to easily import a Photoshop image sequence or a FreeHand file that has a blend animation.

Adjust frame delay

1. Click the **Play button** 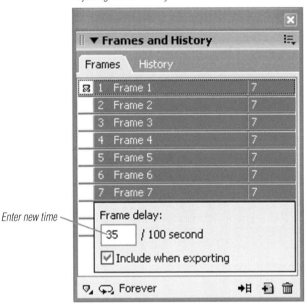 on the bottom of the Document window, then click the **Stop button** ■ after the animation has played a couple of times.

2. Click **Frame 1** on the Frames panel, press and hold **[Shift]**, then click **Frame 7**.

   Frames 1-7 are selected.

3. Double-click the **frame delay column**, type **35** in the Frame delay dialog box, verify that the **Include when exporting check box** is selected, as shown in Figure 16, then press **[Enter]** (Win) or **[return]** (Mac).

   The frame delay changes to 35 for the selected frames.

4. Double-click the **Frame Delay column** for Frame 9 on the Frames panel, type **100** in the Frame delay dialog box, then press **[Enter]** (Win) or **[return]** (Mac).

   The frame delay times for eight of the nine frames are modified, as shown in Figure 17.

5. Click the **Play button** on the bottom of the Document window, then click the **Stop button** ■ after the animation has played a couple of times.

   The animation pauses at the end when the text is visible.

You set the frame delay for different frames and previewed the animation in Fireworks.

FIGURE 16
Adjusting the frame delay

Enter new time

FIGURE 17
Modified frame delay times

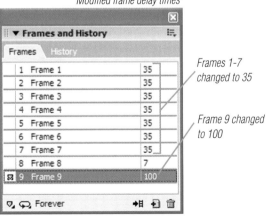

Frames 1-7 changed to 35

Frame 9 changed to 100

FIGURE 18
Onion Skinning dialog box

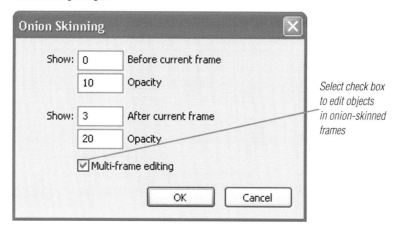

Select check box
to edit objects
in onion-skinned
frames

Use onion skinning

1. Click **Frame 5** on the Frames panel.

2. Click the **Onion Skinning button** ⬭
   on the bottom of the Frames panel, then
   click **Custom** to open the Onion Skinning
   dialog box.

3. Enter the values shown in Figure 18, then
   click **OK**.

   Frame 5 is visible at 100% and the next
   three frames are visible at 20% opacity.

4. Compare your image to Figure 19.

5. Click **Frame 1** and **Frame 6** and view the
   onion skinning setting in those frames.

6. Click the **Onion Skinning button** ⬭ on the
   bottom of the Frames panel, then click **No
   Onion Skinning** to turn off onion skinning.

7. Save your work, then close bearpaw.png.

*You viewed several frames of the animation
simultaneously.*

FIGURE 19
Viewing onion skinning

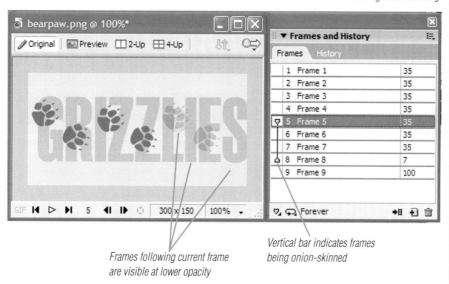

Frames following current frame
are visible at lower opacity

Vertical bar indicates frames
being onion-skinned

ADD TWEENING TO
ANIMATION

What You'll Do

 In this lesson, you will add frames to blend the movement between two instances in an animation.

Understanding Tweening

Animation mimics motion, but the movement may not always seem to flow evenly from one action to the next. The solution is to ease the transition between motion frames—the more frames in an animation, the more smoothly it plays. **Tweening** modifies or blends two or more instances of the same symbol and distributes them to the number of frames you set. As a result, the movement appears more fluid and less erratic. In Fireworks, you can add as many tweened instances of a symbol as you need to create just the animation you want.

Tweening can be very effective when the instances you want to animate are significantly different from instance to instance. For example, you can animate a ball so that it zooms in and out, as shown in Figure 20. When you tween instances, you can determine the number of steps you want to tween using the Tween Instances dialog box, which opens when you click Tween Instances from the Symbol command on the Modify menu. Fireworks creates new objects based on the number of steps you enter. The order in which the instances play is based on

---

Design TIP **History of tweening in animation**

Successful commercial animation began in the early twentieth century. In traditional film animation, a cadre of artists was needed to create just a few seconds of animated film. Senior artists would draw the animated objects' major action points, which were known as keyframes. Junior artists, known as tweeners, were responsible for completing the frames *in between*—from 8 to 24 frames were required for one second of film. In contrast, computer animation usually displays 10 to 20 frames per second. The largely unsung Disney animators of the 1930s and 1940s were among the most creative artists and innovative technology users of their time.

---

their stacking order on the Layers panel, with the lowest object on the Layers panel playing first.

In the Tween Instances dialog box, you can also choose whether to distribute the tweened objects to frames or display the tweening in a single frame. When you distribute objects to frames, each object appears in its own frame. For example, in Figure 20, each tweened instance of the five beach balls plays in five frames, so the animation totals 25 frames. If you do not select the Distribute to frames check box, shown in Figure 21, the tweened instances will appear in one frame. In fact, the image will look just like animation does when you turn

on onion skinning to show all frames at 100%. Depending on the animation, precise alignment of the instances might be crucial. You can duplicate an instance by cloning it, which places an exact copy directly on top of the original. For example, if you move the clone with the arrow keys, you can ensure smooth flow in your animation.

You can break apart an instance and remove its link to the symbol. Breaking apart an instance creates a grouped object and removes any animation or button symbol properties. To break the link between an instance and its symbol, click the Break Apart command from the Symbol command on the Modify menu.

Modifying Canvas Size

When you've completed an animation or any graphic, you may want to modify the size of the canvas. If an object extends beyond the canvas, you can use the Fit Canvas command from the Canvas command on the Modify menu to expand the canvas to fit the object. You can trim the canvas to the edge of objects on the canvas by using the Trim Canvas command. You can also use the Crop tool on the Tools panel to define the area that you want to crop, such as cropping the sides, but not the top, and so on.

FIGURE 20
Sample tweening

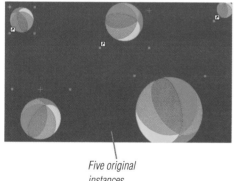

Five original
instances

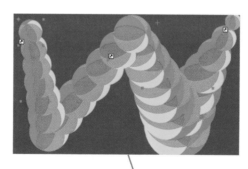

Original instances
tweened five steps and
distributed to frames

FIGURE 21
Tween Instances dialog box

Add tweening to an animation

1. Open fw6_3.png, then save it as **snowcruncher.png**.

2. Drag an instance of the **cruncher graphic symbol** to the middle top of the canvas.

3. On the Property inspector, type **12** in the **X text box**, type **0** in the **Y text box**, then press **[Enter]** (Win) or **[return]** (Mac).

4. Click **Edit** on the menu bar, then click **Clone** to duplicate the symbol and place it on top of the original.

   TIP You can also clone an instance by pressing [Ctrl][Shift][D] (Win) or ⌘ [Shift][D] (Mac).

5. Type **100** in the Y text box on the Property in-spector, press **[Enter]** (Win) or **[return]** (Mac), then compare your image to Figure 22.

6. Press and hold **[Shift]**, then click the **original instance** to select both instances.

7. Click **Modify** on the menu bar, point to **Symbol**, then click **Tween Instances** to open the Tween Instances dialog box.

   TIP You can also press [Ctrl][Alt][Shift][T] (Win) or ⌘ [option][Shift][T] (Mac) to open the Tween Instances dialog box.

8. Type **4** in the **Steps text box**, verify that the **Distribute to frames check box** is selected, then click **OK**.

   The tweened instance appears at the top of the canvas and Fireworks adds frames to the Frames panel.

   (continued)

FIGURE 22
Cloned instance positioned on canvas

Cloned instance

Importing animation files

You can open several files at once and set up a document for animation. First place the files you want to use in a folder, then, in Fireworks, click Open, select all of the files you want in the Open dialog box, then select the Open as animation check box. Fireworks opens the files en masse, placing them on one layer on the Layers panel as a bitmap and each in its own frame on the Frames panel. Fireworks imports files in alphabetical order unless they are numbered.

FIGURE 23
Animation in Frame 6

*Animation ends
with instance at
bottom of canvas*

FIGURE 24
Modified instance

9. Click the **Play button** ▷ on the bottom of the Document window, then click the **Stop button** ■ after the animation has played a couple of times.

 The animation drops down from the top to the bottom of the canvas.

10. Click the **Last frame button** ▶▌ on the bottom of the Document window (if necessary), then compare your image to Figure 23.

You cloned an instance and applied tweening to two instances.

Enhance animation

1. Verify that **Frame 6** is selected, then drag it on top of the **New/Duplicate Frame button** on the Frames panel.

2. Click the **instance** on the canvas to select it.

3. Press **[Ctrl][T]** (Windows) or ⌘ **[T]** (Mac) to free transform the object, then drag to resize it to approximately **285 W** by **65 H** on the Property inspector.

 The instance becomes wider and shorter. The slight distortion of the instance shape will make it appear to crunch during animation.

4. Type **7** in the **X text box** on the Property inspector, type **132** in the **Y text box**, press **[Enter]** (Win) or **[return]** (Mac), then compare your image to Figure 24.

(continued)

5. Double-click the **frame delay column** for Frame 7 on the Frames panel, type **50** in the Frame delay dialog box, then press **[Enter]** (Win) or **[return]** (Mac).

6. Click the **Play button** ▷ on the Document window, then click the **Stop button** ■ after the animation has played a couple of times.

The animation crunches slightly when it reaches the bottom of the canvas.

You copied a frame, modified an instance, and set frame delay.

Trim and crop the canvas

1. Click the **First frame button** ◄ on the Document window (if necessary).

2. Click **Modify** on the menu bar, point to **Canvas**, click **Trim Canvas**, then notice the canvas size at the bottom of the Document window.

The width of the canvas becomes 285 pixels as excess space around the text is trimmed See Figure 25.

TIP You can also press [Ctrl][Alt][T] (Win) or ⌘ [option][T] (Mac) to trim the canvas.

3. Click the **Crop tool** 🗗 on the Tools panel, then draw a bounding box that resembles the box shown in Figure 26.

(continued)

FIGURE 25
Trimmed canvas

FIGURE 26
Using the Crop tool

Bounding box created with Crop tool

FIGURE 27

Trimmed and cropped canvas

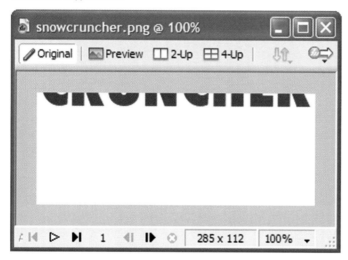

4. Type **285** in the W **text box** on the Property inspector, type **112** in the H **text box**, type **0** in the X **text box**, type **87** in the Y **text box**, then press **[Enter]** (Win) or **[return]** (Mac).

5. Position the **Crop tool pointer** above the bounding box on the canvas, press **[Enter]** (Win) or **[return]** (Mac), then compare your image to Figure 27.

   The height of the canvas becomes 112 pixels and only the bottom portion of the instance is visible on the canvas in Frame 1.

6. Click the **Play button** on the Document window, then click the **Stop button** after the animation has played a couple of times.

   The animation now appears to enter from the top of the canvas, then fall to the bottom of the canvas, and then crunch as it reaches the bottom point.

7. Save your work.

You trimmed and cropped the canvas.

OPTIMIZE, SAVE, AND
EXPORT FILES

What You'll Do

 In this lesson, you will optimize a file, set how many times an animation will play in a browser, and save the file in another file format.

Learning about Optimizing, Saving, and Exporting

After your document reflects your full creative genius, it's time to take it to the next level: optimize the items, and then save them or export them in the proper format. For print media, you'll want to ensure the highest visual quality of your images. However, if the final destination is the Web, you need to configure the file so that it both performs and displays itself in an ideal state. If you want to save a simple graphic (one that does not contain slices, hotspots, or image maps), you can simply use the Save As command to select the file format in which you want to save the file. You can save files in 10 different formats, including animated GIFs, Shockwave Files (SWF), JPEG, and so on. Fireworks applies the current optimization settings to the Save As file format. If your document contains Web objects, you must use the Export command to ensure that the HTML properties are set properly.

Choosing the Number of Times a Movie Will Play

Web designers often assume that viewers will want or need to watch an animation repeatedly. For example, an e-mail image, such as an animated envelope or mailbox, may continuously open and close, in a process known as **looping**. You can choose how many times your animation will play by clicking the GIF animation looping button in the Frames panel, then clicking a number or an option in the list. For example, None means the movie will play once and then stop; 5 means it will play five additional times after the first time, and Forever means it will never stop.

Understanding the Basics of Optimization

Fireworks has specific tools you can use to optimize your graphics. When you **optimize** a graphic, you match the format best suited for the type of graphic with the smallest file size that maintains image quality. The Optimize panel contains settings for the file type, compression, and properties specific to the selected file type. For example, if you choose GIF as the file type, you can adjust the number of colors in the exported graphic, known as **color depth**. If you choose JPEG as the file type, you can adjust the quality of the image using a slider control.

The Preview, 2-Up, and 4-Up buttons on the Document window allow you to preview the results of the optimization controls you've set on the Optimize panel. The 2-Up and 4-Up previews offer the advantage of being able to compare different settings side by side, so you can experiment with different settings to determine the point at which you finally sacrifice image quality for decreased file size. Figure 28 shows different optimization settings for a GIF file.

QUICKTIP

Note that download times are based on the maximum possible throughput; your dial-up modem times will definitely vary.

The Optimize panel contains the following list of preset optimization choices:

- **GIF Web 216**—Makes all colors Web-safe.
- **GIF WebSnap 128** or **GIF WebSnap 256**—Converts non-Web-safe colors to their closest Web-safe equivalent, up to 128 or 256 colors, respectively.
- **GIF Adaptive 256**—Contains up to 256 actual colors used in the graphic.
- **JPEG—Better Quality** and **JPEG—Smaller File**—Sets the quality higher or lower: the lower the setting, the

more quality you lose during compression, but the file size is smaller.
- **Animated GIF WebSnap 128**—Sets the file format to animated GIF and Web-safe colors.

QUICKTIP

You can customize an optimization setting and add it to the list of presets using the Save current settings button on the Optimize panel.

When you choose GIF as the optimization setting, you can choose from several palettes, from black and white to palettes specific to your Windows or Macintosh system. You can also optimize each slice in your document

FIGURE 28
Comparing GIF optimization settings

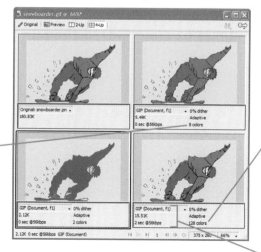

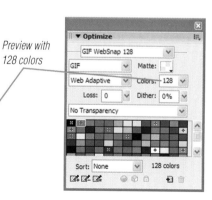

Preview with 8 colors

Preview with 128 colors

File size and download time

individually. For example, you can optimize a slice that contains a photographic image as a JPEG, or even selectively optimize areas of the slice so that the background can be compressed with a lower quality setting. You can optimize other slices in your document, such as text, as GIF files with only the colors necessary to display the text color.

You can further reduce file size by selecting the Remove Unused Colors option, and the Interlaced option (for GIF and PNG file types) on the Optimize panel. **Interlacing** allows the file to download gradually from low to high resolution. You can accomplish the same result for JPEG files by selecting Progressive JPEG from the Layers panel Options menu. If you lower the quality setting for JPEG images, you can increase the

smoothing setting in small increments to help maintain appearance.

Understanding Transparency

Regardless of the shape of the image, JPEG files and other file formats are rectangular. The image appears against its own background color, and the graphic's boundary is the rectangle, not the individual features of the image. GIF file formats permit a transparent background—the image appears to blend with the background of your Web page, creating the appearance of an image boundary. Having a transparent background is particularly effective when you save an animation as an animated GIF. You can select three types of transparency: No Transparency, which includes the canvas color and appears similar to a JPEG; Index Transparency, which allows you to set a specific color or colors as the transparent color or colors and affects both the canvas and the graphic; and Alpha Transparency, which sets the background color or any other selected color to be transparent. After you select the

transparency type, you can select the color in your document that you want to become transparent using the Select Transparency Color button on the Optimize panel.

Understanding Exporting

Exporting an interactive file to the Web involves creating HTML, CSS, or JavaScript code—and often lots of it. The export process is two-fold: optimize the document, and create the code necessary to reconstitute the graphics properly. In Fireworks, this is an effortless process when you use the Export dialog boxes. You can also use the Export Wizard, which guides you through optimizing and exporting.

You can set HTML and CSS code export options using tabs on the HTML Setup dialog box, which you can open from the

File menu. The Export feature generates the files necessary to view a graphic on the Web, or in other applications, such as Macromedia Flash, Dreamweaver, or Adobe Photoshop. You can export the entire document or just portions of it. For example, you can export a single image, the document as an HTML file with its related images, one or more slices, or frames and layers as separate image files.

Depending on whether your file contains slices or image maps, you need to control different aspects of the export. For example, a simple graphic is a simple export: you name the file, accept the default settings, and then select the folder in which you want to save it. Options in the Export dialog box are shown in Figure 29.

QUICKTIP

You should review the specific exporting options for files in Fireworks Help.

The Export Preview dialog box provides all the optimization and export features from the Optimize panel and more in a consolidated location. The Export Preview dialog box consists of three tabs: Options, which contains optimization and view settings; File, where you can scale and crop the image; and Animation, where you can modify animated GIF files, although usually the default settings are adequate. You can open the Export Preview dialog box from the File menu, from the Optimization panel Options menu, or from the Export Wizard.

FIGURE 29
Save as type list in the Export dialog box

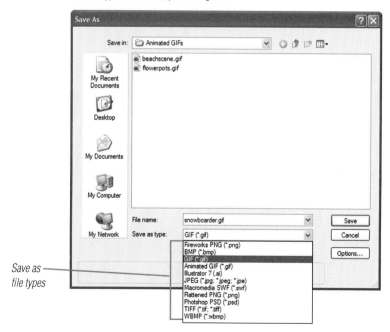

Save as file types

Figure 30 shows the Image Preview dialog box.

If you prefer, you can use the Export Wizard from the File menu to lead you through the export process. The Export Wizard is a logical amalgam of the Optimize panel and Image Preview and Export dialog boxes, combined with some behind-the-scenes analysis to help you choose the best settings for your file. When you open the Export Wizard, Fireworks evaluates the file, asks you questions specific to that file type, and then recommends choices based on its analysis of your file and your responses. You can adjust settings in the panels and dialog boxes as you would if you opened them alone, without using the Wizard.

QUICKTIP

You can export an image to another application using the Quick Export button at the top of the Document window.

Selecting Specific Areas to Export

In addition to exporting a file or graphic in its entirety, you can select different quality settings for portions of a JPEG graphic, or select a specific area in your document to export.

You can use the Selective JPEG commands on the Modify menu to select and set the quality of one or more areas of a JPEG image. Generally, you may find it useful to use this command to minimize the quality setting of the selected areas. To select a part of an image, select a Marquee tool, then click the Save Selection as JPEG Mask command under the Selective JPEG command. Drag a marquee over the area (or select its inverse), then click the Selective Quality options on the Optimize panel (first verify that JPEG is the selected export file type) to open the Selective JPEG Settings dialog box. When you change the quality setting, Fireworks places an overlay on top of the selected area on the canvas.

You can use the Export Area tool on the Tools panel to drag a bounding box around the area you want to export. The Export Area tool, located with the Crop tool, creates a box that resembles and functions similarly to the bounding box you create with the Crop tool. After it is selected, you can double-click the bounding box to open the Image Preview dialog box, where you can then export the image.

FIGURE 30
Image Preview dialog box

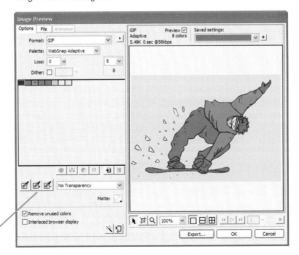

Add, delete, and set transparency buttons

FIGURE 31

Changing the looping setting

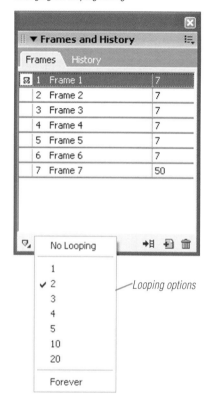

Looping options

FIGURE 32

Settings on the Optimize panel

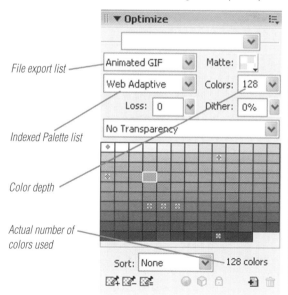

File export list

Indexed Palette list

Color depth

Actual number of colors used

Set options on the Optimize panel and preview the animation in a browser

1. Click the **GIF Animation Looping button** on the bottom of the Frames panel, then click **2**, as shown in Figure 31.

   The looping setting is not noticeable until the animation plays on the Web. To view the setting change, you'll view the animation in your browser.

2. Click **Window** on the menu bar, then click **Optimize** to open the Optimize panel.

   TIP   You can also press [F6] to open the Optimize panel.

3. Click the **Export file format list arrow**, then click **Animated GIF**.

4. Click the **Indexed Palette list arrow**, click **Web Adaptive**, then compare your Optimize panel to Figure 32.

   TIP   If a number is not visible on the bottom of the Optimize panel, click Rebuild.

   (continued)

5. Click the **First frame button** 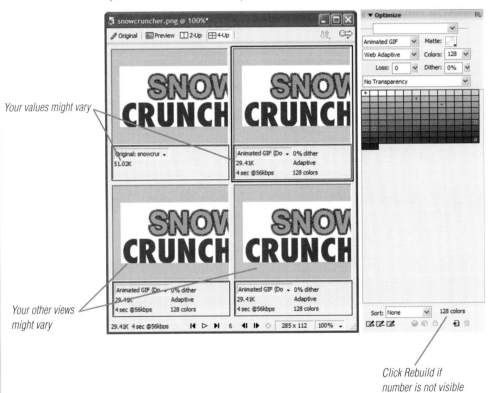 on the Document window (if necessary).

6. Click **File** on the menu bar, point to **Preview in Browser**, then click your browser.

   The animation plays the specified number of times, and then stops.

7. Close your browser.

You specified the number of times the animation should play, set the file format, and previewed the animation in a browser.

Change the color depth

1. Verify that **128** is the Colors setting on the Optimize panel and that a colors used number appears at the bottom right of the panel, then click **Rebuild** if a colors used number does not appear.

   The number at the bottom of the panel is the actual number of colors used in the file.

2. Click **Frame 6** on the Frames panel.

3. Click the **4-Up button** 4-Up on the Document window, click the view in the top-right corner to select it, then compare your image to Figure 33.

   (continued)

FIGURE 33
Optimization viewed at 128 color depth

Your values might vary

Your other views might vary

Click Rebuild if number is not visible

FIGURE 34
Optimization comparison

File size and
time savings
with 32 colors

FIGURE 35
Selecting a transparency option

Type of transparency list

4. Click the view in the lower-right corner to select it, click the **Maximum number of colors list arrow** on the Optimize panel, click **32**, then compare your image to Figure 34.

The file size is smaller and the download time is less, but the image quality is still acceptable.

> TIP   If the file size and download times are not visible on the Optimize panel, click Rebuild or reselect the color depth.

You changed the color depth to reduce file size and download time.

Change the transparency of an animated GIF

1. Click the **Choose type of transparency list arrow** on the Optimize panel, then click **Index Transparency**, as shown in Figure 35.

Because the transparency setting is not visible until you preview the animation, the canvas still appears white in Original view, although a checkerboard pattern is visible in the selected view.

2. Click the **Preview button** ⬛ Preview on the Document window.

The canvas color consists of a gray and white checkerboard pattern, indicating that it is transparent.

(continued)

3. Compare your image to Figure 36, then save your work.

4. Click **File** on the menu bar, point to **Preview in Browser**, then click your browser.

   The animation plays against the background color of your browser window.

5. Close your browser.

You changed the transparency of an animated GIF to index transparency.

Export an optimized file

1. Click the **Original button** ✎ Original on the Document window.

2. Click **File** on the menu bar, then click **Save As** to open the Save As dialog box.

   TIP   You can also open the Save As dialog box by clicking [Ctrl][Shift][S] (Win) or ⌘ [Shift][S] (Mac).

   (continued)

FIGURE 36
Modified transparency setting

Checkerboard pattern indicates transparency

FIGURE 37

Save As dialog box

Your folder might vary —

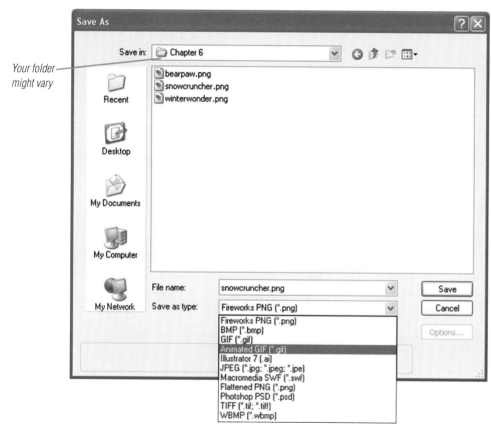

3. Navigate to the drive and folder where your Solution Files are stored, click the **Save as type list arrow**, point to **Animated GIF**, compare your dialog box to Figure 37, then click **Save**.

4. Close snowcruncher.gif, then when prompted save your changes to snowcruncher.png in the drive and folder where your Solution Files are stored.

5. Open the file management tool on your operating system, adjust the settings to display extensions (if necessary), then navigate to the drive and folder where your Solution Files are stored.

6. Notice the newly saved file named snowcruncher.gif, then compare its file size to snowcruncher.png.

   TIP Depending on the file association for GIF files on your computer, you might be able to view the animated GIF by opening it from your file manager or you might need to first open your browser and then play the animated GIF by opening it from the browser.

7. Close your file management.

You saved the optimized file in another file format, an animated GIF.

Create basic animation.

1. Open fw6_4.png, save it as **birthdaymsg.png**, then open the Library, Info, and Frames panels.
2. Create a new layer and change the name to **helium**.
3. Drag an instance of the balloon symbol to the lower-right corner of the canvas at the following coordinates: X: 410, Y: 95. (*Hint*: The balloon will be partly off-canvas.)
4. Add an Adjust Color filter to the instance in the Filters section of the Property inspector, then select the Hue/Saturation filter with the following settings: Colorize option selected, Hue: 253, Saturation: 100, and Lightness: 30.
5. Animate the instance with the following settings: Frames: 5, Move: 157, Direction: 77, Scale to and Opacity: 100, and Rotate: 0.
6. Change the name of the animation symbol in the Library panel and the Animation symbol object on the Layers panel to **heliumballoon**.
7. Play the animation in the Document window.
8. Select Frame 1, then save your work.

Modify and preview an animation.

1. Change the scale of the animation to 40, the opacity to 74, and add a rotation of 25 CCW.
2. Select the objects on Layer 1 in the Layers panel and share them with layers.

3. Play the animation in the Document window.
4. Play the animation in Preview view.
5. Save your work, then compare your image to Figure 38. (*Hint*: For illustrative purposes, the animation is shown in its entirety.)
6. Close birthdaymsg.png.

Create frame animation.

1. Open fw6_5.png, then save it as **gifts.png**. (*Hint*: Show guides, if they are not visible.)
2. Duplicate Frame 1, then drag the i symbol to the canvas. (*Hint*: Use the guide line to align the bottom of the instances.)
3. Repeat for the remaining letters until you have "Gifts" spelled out over five frames.
4. Duplicate Frame 5, then group the objects.

5. Add a Zoom Blur filter using default settings, and a Glow filter using the first bright green color swatch and default settings.
6. Adjust the frame delay of Frames 1–5 to 20, and the frame delay of Frame 6 to 50.
7. Turn off guides, save your work, then preview the animation in Fireworks.
8. In Original view, select Frame 4.
9. Set a custom onion skinning that displays one frame before the current at 20% and two frames after at 50%.
10. Compare your image to Figure 38, then save your work and close gifts.png.

FIGURE 38
Completed Skills Review (1)

Add tweening to an animation.

1. Open fw6_6.png, then save it as **birthdaysmile.png**.
2. Drag an instance of the big smile symbol to the middle of the canvas at the following coordinates: X: 108, Y: 61.
3. Clone the instance, scale it numerically to 25%, then move it to the upper-right corner of the canvas, X: 400, Y: 0.
4. Move the scaled graphic symbol to the bottom of the Layers panel.
5. Tween the two instances with 5 steps and select the Distribute to frames check box.
6. Select Frame 7, select the instance, and add an Outer Bevel filter with a smooth Bevel edge shape, #FFCC99 color, 51% contrast, 10 softness, and the rest default settings; and a Glow filter with default settings.
7. Preview the animation in Fireworks.
8. Save your work.

Set frame delay, trim, and crop the canvas.

1. Set the frame delay for Frames 1-6 to 15 and for Frame 7 to 75.
2. Trim the canvas.
3. Select Frame 1.
4. Create a crop bounding box that measures 375 × 290 and X: 79 and Y: 27. (*Hint*: The top of the face will be outside the bounding box.)
5. Crop the canvas, then save your work.

Optimize, save, and export files.

1. Set the Looping to 5 on the Frames panel, then open the Optimize panel.
2. Set the Export file format to Animated GIF, then set the Indexed Palette to Web Adaptive, if necessary.
3. Preview the animation in a browser, then save your work.
4. Select Frame 7, set the color depth to 128, then compare color depths of 128 and 32 in 4-Up preview.
5. Select the 32 color depth in the 4-Up window, then save your work.
6. Set the transparency to Index Transparency, then preview the animation in a browser.
7. Export the .gif file to the drive and folder where your Solution Files are stored.
8. Save your work, then compare your image to Figure 39.

FIGURE 39
Completed Skills Review (2)

Your friends insisted on putting all 21 candles and 1 for good luck on your birthday cake. After wiping up butter cream frosting for weeks, you've decided to create a reenactment of the event using your Fireworks skills. Your goal is to use animation to convince your friends never to try to light so many candles again.

1. Obtain images that will reinforce your birthday theme. You can obtain images from your computer, from the Internet, from a digital camera, or from scanned media. You can use images from the Web that are free for both personal and commercial use (check the copyright information for any such file before downloading it).

2. Create a new document and save it as **birthdaycake.png**.

3. Import the following files and the files you obtained in Step 1 into your document.
   - cake.gif
   - candle.gif

4. Convert objects to symbols as necessary.

5. Create frame-by-frame animation using at least one of the symbols, and modify instances as needed. (*Hint*: The candles were modified from one symbol and were created frame by frame.)

6. Build at least one animation that involves tweening. (*Hint*: The cake instance with glowing candles was created by adding tweening to two instances of the glowing cake and modifying the amount of glow.)

7. Trim, crop, or adjust frame delay, looping, and transparency as desired.

8. Optimize and export the file. (*Hint*: The sample is an animated GIF with 16 colors.)

9. Preview the animation, save your work, then examine the sample shown in Figure 40.

FIGURE 40
Sample Completed Project Builder 1

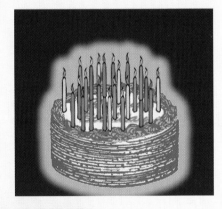

One of your parents has donated to a fund that rewards elementary students who improve their reading skills. In addition to a monetary donation, they volunteered you to design a banner ad for the local library Web site.

1. Obtain images of books or other reading material that will fit your theme. You can obtain images from your computer, from the Internet, from a digital camera, or from scanned media. You can use files from the Web that are free for both personal and commercial use (check the copyright information for any such file before downloading it).
2. Create a new document and save it as **readbooks.png**.
3. Copy or import the files into your document and convert objects to symbols as necessary.
4. Build at least two animations using the techniques of your choice. (*Hint*: The sliding and tumbling book and the blur-to-sharp text are examples of tweening.)
5. Trim, crop, or adjust frame delay, looping, and transparency as desired.
6. Optimize and export the animation. (*Hint*: The sample is an animated GIF with 16 colors.)
7. Preview the animation, save your work, then examine the sample shown in Figure 41.

FIGURE 41
Sample Completed Project Builder 2

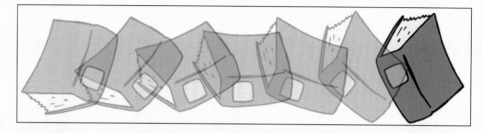

Your interest in creating animation for the Web can easily become an avid interest and even an obsession. Learning to use your animation powers for good or evil is often best learned through experience, not theory. Animation can be used as a spot effect or can encompass the site. Because dynamic Web sites are updated frequently to reflect current trends, this page might be different from Figure 42 if you open it online.

1. Connect to the Internet and go to *www.course.com*. Navigate to the page for this book, click the Student Online Companion, then click the link for this chapter.
2. Open a document in a word processor, or open a new Fireworks document, then save the file as **animation**. (*Hint*: You can also use the Text tool in Fireworks to answer the questions.)
3. Scroll down the page to find winners and nominees in the Best Use of Animation or Moving Images category. You can also select a site from any of the other categories, providing it has animation.
4. Explore several sites, then, when you find one or two that interest you, type the URL in your document, then answer the following questions:
   - What seems to be the purpose of this site?
   - Who is the target audience?
   - What animation is present? How does it serve the site?
   - How might an animation symbol, frame-by-frame animation, or tweened instances be used in this site?
   - Discuss how frame rate or looping might be used.
   - How would you change the animation in this site?
5. Save your work.

FIGURE 42
Design Project

Your class on popular culture just read an article about the staggering debt rate of people aged 18–30. Your group has been assigned to write a response and give a presentation on this topic. As an introduction to your online slide presentation, you first want to prove or dispel common myths about money. The sample shown in Figure 43 demonstrates that yes, money does grow on trees. Your group can choose the financial myth or misconception of its choice and then prove it or dispel it.

1. Obtain images of the financial myth or misconception you've chosen. You can obtain images from your computer, from the Internet, from a digital camera, or from scanned media. You can use files from the Web that are free for both personal and commercial use (check the copyright information for any such file before downloading it).
2. Create a new document and save it as **mymoneymyth.png**.
3. Copy or import the files into your document.
4. Convert objects to symbols as necessary. (*Hint*: There are two dollar bill symbols and one tree symbol in the sample.)

5. Build animation using the techniques of your choice. (*Hint*: The dollar bill animation in the sample is frame-by-frame animation.)
6. Trim, crop, or adjust frame delay, looping, and transparency as desired.

FIGURE 43
Sample Completed Portfolio Project

7. Optimize and export the animation. (*Hint*: The sample is an animated GIF with 64 colors.)
8. Preview the document, save your work, then examine the sample shown in Figure 43.

a.

7

CREATING SOPHISTICATED
WEB PAGE NAVIGATION

1. Create a pop-up menu.

2. Create a navigation bar.

3. Integrate Fireworks HTML into an HTML editor.

7 CREATING SOPHISTICATED
WEB PAGE NAVIGATION

Pop-up Menus and Navigation Bars

A successful Web site helps visitors find the information they want and then navigate to the relevant URL. You can design a Web site so that a pop-up menu and any submenus appear when triggered by a mouse action. By filling out a series of dialog boxes, you can tailor the pop-up menu to look and function exactly the way you want.

Similarly, you can assemble button symbol instances to create a navigation bar with up to four states: Up, Over, and, if you want them, Down and Over While Down.

Integrating HTML

After you create a great-looking rollover, pop-up menu, or navigation bar, you might be challenged to export the document so that the HTML code integrates with your HTML editor. Fireworks makes it easy to export in the HTML style you need, or to copy HTML code into your HTML editor.

Tools You'll Use

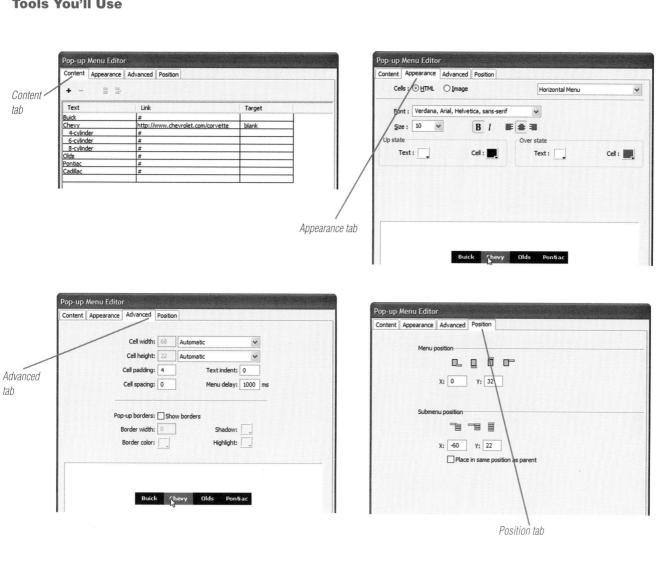

Content tab

Appearance tab

Advanced tab

Position tab

CREATE A
POP-UP MENU

What You'll Do

 In this lesson, you will add and edit a pop-up menu and submenu, and export the document.

Understanding Pop-up Menus

You've seen how rollovers can instantly infuse your site with change or information, or how you can link to another Web page. Many times, the information in your Web page consists of title topics and subtopics. You could create individual buttons for each entry, but that could easily clutter up your Web page and still not be easy for your users to understand or navigate. One solution is to create a pop-up menu that organizes and displays the topics hierarchically. A **pop-up menu** is a menu that appears when you move the mouse pointer over a trigger image in a browser. It contains a list of items that link to other Web pages. Within the greater Web community, pop-up menus are also known as pop-down or drop-down menus.

In addition to rollovers and swapped images, pop-up menus are one of the main categories of Fireworks behaviors. In fact, because it has Up and Over states, you create a pop-up menu by attaching it to a Web object: a slice or a hotspot. You can access the Pop-up Menu Editor by opening the Behaviors panel, clicking the Add behavior button, and then clicking Set Pop-Up Menu. The Pop-up Menu Editor consists of four tabs: Content, Appearance, Advanced, and Position. To create a pop-up menu, you just fill out the information on each tab. Depending on the look and function of

Using a custom style as the cell background

In addition to selecting the default styles on the Appearance tab, you can create a custom style and then select it from the Styles panel. Click the Options menu button, click Export Styles, then save the style in the Nav Menu folder on the drive where Fireworks is loaded. The Nav Menu folder contains the custom style files for pop-up menus. The location of the Nav Menu folder depends on your computer platform and operating system. To locate it on your system, search Fireworks Help for "configuration files."

your pop-up menu, you might not need to complete more than the Content tab.

The Content tab, shown in Figure 1, is where you add the items in a menu or submenu, enter their URL links (the addresses), if any, and the URL targets (how they will appear in the browser). You can add menu or submenu items and then drag the entries to a new location in the list, similar to how you drag an object or layer in the Layers panel. By default, each item in the list is a menu item. To convert a menu item into a submenu item, select the item, and then click the Indent Menu button. You can turn a submenu item back to a menu item by clicking the Outdent Menu button. Figure 2 shows a sample menu and submenu.

You can set and preview the style and overall look of the pop-up in its Up and Over states using settings on the Appearance tab. You can think of a pop-up menu as a small table whose cells you format in a variety of ways. For example, you can set the pop-up menu to appear vertically or horizontally, use HTML code or an image as the cell background in the menu, select font attributes, and choose a style for the pop-up menu in both states. Note that when you use an image as the cell background instead of HTML code, you increase the size of your file. Also keep in mind how a long menu or submenu will look on your Web page.

FIGURE 1
Content tab in the Pop-up Menu Editor

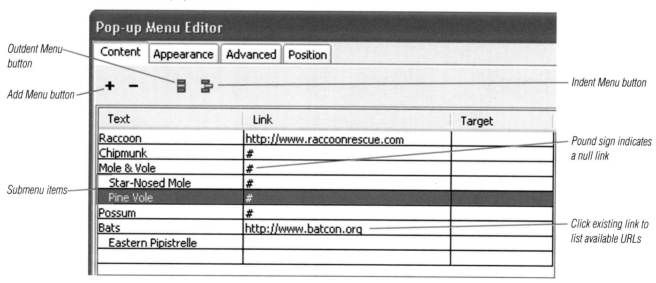

The Advanced tab allows you to apply HTML table-specific values for the pop-up menu. For example, you can set cell dimension, padding, and spacing, as well as the width and color of the cell border, the length of time the menu remains visible after the mouse pointer moves away from it, and the indentation of the text. The Position tab enables you to set how the menu and submenu items appear on screen, such as above, below, or offset from the menu. You can select a preset position button or enter X and Y coordinates.

Exporting Pop-up Menus

Although creating and positioning a pop-up menu in Fireworks is simple, the code required to make the menu function correctly in a Web browser is complex. Fortunately, when you export a document that contains a pop-up menu into HTML, Fireworks automatically generates the necessary JavaScript. Fireworks can also export pop-up menus using a combination of JavaScript and Cascading Style Sheets (CSS). CSS is easier to understand and maintain, and you'll be able to index the menus and update the links within the code using Dreamweaver or another HTML editor. When you complete the export process, you will notice that Fireworks exports a JavaScript file, mm_menu.js or mm_css_menu.js, to the same folder as the HTML file. Every time you add a behavior to your Fireworks document (anything from the Behaviors panel), Fireworks must generate JavaScript to create the interactivity. Fireworks behaviors make it easy to add JavaScript functionality to your documents without having to write any code yourself.

QUICKTIP

For a menu, X and Y coordinate values of zero align the upper-left corner of the menu with that location on the slice. For a submenu, the X and Y values position the upper-left corner of the submenu with the upper-right corner of its parent menu item when the Place in same position as parent check box is not selected.

FIGURE 2
Sample menu and submenu

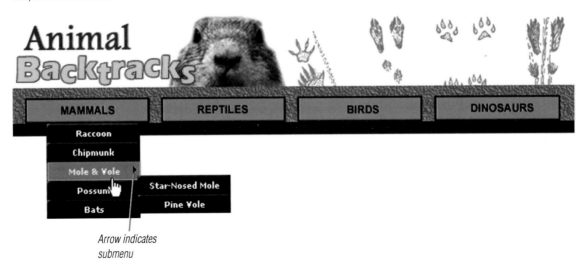

Arrow indicates submenu

FIGURE 3

Selecting the Set Pop-Up Menu behavior

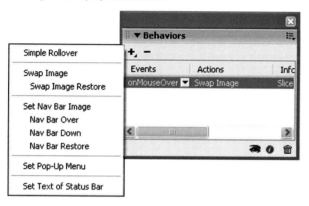

FIGURE 4

Menu items added to Content tab

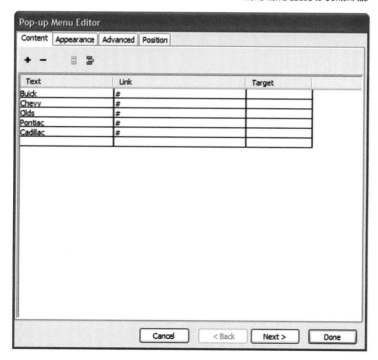

Create a pop-up menu

1. Open fw7_1.png, then save it as **gmparts.png**.

   TIP   Click Maintain Appearance if Fireworks displays the Replace Fonts dialog box.

2. Click the **Show slices and hotspots button** 🔲 on the Tools panel, then click the **engines slice** to select it.

3. Open the Behaviors panel.

   A Swap Image behavior already applied to the engine slice appears in the Behaviors panel.

4. Click the **Add behavior button** ➕ in the Behaviors panel, then click **Set Pop-Up Menu**, as shown in Figure 3, to open the Pop-up Menu Editor.

5. Double-click the **empty menu item** under Text (if necessary), type **Buick**, press **[Tab]**, then type # to add a null value as the URL link.

   A new empty menu item appears when you tab to the Link column. In this instance, a null value indicates that the Link field is a dummy link, which serves as a placeholder for the actual link.

   TIP   You can also click the Add Menu button to create a new, empty menu item.

6. Repeat Step 5, but type **Chevy**, **Olds**, **Pontiac**, and **Cadillac** as separate menu items with null links, then compare your Content tab to Figure 4.

   TIP   If you enter a URL link and leave the Target box blank, by default the URL link replaces the current page in the browser.

You created and added items to a pop-up menu.

Add a pop-up submenu

1. Click the **Chevy menu item**, then click the **Add Menu button** ✚ to add an empty menu item beneath Chevy.

2. Double-click the empty cell under Text, type **4-cylinder**, press **[Tab]**, type **#**, press **[Enter]** (Win) or **[return]** (Mac), then click **4-cylinder** to select the entire menu item, as shown in Figure 5.

3. Click the **Indent Menu button** 📑 to make 4-cylinder a submenu item of Chevy.

4. Click the **Add Menu button** ✚ to add an empty menu item beneath 4-cylinder.

5. Double-click the empty cell, type **6-cylinder**, press **[Tab]**, type **#**, then click **6-cylinder** to select the menu item.

   The new menu item is indented.

6. Repeat Steps 4 and 5, but type **8-cylinder**.

7. Compare your Content tab to Figure 6.

You added items to a submenu.

FIGURE 5
Selecting a menu item

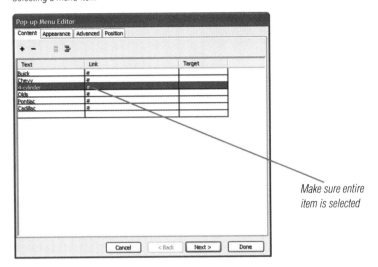

*Make sure entire
item is selected*

FIGURE 6
Submenu items added to menu

Indent Menu button

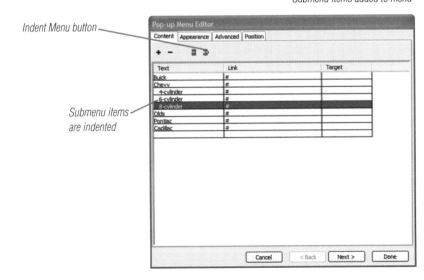

*Submenu items
are indented*

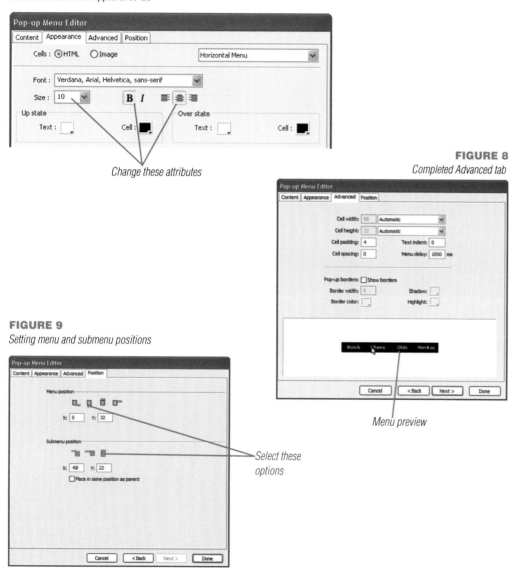

FIGURE 7

Font attributes on the Appearance tab

Change these attributes

FIGURE 8

Completed Advanced tab

Menu preview

FIGURE 9

Setting menu and submenu positions

Select these options

Set menu appearance, table construction, and position

1. Click **Next** to display the Appearance tab.

   TIP You can also click the tab name to open it.

2. Click the **HTML option**, click the **Choose alignment of the pop-up menu list arrow**, click **Horizontal Menu**, then change the font attributes so that your values match those shown in Figure 7.

3. Verify that white appears in the **Text color box**, and that black appears in the **Cell color box** in both the Up state and the Over state sections.

4. Click **Next** to open the Advanced tab.

5. Modify the settings so that your values match those shown in Figure 8.

6. Click **Next** to open the Position tab.

7. Click the **bottom of slice button** (2nd button) in the Menu position section.

8. Click the **bottom of menu button** (3rd button) in the Submenu position section, verify that the **Place in same position as parent check box** is not selected, then compare your Position tab to Figure 9.

9. Click **Done** to close the Pop-up Menu Editor.

You used the Pop-up Menu Editor to set options for the pop-up menu's appearance and the position of the pop-up menu.

Lesson 1   Create a Pop-up Menu

FIREWORKS 7-9

Preview the pop-up menu

1. Notice that the slice behavior line is an outline of the pop-up menu.

   TIP   You can drag the menu outline to reposition the menu around the slice on the canvas.

2. Click the **Hide slices and hotspots button** on the Tools panel.

3. Click the **Preview button** Preview on the Document window, then roll the mouse pointer over the engines button.

   The rollover is visible but the pop-up menu is not. Pop-up menus are not visible in a Fireworks preview.

4. Click **File** on the menu bar, point to **Preview in Browser**, then click the first browser in the list to open the primary browser.

5. Roll the mouse pointer over the **engines button**, roll the mouse pointer over the **Chevy button**, then compare your image to Figure 10.

   The menu and submenu are visible, but the submenu is not centered beneath the Chevy menu and there is no differentiation when you move the mouse pointer over the cylinder choices.

6. Close the browser.

You previewed the pop-up menu in Fireworks and in a browser.

FIGURE 10
Previewing the pop-up menu in a browser

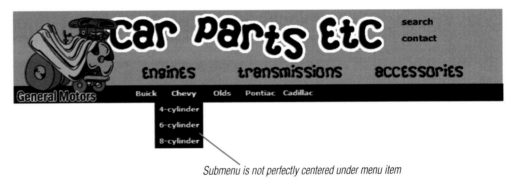

Submenu is not perfectly centered under menu item

FIGURE 11
Changing the target on the Content tab

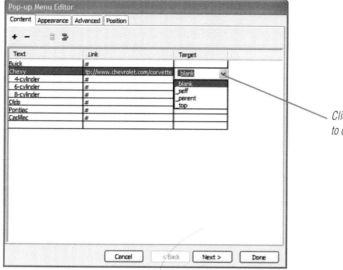

*Click list arrow
to display list*

FIGURE 12
Previewing the modified pop-up menu

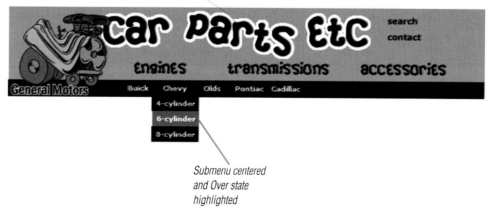

*Submenu centered
and Over state
highlighted*

Edit the pop-up menu

1. Click the **Show slices and hotspots button** on the Tools panel, click the **Original button** *Original* on the Document window, then click the **engines slice**.

2. Double-click the **Show Popup Menu behavior** in the Behaviors panel to open the Pop-up Menu Editor.

3. Double-click the **Link box** for Chevy, then type **http://www.chevrolet.com/corvette**.

4. Click the **Target box**, click the **Target list arrow**, then click **_blank** to open the URL in a separate window, as shown in Figure 11.

5. Click the **Appearance tab**, click the **Over State Cell color box**, type **#CC3300** in the hexadecimal text box, then press **[Enter]** (Win) or **[return]** (Mac).

6. Click the **Position tab**, change the value in the **Submenu position X text box** to **-60**, then click **Done**.

7. Preview the menu in your primary browser, then test the pop-up menu, as shown in Figure 12.

8. Click the **Chevy button**, view the Web page, then close both browser windows.

   | TIP   If you are not online, the Chevy site will not open.

You modified the pop-up menu and then previewed it in a browser.

Optimize and export the document

1. Click **Select** on the menu bar, then click **Deselect** to deselect all the slices.

2. Open the Optimize panel (if necessary).

3. Click the **Saved settings list arrow** in the Optimize panel, then click **GIF WebSnap 128** (if necessary).

4. Click **File** on the menu bar, then click **Export**.

5. Navigate to the drive and folder where your Data Files are stored, create a new folder named **gmparts**, then open the folder (Win).

6. Click the **Export list arrow**, click **HTML and Images** (if necessary), click the **Put images in subfolder check box** to select it, then verify that your Export dialog box resembles Figure 13.

7. Click **Options** to open the HTML Setup dialog box. Click the **Use CSS For Popup Menus check box** to select it, then click the **Write CSS to an external file check box** to select it.

   When the document is exported, Fireworks generates an external Cascading Style Sheets (CSS) file that controls the appearance of the pop-up menu.

8. Verify that your HTML Setup dialog box resembles Figure 14, click **OK**, then click **Export** in the Export dialog box.

   Fireworks exports the images to the images subfolder in the gmparts folder and places the gmparts.htm file and the related mm_css_menu.js and gmparts.css files in the gmparts folder.

   (continued)

FIGURE 13
Options in the Export dialog box

Select these two check boxes

FIGURE 14
HTML Setup dialog box

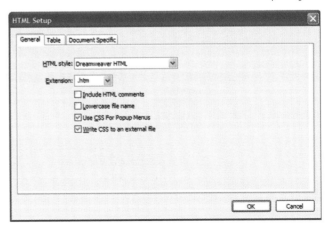

9. Open the file management tool that is on your operating system, adjust the settings to display extensions, then navigate to the drive and folder where you created the gmparts folder.

10. Compare your image to Figure 15, then close your file management tool.

11. Save your work, then close gmparts.png.

You optimized and exported the document containing a pop-up menu and viewed the associated export files.

FIGURE 15

Exported pop-up menu files

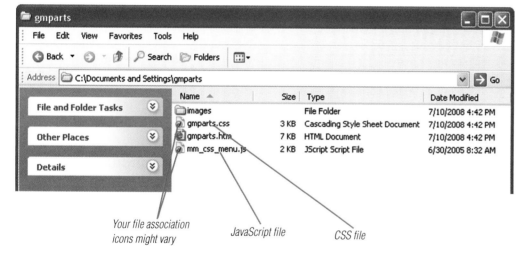

Your file association icons might vary   JavaScript file   CSS file

CREATE A
NAVIGATION BAR

What You'll Do

 In this lesson, you will create a navigation bar and optimize and export the document.

Understanding Navigation Bars

When you created buttons in previous units, you were building efficient navigation tools for your users. You can easily create buttons that are part of a navigation system known as a navigation bar, or nav bar. A **navigation bar** is a group of buttons that link to different areas inside or outside the Web site.

A nav bar can be positioned along any perimeter of the main Web page, usually along the top or left side, although many creative designers incorporate the nav bar as part of the overall design, as shown in Figure 16. A nav bar can be simple text, an image, or any combination thereof, depending on your design and file size requirements. Whatever its appearance, even if it appears to be melded into the overall design, the purpose of a nav bar remains constant: to maintain the same look from page to page, even though the functions may be page-specific. A well-functioning, uniform-looking nav bar is a good foundation for any successful site.

In Fireworks, you can create a nav bar by creating instances of button symbols that contain Down and Over While Down states in addition to an Up and Over state. When you create the Down and Over While Down states in the Button Editor, Fireworks adds a navigation bar image behavior to the Behaviors panel. Fireworks automatically inserts a slice when you drag a button instance to the canvas or when you convert an object to a button symbol.

You can also create a navigation bar by creating individual frames for each rollover state, and adding a Simple Rollover behavior to them. You can add slices to the rollover button, and then select the slices and use the Set Nav Bar Image behavior in the Behaviors panel. Figure 17 shows the Set Nav Bar Image dialog box. If you do not first add slices or hotspots to objects, Fireworks prompts you and adds them for you.

Building Efficient Navigation Bars

Creating a nav bar for your users helps make your site efficient and easy to use. You can make the process of creating a nav bar in Fireworks equally easy and efficient. The buttons in a nav bar are interrelated in function and appearance; therefore, you want to minimize the opportunity for error if you need to edit the nontext portions of a button, and you want to maximize your speed in doing so.

You've seen how easy it is to create a button, then an instance, then add text, and then modify the button's appearance in different states. When you're creating buttons that will serve as a nav bar, you can also create different button states for the button object, duplicate button instances on the canvas, and then just edit the text label for each different button instance as desired.

Fireworks allows you to export the navigation bar for the Down state image of each button of the page that you are currently viewing. The Down state image is displayed when you select the Export multiple nav bar HTML files check box in the Document Specific tab of the HTML Setup dialog box. To enable this feature, you must also ensure that the button object name is identical to the URL link prefix filename. For example, a Contact Us navigation button would have the following properties: text label: Contact Us (the text label can be any text or image), button object name: contact, and URL link: contact.htm. You can easily enter the button object name and URL link filename in text boxes on the Property inspector.

FIGURE 16

Sample navigation bar

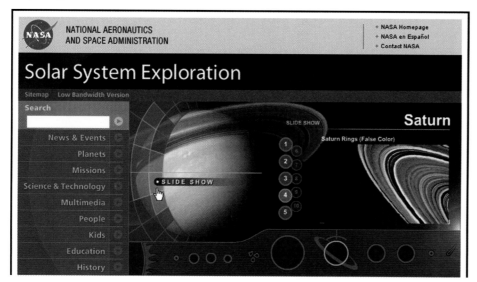

FIGURE 17

Set Nav Bar Image dialog box

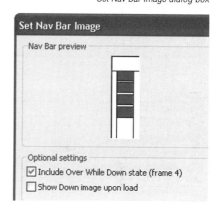

Create a generic button symbol with an Up state

1. Open fw7_2.png, save it as **recipes.png**, then make sure the Library and Behaviors panels are open.

2. Click the **Pointer tool** on the Tools panel (if necessary), then click the **small pale yellow rectangle** on the canvas.

3. Click **Modify** on the menu bar, point to **Symbol**, then click **Convert to Symbol** to open the Symbol Properties dialog box.

4. Type **generic button** in the Name text box, click the **Button option**, then click **OK**.

5. Double-click the **instance** on the canvas to open the Button Editor.

6. Click the **Text tool** A on the Tools panel, then enter the attributes shown in Figure 18.

7. Click the pointer over the crosshair, then type **MY LABEL**.

8. Click the **Pointer tool** on the Tools panel, press and hold **[Shift]**, click the **rectangle** to select both objects, click **Modify** on the menu bar, point to **Align**, then click **Center Vertical**.

9. Click **Modify** on the menu bar, point to **Align**, click **Center Horizontal**, then compare your Button Editor to Figure 19.

You created a button symbol and added text to it in the Up state.

FIGURE 18
Font attributes for the generic button

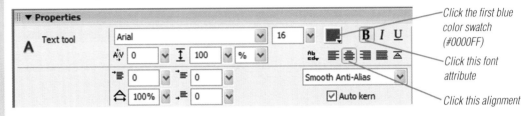

Click the first blue color swatch (#0000FF)

Click this font attribute

Click this alignment

FIGURE 19
Text added to Up state

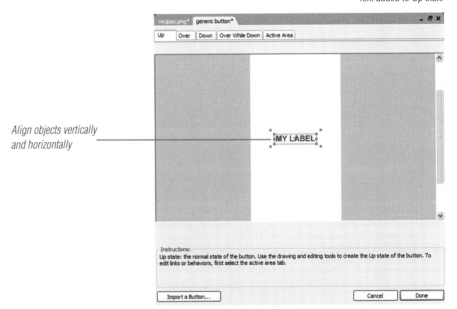

Align objects vertically and horizontally

FIGURE 20

Navigation bar behavior added to Down state

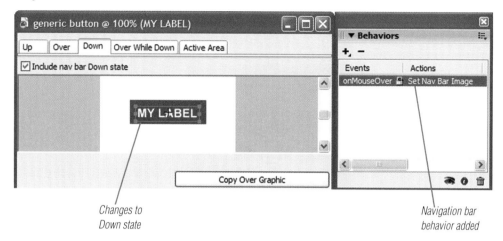

Changes to
Down state

Navigation bar
behavior added

Create other states for the button symbol

1. Click the **Over tab**, then click **Copy Up Graphic**.

2. Click the **rectangle**, click the **Fill Color box** on the Property inspector, type **#FFCC33** in the hexadecimal text box, then press **[Enter]** (Win) or **[return]** (Mac).

3. Click the **Down tab**, click **Copy Over Graphic**, click the **rectangle**, click the **Fill Color box** on the Property inspector, type **#9900CC** in the hexadecimal text box, then press **[Enter]** (Win) or **[return]** (Mac).

4. Click the **text object**, click the **Color box** on the Property inspector, click the first white color swatch in the color pop-up window, then compare your Button Editor to Figure 20.

5. Click the **Over While Down tab**, click **Copy Down Graphic**, click the **rectangle**, click the **Fill Color box** on the Property inspector, then click the blue color swatch (#0000FF) in the second column of the color pop-up window.

6. Click the **Active Area tab**, then verify that the slice covers the button exactly.

7. Click **Done**, then compare your image to Figure 21.

You created a button symbol.

FIGURE 21
Newly created button symbol

Menu preview

Create instances of the generic button symbol

1. Click **View** on the menu bar, point to **Grid**, then verify that **Snap to Grid** is selected.

   | TIP   Objects will snap to the grid even when Show Grid is not selected.

2. Press and hold **[Alt]** (Win) or **[option]** (Mac), then drag an instance of the button instance below the original.

3. Click **Edit** on the menu bar, then click **Repeat Duplicate** to duplicate and place another instance on the canvas.

4. Verify on the Property inspector that the coordinates of the middle instance are **35 X, 180 Y.**

5. Verify on the Property inspector that the coordinates for the bottom instance are **35 X, 235 Y,** then compare your image to Figure 22.

6. Click the **top button instance** to select it, select the text in the Button Name text box on the left side of the Property inspector, type **starters**, then press **[Enter]** (Win) or **[return]** (Mac).

7. Select the text in the **Text text box** on the Property inspector, type **Starters**, then press **[Enter]** (Win) or **[return]** (Mac).

(continued)

FIGURE 22
Duplicated button instances

FIGURE 23
Edited button instance properties

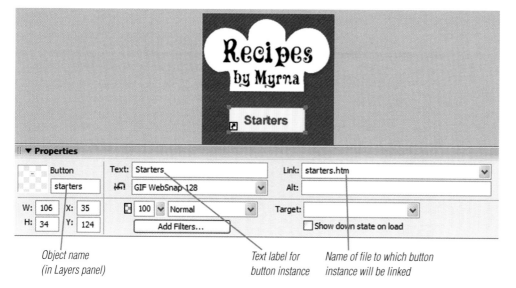

▼ Properties

	Button	Text:	Starters	Link:	starters.htm
	starters		GIF WebSnap 128	Alt:	
W: 106 X: 35			100 Normal	Target:	
H: 34 Y: 124			Add Filters...		☐ Show down state on load

Object name
(in Layers panel)

Text label for
button instance

Name of file to which button
instance will be linked

FIGURE 24
Aligning nav bar slices

Align slices
(to the left)
with arrow
keys to avoid
extraneous
slices

8. Click the **Link text box** on the Property inspector, type **starters.htm**, then compare your Property inspector to Figure 23.

   TIP   To export an HTML file for the Down state of each page, the button name must match the link filename.

9. Repeat Steps 6, 7, and 8 for the middle instance, changing the name of the Button to **entrees**, the Text to **Entrees**, and the Link to **entrees.htm**.

10. Repeat Steps 6, 7, and 8 for the bottom instance, changing the name of the Button to **desserts**, the Text to **Desserts**, and the Link to **desserts.htm**.

11. Click in a blank area of the canvas to deselect the Desserts button.

You created duplicate instances and changed their properties.

Optimize and export the document and nav bar

1. Click the **Show slices and hotspots button** 🔲 on the Tools panel, then align the slices of the nav bar until your image resembles Figure 24 (if necessary).

2. Click the **Hide slices and hotspots button** 🔲 on the Tools panel.

3. Open the Optimize panel (if necessary).

4. Click the **Saved settings list arrow**, then click **GIF WebSnap 128**.

5. Click **File** on the menu bar, then click **Export**.

   (continued)

6. Navigate to the drive and folder where your Data Files are stored, create a new folder named **recipes**, then open the folder (if necessary).

7. Click the **Export list arrow**, click **HTML and Images** (if necessary), then verify that your Export dialog box resembles Figure 25.

8. Click **Options** to open the HTML Setup dialog box, verify that **.htm** is the Extension, then click the **Document Specific tab**.

> TIP   On the Mac, the Export dialog box does not appear when the HTML Setup dialog box is open. It reappears when you close the HTML Setup dialog box.

9. Verify that the **Export multiple nav bar HTML files check box** and the **Include areas without slice objects check box** are selected.

10. Compare your dialog boxes to Figure 25, then click **OK** to close the HTML Setup dialog box.

11. Click **Export** to open the file management tool that is on your operating system, adjust the settings to display extensions (if necessary), then navigate to the drive and folder where you created the recipes folder.

The folder contains recipes.htm, the Down state .htm files for the nav bar, and the images folder.

12. Compare your image to Figure 26, then close your file management tool.

You optimized and exported the document containing the nav bar, then viewed the associated export files.

FIGURE 25
Options in the Export and HTML Setup dialog boxes

FIGURE 26
Exported nav bar and image files

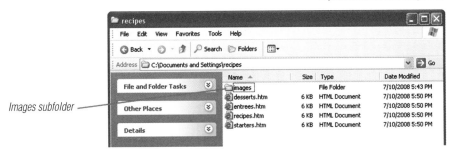

Images subfolder

FIGURE 27
Previewing the nav bar in a browser

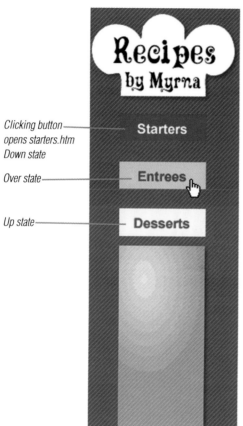

Clicking button opens starters.htm Down state

Over state

Up state

Preview the document and nav bar

1. Open your browser, then open recipes.htm.

2. Roll the mouse pointer over the **Starters button**, click the **button**, roll the mouse pointer over the **Entrees button**, then compare your image to Figure 27.

   The starters.htm file opens in response to the mouse click and the Over state of the Entrees button responds to the rollover.

3. Roll the mouse pointer over the **Starters button**.

   The button turns blue, reflecting the Over While Down state.

4. Close your browser, save your work, then close recipes.png.

You previewed the nav bar in your browser.

INTEGRATE FIREWORKS
HTML INTO AN HTML EDITOR

What You'll Do

```
<!DOCTYPE html PUBLIC "-//W3C//DTD XHTML 1.0 Transitional//EN" "http://www.w3.org/TR/xhtml1/DTD/xhtml1-transitional.dtd">
<html xmlns="http://www.w3.org/1999/xhtml">
<head>
<meta http-equiv="Content-Type" content="text/html; charset=iso-8859-1" />
<title>Untitled Document</title>
<style type="text/css" media="screen">
<!--
@import "../data/Revealed Series/Barbara Waxer/pqparts.css";
-->
</style>
<script language="JavaScript1.2" type="text/javascript" src="mm_css_menu.js"></script>
<script type="text/JavaScript">
<!--
function MM_swapImgRestore() { //v3.0
var i,x,a=document.MM_sr; for(i=0;a&&i<a.length&&(x=a[i])&&x.oSrc;i++) x.src=x.oSrc;

function MM_preloadImages() { //v3.0
var d=document; if(d.images){ if(!d.MM_p) d.MM_p=new Array();
var i,j=d.MM_p.length,a=MM_preloadImages.arguments; for(i=0; i<a.length; i++)
if (a[i].indexOf("#")!=0){ d.MM_p[j]=new Image; d.MM_p[j++].src=a[i];}}

function MM_findObj(n, d) { //v4.01
var p,i,x; if(!d) d=document; if((p=n.indexOf("?"))>0&&parent.frames.length) {
d=parent.frames[n.substring(p+1)].document; n=n.substring(0,p);}
if(!(x=d[n])&&d.all) x=d.all[n]; for (i=0;!x&&i<d.forms.length;i++) x=d.forms[i][n];
for(i=0;!x&&d.layers&&i<d.layers.length;i++) x=MM_findObj(n,d.layers[i].document);
if(!x && d.getElementById) x=d.getElementById(n); return x;}

function MM_swapImage() { //v3.0
var i,j=0,x,a=MM_swapImage.arguments; document.MM_sr=new Array; for(i=0;i<(a.length-2);i+=3)
if ((x=MM_findObj(a[i]))!=null){document.MM_sr[j++]=x; if(!x.oSrc) x.oSrc=x.src; x.src=a[i+2];}}
//-->
</script>
</head>
```

 In this lesson, you will learn about the basic relationship between the HTML code Fireworks creates when you export a document, and the HTML editor that will turn it into a Web page.

Understanding Web Page Structure and Basic HTML Code

A Web browser determines the appearance of a Web page by interpreting **Hypertext Markup Language (HTML)** code. HTML is the *lingua franca* that stipulates how a Web browser formats and displays text, graphics, sound, and other content so your browser can read it. HTML consists of **tags** that describe how the text should be formatted when a browser displays it. The tags are used in pairs, as shown next, and contain data in between. For example, the tags *<title> Car Parts, Etc </title>* include the Web page's title, Car Parts, Etc.

HTML files are divided into two segments: a head and a body. The body contains the content of the Web page that the browser will display to the viewer. The head content is generally not viewed, except for the title. The head contains important information that the Web page needs to function properly: the language encoding, JavaScript and VBScript functions and variables, and keywords and content indicators for search engines. JavaScript is a **client-side scripting language**, which means that it runs within a Web browser. Every time you add a behavior to a slice or hotspot, Fireworks automatically generates the JavaScript necessary for the interactivity in an HTML page.

JavaScript generally sits inside the HTML page, between the open <script> tag and the close </script> tag. These script tags can be in the head or body section of the HTML, or both. JavaScript can also be in its own file, separate from the HTML document. In this case, the JavaScript file has the .js extension, and the HTML file has a script tag that calls on the external file, such as the mm_menu.js or mm_css_menu.js file that Fireworks creates when you export a pop-up menu. In Fireworks, the Set Pop-Up Menu behavior places JavaScript code in a separate .js file.

Using Exported Fireworks HTML

When you generate HTML by exporting files in Fireworks, you will probably want to integrate it and be able to edit it with the content you've created in an HTML editor, such as Dreamweaver. Depending on the kind of Web page you want to create, your HTML editor of choice, and your work preferences, you can accomplish this in several ways.

Fireworks generates two kinds of HTML code: one for an image map and one for a table for sliced images. An image map is HTML code that identifies hotspots in an image for linking. A table is HTML code that divides an area of the page into rows and columns for display. Every time you export slices in Fireworks, the program generates individual images based on your slices, and it must generate the HTML code for a table to reassemble those images into a single unit. For example, when you export HTML and Images as the type, the code in <body> contains an image map and/or table code, along with comments that allow you to round-trip the code back to Fireworks from Dreamweaver.

Building a Content Page Around a Fireworks HTML Page

If your Fireworks HTML includes Fireworks-generated JavaScript, such as from behaviors you added using the Behaviors panel, you need to ensure that the HTML editor will recognize it. You can achieve this by selecting an HTML style, shown in Figure 28. Use the following settings in the Export dialog box: verify that Export HTML File is the HTML selection, click Options to open the HTML Setup dialog box, and then select the HTML Style that matches your HTML editor. JavaScript is inserted in between the open <script> tag and the close </script> tag.

QUICK TIP
You can also open the HTML Setup dialog box from the File menu.

When you export a document with HTML and Images as the type, you can open the HTML document that Fireworks generated in your HTML editor and then edit it as though you had created it from scratch in that program. Because HTML is an **open standard**, all HTML editors can read one another's code. However, some HTML editors, such as Dreamweaver, Adobe GoLive, and FrontPage, have special interfaces for creating and applying JavaScript interactivity.

FIGURE 28
HTML Style export options

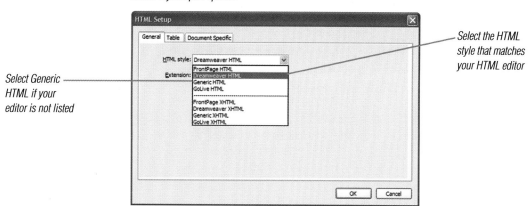

Select Generic HTML if your editor is not listed

Select the HTML style that matches your HTML editor

Figure 29 shows the HTML generated by Fireworks during export. JavaScript also appears differently depending on the style.

Inserting a Fireworks HTML Table into an Existing HTML Page

There will be many occasions when you need to insert a sliced image, image map, nav bar, or pop-up menu you created in Fireworks into the page layout of your HTML editor. When you open the HTML Setup dialog box in Fireworks and select either Dreamweaver HTML or XHTML as the style, Dreamweaver recognizes special code in the HTML. After you're in Dreamweaver, you can just place the insertion pointer where you want the element to appear and follow the directions in Dreamweaver for inserting Fireworks HTML. For other editors, you might need to be a bit more resourceful.

You can copy HTML code onto the Clipboard and then paste it in your HTML editor. When pasting HTML code onto the Clipboard, be sure to select the Include HTML comments check box on the General tab of the HTML Setup dialog box, and then choose the relevant HTML style. Fireworks HTML code works quite seamlessly in Dreamweaver. For other editors, when you copy Fireworks HTML code containing JavaScript code that enables interactivity, such as rollovers, behaviors, or buttons, the functions might not always operate as you intended.

FIGURE 29
Viewing Fireworks HTML

HTML style selected during export

JavaScript

```
<!DOCTYPE HTML PUBLIC "-//W3C//DTD HTML 4.01 Transitional//EN" "http://www.w3.org/TR/html4/loose.dtd">
<!-- saved from url=(0014)about:internet -->
<html>
<head>
<title>gmparts.gif</title>
<meta http-equiv="Content-Type" content="text/html;">
<!--Fireworks 8 Dreamweaver 8 target.   Created Thu Jul 10 16:42:48 GMT-0600 (Mountain Standard Time) 2008-->
<script language="JavaScript">
<!--
function MM_findObj(n, d) { //v4.01
  var p,i,x;  if(!d) d=document; if((p=n.indexOf("?"))>0&&parent.frames.length) {
    d=parent.frames[n.substring(p+1)].document; n=n.substring(0,p);}
  if(!(x=d[n])&&d.all) x=d.all[n]; for (i=0;!x&&i<d.forms.length;i++) x=d.forms[i][n];
  for(i=0;!x&&d.layers&&i<d.layers.length;i++) x=MM_findObj(n,d.layers[i].document);
  if(!x && d.getElementById) x=d.getElementById(n); return x;
}
function MM_swapImage() { //v3.0
  var i,j=0,x,a=MM_swapImage.arguments; document.MM_sr=new Array; for(i=0;i<(a.length-2);i+=3)
   if ((x=MM_findObj(a[i]))!=null){document.MM_sr[j++]=x; if(!x.oSrc) x.oSrc=x.src; x.src=a[i+2];}
}
function MM_swapImgRestore() { //v3.0
  var i,x,a=document.MM_sr; for(i=0;a&&i<a.length&&(x=a[i])&&x.oSrc;i++) x.src=x.oSrc;
}
function MM_preloadImages() { //v3.0
  var d=document; if(d.images){ if(!d.MM_p) d.MM_p=new Array();
    var i,j=d.MM_p.length,a=MM_preloadImages.arguments; for(i=0; i<a.length; i++)
    if (a[i].indexOf("#")!=0){ d.MM_p[j]=new Image; d.MM_p[j++].src=a[i];}}
}
//-->
</script>
<script language="JavaScript1.2" type="text/javascript" src="mm_css_menu.js"></script>
<style type="text/css" media="screen">
       @import "./gmparts.css";
</style>
</head>
```

For the HTML and JavaScript code, open the Fireworks HTML file, copy the open <script> tag and continue copying the code through the close </script> tag. Next, paste this code inside the head section of the new HTML page, right before the close </head> tag. To insert the body of the Fireworks HTML, copy everything between, but do not include the open <body> tag and close </body> tag, then paste it where it should appear in the new HTML page. Figure 30 shows the CSS style in Fireworks HTML after it has been inserted and saved in Dreamweaver.

FIGURE 30
Viewing CSS style

CSS style

CSS JavaScript file

```
<!DOCTYPE html PUBLIC "-//W3C//DTD XHTML 1.0 Transitional//EN" "http://www.w3.org/TR/xhtml1/DTD/xhtml1-transitional.dtd"
<html xmlns="http://www.w3.org/1999/xhtml">
<head>
<meta http-equiv="Content-Type" content="text/html; charset=iso-8859-1" />
<title>Untitled Document</title>
<style type="text/css" media="screen">
        @import "../data/Revealed Series/Barbara Waxer/gmparts.css";
</style>
<script language="JavaScript1.2" type="text/javascript" src="mm_css_menu.js"></script>
<script type="text/JavaScript">
<!--
function MM_swapImgRestore() { //v3.0
  var i,x,a=document.MM_sr; for(i=0;a&&i<a.length&&(x=a[i])&&x.oSrc;i++) x.src=x.oSrc;
}

function MM_preloadImages() { //v3.0
  var d=document; if(d.images){ if(!d.MM_p) d.MM_p=new Array();
    var i,j=d.MM_p.length,a=MM_preloadImages.arguments; for(i=0; i<a.length; i++)
    if (a[i].indexOf("#")!=0){ d.MM_p[j]=new Image; d.MM_p[j++].src=a[i];}}
}

function MM_findObj(n, d) { //v4.01
  var p,i,x;  if(!d) d=document; if((p=n.indexOf("?"))>0&&parent.frames.length) {
    d=parent.frames[n.substring(p+1)].document; n=n.substring(0,p);}
  if(!(x=d[n])&&d.all) x=d.all[n]; for (i=0;!x&&i<d.forms.length;i++) x=d.forms[i][n];
  for(i=0;!x&&d.layers&&i<d.layers.length;i++) x=MM_findObj(n,d.layers[i].document);
  if(!x && d.getElementById) x=d.getElementById(n); return x;
}

function MM_swapImage() { //v3.0
  var i,j=0,x,a=MM_swapImage.arguments; document.MM_sr=new Array; for(i=0;i<(a.length-2);i+=3)
   if ((x=MM_findObj(a[i]))!=null){document.MM_sr[j++]=x; if(!x.oSrc) x.oSrc=x.src; x.src=a[i+2];}
}
//-->
</script>
</head>
```

Create a pop-up menu and submenu on the Content tab.

1. Open fw7_3.png, then save it as **literary_cat.png**.
2. Show slices, select the books slice, then open the Behaviors panel.
3. Add a Set Pop-Up Menu behavior to the books slice.
4. Add the following menu items with null link values in the Pop-up Menu Editor: Fiction, Biography, Kids, Coffee Table, and Hobbies.
5. Add the following submenu items to the Coffee Table menu item with a null value: Art, Nature, and Travel.

Set the appearance.

1. Click the Appearance tab.
2. Select the HTML option and Vertical Menu as the orientation.
3. Enter the following font attributes: Font: Times New Roman, Times, Serif; Font Size: 14; Bold, and Left alignment.
4. Make sure that the text color is white and that the cell color is black for the Up state and Over state.

Set table attributes and menu position.

1. Click the Advanced tab.
2. Enter the following cell attributes: Cell width and Cell height: Automatic, Cell padding: 6, Text indent: 0, Cell spacing: 0, Menu delay: 1000, select the Show borders check box, then accept the default values.
3. Click the Position tab.

4. Set the menu position to the bottom of the slice and the submenu position to the upper right of the menu.
5. Click Done to close the Pop-up Menu Editor.
6. Save your work.

Preview and test the pop-up menu.

1. Preview the document in a browser.
2. Test the pop-up menu and submenu, then close the browser.

Edit the pop-up menu.

1. Open the Pop-up Menu Editor from the Behaviors panel.
2. Add the following URL to the Biography link: *http://www.biography.com*, then set the target to _blank.
3. Press [Spacebar] twice after the coffee table entry.
4. Click the Appearance tab, then change the Up state cell color to #FF9933 and the Over state cell color to #996600.
5. Click the Position tab, then change the Menu position X coordinate to 22 and Y to 47.
6. Click Done to close the Pop-up Menu Editor.
7. Save your work.
8. Test the pop-up menu in a browser, then close the browser.

Optimize and export the document.

1. Verify that no slices are selected.
2. Open the Optimize panel and make the Saved setting GIF WebSnap 128.

3. Open the Export dialog box, create a new folder named **litcat**, then open the folder (Win).
4. Verify the following settings: Export: HTML and Images; HTML: Export HTML File; Slices: Export Slices; and that the Include areas without slices and Put images in sub-folder check boxes are selected.
5. Click Options to open the HTML Setup dialog box, then select the Use CSS For Popup Menus check box and the Write CSS to an external file check box.
6. Export the file, then save your work.
7. Use your file management tool to view the files created during export.
8. Preview the file in a browser, compare your image to Figure 31, then close the browser and literary_cat.png.

Create a button symbol.

1. Open fw7_4.png, then save it as **technodude.png**.
2. Select the black rectangle on the canvas and convert it to a button symbol named **generic button**.
3. Edit the symbol in the Button Editor, select the Text tool with the following attributes: Font: Tahoma, Font Size: 13, Color: white, Bold, and Center alignment.
4. Center the pointer over the crosshair, then type **MY LABEL**.
5. Select both objects, then align them vertically and horizontally.

Create other button states.

1. Click the Over tab, then copy the Up graphic.
2. Change the rectangle color to #999999 and add a black Inner Glow effect with default settings.
3. Change the text color to #00FF00.
4. Click the Down tab.
5. Copy the Over graphic, change the color of the rectangle to black and the Inner Glow color to #00FF00.
6. Click the Over While Down tab, then copy the Down graphic.
7. Change the rectangle color to #666666, remove the Inner Glow effect, and change the text color to #CCCCCC.
8. Click the Active Area tab, then make sure the slice covers the rectangle.
9. Click Done to close the Button Editor.
10. Save your work.

Create button instances.

1. Turn on Snap to Grid (if necessary).
2. Drag two duplicate instances of the generic button symbol instance to the right of the button instance on the canvas to form a horizontal bar.
3. Change the text of the left instance to **TECH SUPPORT**, the name of the button instance object to **techsupport**, and the link to techsupport.htm.
4. Repeat Step 4 for the middle instance, changing the text to **PROGRAMMING**, the name of the button instance object to **programming**, and the link to programming.htm.

5. Repeat Step 4 for the right instance, changing the text to **TUTORIALS**, the name of the button instance object to **tutorials**, and the link to tutorials.htm.
6. Save your work.

Optimize, export, and preview.

1. Verify that no slices are selected.
2. Open the Optimize panel, then select GIF WebSnap 128 as the Saved setting.
3. Open the Export dialog box, create a new folder named **techno**, then open the folder (Win).
4. Enter the following: Save as type: HTML and Images, HTML: Export HTML File, Slices: Export Slices, and the Include areas without slices and Put images in subfolder check boxes should be selected.
5. Click the Options button and verify that the Extension on the General tab is .htm, that the Export multiple nav bar HTML files check box and the Include areas without slice objects check box are selected on the Document Specific tab, then close the HTML Setup dialog box.
6. Export the file, then save your work.
7. Open the technodude.htm file in a browser, then test the nav bar.
8. Compare your image to Figure 31, then close your browser and technodude.png.

FIGURE 31
Completed Skills Review

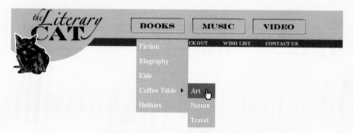

Some friends of yours own a successful specialty food delivery business, Snack of the Month. Business has been booming, so now they're ready to expand to more items. They've asked you to design their new Web site, Stuff of the Month.

1. Obtain images that will reinforce your food theme. You can obtain images from your computer, from the Internet, from a digital camera, or from scanned media. You can use images from the Web that are free for both personal and commercial use (check the copyright information for any such file before downloading it).

2. Create a new document and save it as **stuffomonth.png**.

3. Import the following file and the files you obtained in Step 1 into your document.
   - box.jpg

4. Create at least three buttons.

5. Create a pop-up menu and two submenus for at least one button.

6. Select the appearance of the pop-up menu items. Choose Image as the Cells type in the Appearance tab, then select styles of your choice.

7. Optimize and export the file in a folder named **stuffomonth**.

8. Open the stuffomonth.htm file in a browser, then test the pop-up menu.

9. Save your work, then examine the sample shown in Figure 32.

FIGURE 32
Sample Completed Project Builder 1

One of your good friends is a home project/crafts maven—she can transform any object into another object that someone will buy. You recently met someone who is a broker of large broken palette orders from discount and wholesale stores. Talking to her gave you the idea of starting a little side business: partner with your friend to buy up quantities of something and show how it can be transformed into a marketable item. You'll name the business Trash to Cash. You've already transformed your first item and are ready to use your Fireworks skills to advertise the business. Your Web page will convey your message.

1. Obtain images of the bulk item or end product that will fit your theme. You can obtain images from your computer, from the Internet, from adigital camera, or from scanned media. You can use images from the Web that are free for both personal and commercial use (check the copyright information for any such file before downloading it).
2. Create a new document and save it as **trash2cash.png**.
3. Copy or import the files into your document and convert objects to symbols as necessary.
4. Create a navigation bar for the site.
5. Optimize and export the file. (*Hint*: Create a folder named trash2cash.)
6. Open the trash2cash.htm file in a browser, then test the nav bar.
7. Save your work, then examine the sample shown in Figure 33.

FIGURE 33
Sample Completed Project Builder 2

Typically, when you navigate a Web page, you only use the navigation bar to get to the next page or link. However, navigation bars and pop-up menus can easily become part of the Web page design, and thus affect how you experience the site.

1. Connect to the Internet and go to *www.course.com*. Navigate to the page for this book, click the Student Online Companion, then click the link for this chapter. (*Note*: Web sites are updated frequently to reflect current trends, so this page might be different from Figure 34 if you open it online.)
2. Open a document in a word processor, or open a new Fireworks document, then save the file as **navigation**. (*Hint*: You can also use the Text tool in Fireworks to answer the questions.)
3. Explore several pages in the site, then, when you find one or two that interest you, answer the following questions:
    ■ What seems to be the purpose of this site?
    ■ Who is the target audience?
    ■ How is navigation used in the site? How many navigational elements are there?
    ■ How do the navigation system and pop-up menus fit the Web design? How are they configured?
    ■ Are navigation bars and pop-up menus subtle or obvious? Do you find them intuitive and useful? Do you like them? Discuss why or why not.

FIGURE 34
Design Project

    ■ How would you change the navigation or pop-up menus at this site?
4. Save your work.

Your group can assign elements of the project to individual members, or work collectively to create the finished product.

You've been asked to determine how the study or work environment affects performance. You can examine the related variable of your choice, such as the neatness of a desk, the aesthetic trappings, the quality of office supplies, and so on. Your group can choose the environmental variable of your choice and use your Fireworks skills to present a marketing solution.

1. Obtain images of the study or work variable you've chosen. You can obtain images from your computer, from the Internet, from a digital camera, or from scanned media. You can use images from the Web that are free for both personal and commercial use (check the copyright information for any such file before downloading it).
2. Create a new document and save it as **desktop_theory.png**.
3. Copy or import the files into your document.
4. Convert objects to symbols as necessary.
5. Create a pop-up menu and submenus.
6. Create a nav bar.

7. Optimize and export the document. (*Hint*: Create a folder named desktop_theory.)
8. Open the desktop_theory.htm file in a browser, then test the pop-up menu and nav bar.

FIGURE 35
Sample Completed Portfolio Project

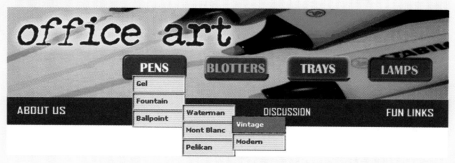

9. Save your work, then examine the sample shown in Figure 35. Note that part of the figure is a compilation of the nav bar and buttons in each state.

chapter

8 ENHANCING
PRODUCTIVITY

1. Tailor and customize work.

2. Make global changes.

3. Integrate Fireworks with other applications.

4. Understand intellectual property issues.

M A C R O M E D I A   F I R E W O R K S   8

Making Your Job Easier

Inevitably, in the course of design, you are going to need to make a global change to one thing or another. Regardless of who your client is (and especially if it's yourself), change might be necessary even after you think the project is complete.

Fireworks makes it easy to change many attributes in one or more documents using the Find and Replace feature and the Batch Process feature. You can perform a series of steps on one object, and then use the History panel to replay that series of steps on another object. You can also save steps as commands.

You can further tailor the Fireworks environment to improve your workflow by customizing keyboard shortcuts. Fireworks allows you to use shortcuts from other applications. Because Fireworks is a graphics program, many of its robust (and cool)

features take a hit on your system resources. You can adjust settings in the History panel and in the Preferences dialog box to change the way Fireworks uses system resources.

One of Fireworks' greatest strengths is its ability to interface with other programs. There are several features you can use to instantly integrate your documents with other programs within the Macromedia Studio suite and with other popular programs.

Finally, all Web content, whether it's something you view, download, or create, has some relationship with intellectual property law. You can safely assume that just about every image, video, or sound with which you come in contact in a Web page is protected by copyright law. Understanding the basic principles of copyright, trademark, and other intellectual property issues is essential to effective (and legal) Web page design.

Tools You'll Use

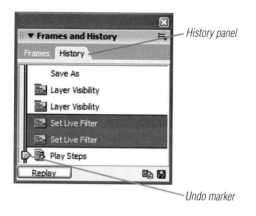

History panel

Undo marker

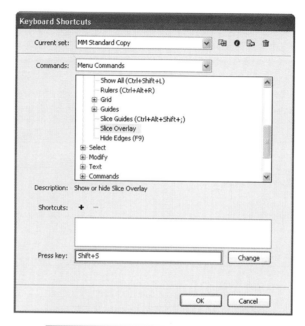

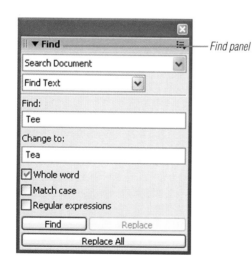

Find panel

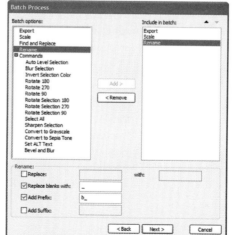

TAILOR AND
CUSTOMIZE WORK

What You'll Do

In this lesson, you will duplicate a set of keyboard shortcuts, create a custom keyboard shortcut command, and then use the History panel to undo a step, replay steps, and save steps as a command.

Customizing Keyboard Shortcuts

The master set of Fireworks keyboard shortcuts shares common functions with other programs. For example, the copy shortcut, [Ctrl][C] (Win) or ⌘[C] (Mac), is found in other major software applications, including the Corel, Adobe, and Microsoft suites. However, some commands or tools do not have shortcuts, whereas others are Macromedia-specific. You can personalize your own set of keyboard shortcuts by creating or modifying the ones you want, or by using a set from another application with which you are familiar.

You can open the Keyboard Shortcuts dialog box from the Edit menu (Win) or Fireworks menu (Mac). Fireworks provides five default sets: Fireworks, FreeHand, Illustrator, Macromedia Standard, and Photoshop. If you want to use a shortcut set from another application, choose a set from the Current Set list. If you want to add a custom shortcut, you must first duplicate a default set, rename it, and then modify shortcuts as you want. You cannot replace or overwrite a default shortcut set, but you can modify custom sets. To view shortcuts, click an option from the Commands list: Menu Commands, Tools, or Miscellaneous. You can then change an existing shortcut or create one for a command that lacks one. Command shortcuts must include a **modifier key**: [Shift], [Ctrl], and [Alt] (Win), or [Shift], ⌘, [option], and [control] (Mac). Tool shortcuts cannot include a modifier key, only a letter or number.

QUICK TIP

You do not have to open a document to edit keyboard shortcuts.

Using the History Panel

The History panel records the steps you've recently performed for the current document. If you close the document and open it later to continue your work, the history is not saved. You can undo recorded steps using the History panel. You can also set the number of undo steps in the History panel by clicking Preferences on the Edit menu (Win) or on the Fireworks menu

(Mac), and then typing a number in the Undo Steps text box on the General tab.

Figure 1 shows steps in the History panel. The undo marker points to the current step. You can step back into the history of your document by dragging the Undo marker up the step history in the panel, undoing each step beneath it. Undone steps are overwritten in the History panel by subsequent edits in the document. The History panel tracks results, not keystrokes.

You can also select one or more steps, select another object and replay the steps, or copy steps to the Clipboard where you can use them to build a custom command script to replay later. If you want to permanently save steps as a command, click the

Save button on the History panel. The custom commands you create on the History panel appear at the bottom of the Commands menu.

Maximizing Available Resources

Every graphics program you use is going to tap into the available resources on your computer to some extent, depending on the program and the operating system. You can search the system requirements Web page for your operating system on hints for optimizing your particular computer.

Within the Fireworks environment, you can reduce the number of undo/redo steps that Fireworks stores by opening the Preferences dialog box from the Edit menu (Win) or

Fireworks menu (Mac). Figure 2 shows the General tab in the Preferences dialog box. You can also clear steps from the History panel by clicking Clear History from the History panel Options menu. Note that when you clear the history, you cannot undo that action; everything you've done in your document to that point is editable within the standard confines of the feature, but not undoable. For example, you can delete effects in the Filters section of the Property inspector to remove them, but you cannot undo the steps that created them.

QUICKTIP

You need to restart Fireworks for the Preferences dialog box and History panel changes to take effect.

FIGURE 1

History panel

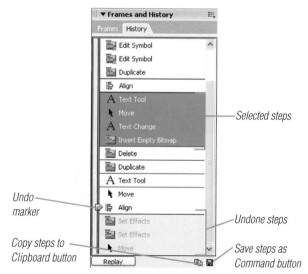

Selected steps

Undo marker

Undone steps

Copy steps to Clipboard button

Save steps as Command button

FIGURE 2

General tab in the Preferences dialog box

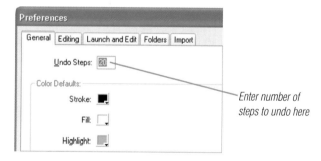

Enter number of steps to undo here

Create a duplicate keyboard shortcut set and custom shortcut

1. Open fw8_1.png, then save it as **rainbowtea.png**.

2. Click **Edit** (Win) or **Fireworks** (Mac) on the menu bar, then click **Keyboard Shortcuts** to open the Keyboard Shortcuts dialog box.

3. Click the **Duplicate Set button**  at the top of the dialog box, type **MM Standard Copy** in the Name text box, as shown in Figure 3, then click **OK**.

4. Verify that **Menu Commands** appears in the Commands box, click the **expand icon** next to View, scroll down the list, then click **Slice Overlay** to select it.

5. Click the **Add a new shortcut button** +, press and hold **[Shift]**, then type **S**.

   Fireworks automatically adds the modifier key, Shift, to the Press key text box.

6. Compare your dialog box to Figure 4, then click **OK**.

7. Verify that the rainbowtea.png window is active, press and hold **[Shift]**, then press **[S]**.

   The slices in the document are visible and the Show slices and hotspots button on the Tools panel is active.

8. Click the **Hide slices and hotspots button** on the Tools panel.

You created a duplicate set of keyboard shortcuts and added a custom shortcut.

FIGURE 3
Naming a duplicate keyboard shortcut set

Type new name here

FIGURE 4
Entering a custom keyboard shortcut

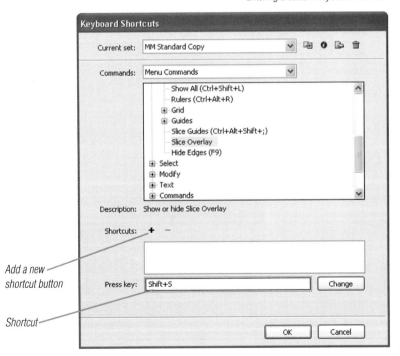

Add a new shortcut button

Shortcut

FIGURE 5
Undoing a step

Move Undo
marker up a step

Step to unbold
text is grayed out

Undo a step in the History panel

1. Open the History panel from the Window menu (if necessary).

   TIP You can also press [Shift][F10] (Win) to open and close the History panel.

2. Click the **Rainbow Stripe Tee text object** on the canvas to select it, then click the **Bold button B** on the Property inspector to unbold the text.

3. Drag the **Undo marker** in the History panel up one step.

   TIP When you undo an action from the Edit menu, the Undo marker moves up one step in the History panel.

4. Compare your image to Figure 5.

   TIP Depending on your system resources, you can set approximately 1000 undo steps. A solid line separates steps that cannot be replayed together. A red X indicates steps that Fireworks cannot record.

You used the History panel to undo a step.

Assigning keyboard shortcuts on the Mac

With the release of Mac OS X 10.4, Apple has reserved some keyboard shortcuts that were previously available to Fireworks. These shortcuts are now assigned to system features, such as Exposé, Dashboard, and Spotlight. Fortunately, you can change or remove these shortcuts by opening System Preferences, choosing the Keyboard & Mouse preference pane, and clicking Keyboard Shortcuts. Dashboard and Exposé shortcuts can also be modified in the Dashboard & Exposé preference pane.

Replay steps in the History panel

1. Click the **top stripe object** on the canvas to select it, then click the **Add live filters button** ![+] in the Filters section of the Property inspector.

2. Point to **Bevel and Emboss**, click **Inner Bevel**, click the **Bevel edge shape list arrow**, click **Smooth**, then press **[Enter]** (Win) or **[return]** (Mac).

3. Click the **Add Filters button** ![+] in the Filters section of the Property inspector, point to **Blur**, click **Blur More**, then compare your image to Figure 6.

4. Press and hold **[Shift]**, then click the **Set Live Filter steps** in the History panel to select them.

   > TIP You must first select steps before you can replay them.

5. Click the **bottom stripe object** on the canvas, then click **Replay** on the History panel.

   The bevel and blur effects are applied to the object.

6. Compare your image to Figure 7.

You selected and then replayed steps on the History panel.

FIGURE 6
Set Live Filter steps in the History panel

Set Effects steps in
the History panel
and applied to object

FIGURE 7
Replaying steps in the History panel

Click button to
replay selected steps

FIGURE 8
Save Command dialog box

FIGURE 9
Command added to Commands menu

Newly saved command

Save steps as a command

1. Press and hold **[Shift]**, then click the **Set Live Filter steps** in the History panel to select them (if necessary).

2. Click the **Save steps as a Command button** 💾 on the bottom of the History panel to open the Save Command dialog box.

3. Type **Bevel and Blur** in the Name text box, as shown in Figure 8, then click **OK**.

4. Click **Commands** on the menu bar, then compare your menu to Figure 9.

   The Bevel and Blur command appears on the Commands menu.

   > TIP   To delete or rename a custom command, click Manage Saved Commands on the Commands menu, then modify a command in the list.

5. Save your work.

You saved a command to the Commands menu.

Accessing extensions and support

The Macromedia Extensions Manager allows you to add, delete, and manage extensions, such as Creative Commands. You can open the Extensions Manager by clicking the Manage Extensions command on the Help or Commands menu. You download extensions on the Fireworks Exchange Web site, which contains JavaScript commands, filters, textures, Auto Shapes, and so on. You can navigate to the Fireworks Exchange Web site from the Start page or from the Help menu. To access tutorials, sample files, and tech notes, click the Fireworks Support Center command on the Help menu.

Lesson 1   Tailor and Customize Work

MAKE GLOBAL
CHANGES

What You'll Do

In this lesson, you will find and replace text, and use the Batch Process feature to rescale several JPEG files.

Using the Find Panel

When you're working with any design, change is unavoidable and in many instances, welcome. However, learning when and how to call a project complete is an important skill, whether it's a Web site or a house design. Because Web content has both visual and experiential dimensions, the content that you can change is significant. A typical Web site can consist of hundreds of individual elements and images. Although the question of whether you should change attributes and elements in a document remains subjective, Fireworks makes it easy to make those changes using the Find feature should you decide they're necessary.

Before you enter criteria to find and replace, you can determine how Fireworks will handle the affected files. When you open the Replace Options dialog box from the Options menu list on the Find panel, you can instruct Fireworks to save and close files after performing the find and replace, or to create backups of original files.

In many documents, the attributes you apply to vector and text shapes add to the overall design and give a document its unique look and feel. You can use the Find feature to change vector and text object attributes, as well as other elements. You can search a current selection, frame, document, project log, or a group of files. After you select what you want to search, you can select what you want to find: text, font, color URL, and non-Web 216 colors. Each item has fields specific to it, as shown in Figure 10. For text searches, in addition to preselected options, you can select the Regular Expressions check box to find patterns in text. A regular expression is a string of characters that tells Fireworks which pattern (string) to seek with and under what parameters. For example, the command `:%s/b[aeio]g/bug/g` will change each occurrence of "bag," "beg," "big," and "bog" to "bug."

Using Batch Process

Batch processing allows you to automatically apply the same modification to multiple files at the same time. You can run a batch process on any file that Fireworks can open. You can open the Batch Process dialog box from the Batch Process command on the File menu. To run a batch process, you select the files you want, select the option(s), add them to the Include in Batch section, adjust settings, click Next, and then click Batch. Figure 11 shows sample settings in the Batch Process dialog box. Fireworks opens the files, makes the changes, and then closes the files. You can also save backups of original files and specify the destination location of the changed files.

You can run the following batch process options:

- **Export**—Select an export setting as you would from the Optimize panel, or click Edit to open the Export Preview dialog box.

- **Scale**—Choose to scale to size, to fit the area, or to a percentage.
- **Find and Replace**—Click Edit to open the Find and Replace panel, then select find and replace criteria.
- **Rename**—Rename files by adding a prefix, adding a suffix, replacing a substring, or replacing blanks.
- **Commands**—Run any or all of the JavaScript commands listed in the Batch Options section.

FIGURE 10
Sample Find settings

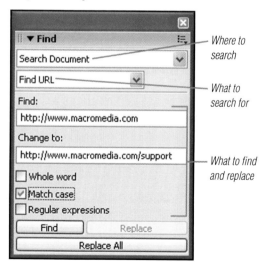

Where to search

What to search for

What to find and replace

FIGURE 11
Sample Batch Process settings

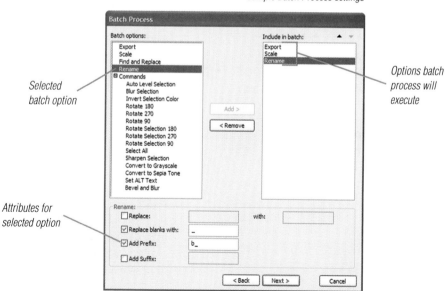

Selected batch option

Attributes for selected option

Options batch process will execute

Find and replace text

1. Click **Window** on the menu bar, then click **Find**. The Find panel opens.

   TIP You can also press [Ctrl][F] (Win) or ⌘ [F] (Mac), or click Edit and then click Find and Replace to open the Find panel.

2. Click the **Search list arrow**, click **Search Document** (if necessary), click the **Find list arrow**, click **Find Text** (if necessary), then enter the values shown in Figure 12.

3. Click **Find**, notice that the word "Tee" is highlighted in the title, click **Replace All**, then compare your image to Figure 13.

   Fireworks searches all the objects in the document, including each state of the button instances, and replaces "Tee" with "Tea." The dialog box tells you the number of replacements that Fireworks made.

   TIP Fireworks does not search Library symbols that are not used in the document.

4. Click **OK** to close the dialog box.

   TIP The results of the find and replace action might alter the alignment of objects on the canvas.

5. Close the Find panel.

You found and replaced text in the document.

FIGURE 12
Text settings in the Find panel

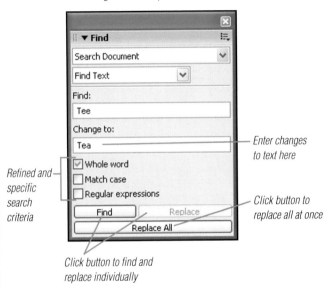

Refined and specific search criteria

Enter changes to text here

Click button to replace all at once

Click button to find and replace individually

FIGURE 13
Completed Find operation

Last replacement is highlighted

FIGURE 14

Selecting files for batch processing

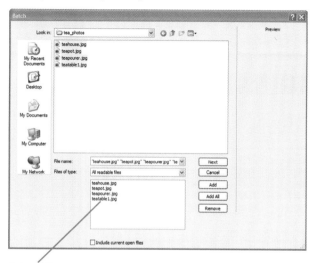

Selected files

FIGURE 15

Selecting scale attributes in the Batch Process dialog box

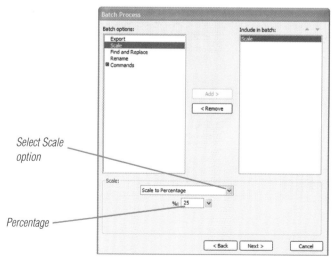

Select Scale option

Percentage

1. Click **File** on the menu bar, click **Import**, navigate to the drive and folder where your Data Files are stored, then locate the tea_photos folder.

2. Import **teapot.jpg**, place the **import pointer** in the upper-left corner of the canvas, then click the mouse.

   The imported bitmap fills the canvas.

3. Delete the newly imported bitmap, click **File** on the menu bar, then click **Batch Process**.

4. Navigate to the tea_photos folder, verify that **All readable files** appears as the Files of type selection (Win), click **Add All**, compare your dialog box to Figure 14, then click **Next**.

5. Click **Scale** in the Batch options section, then click **Add** to add it to the Include in batch section.

6. Click the **Scale list arrow**, click **Scale to Percentage**, double-click the **percentage text box**, type **25**, compare your dialog box to Figure 15, then click **Next**.

7. Verify that **Same location as original file** is selected in the Batch output section and that **Overwrite existing backups** is selected in the Backups section, then click **Batch**.

   Fireworks opens and closes each file as it performs the batch process.

8. Click **OK** to close the Batch Progress dialog box.

You ran a batch process on several files to rescale them at a set percentage.

View the results of batch processing

1. Open the file management tool on your operating system, adjust the settings to display file details, then navigate to the drive and folder where the tea_photos folder is stored.

2. Note the file size for the batch-processed files, open the Original folder, compare the file sizes shown in Figure 16, then close your file management tool.

   The files scaled during the batch process are significantly smaller than the originals.

3. Import the batch-processed teapot.jpg from the tea_photos folder.

   (continued)

FIGURE 16
Comparing file sizes

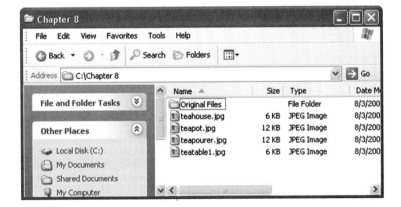

FIGURE 17
Scaled file imported into document

Rainbow Stripe Tea

Red

Green

Wulong

Floral scent

Compressed

Tea links

Rainbow Stripe Tea is a division of Rainbow Stripe Products, Ltd

4. Position the **import pointer** ⌐ in the upper-left corner of the canvas, then click the mouse.

   The imported file is much smaller and fits in a small portion of the canvas.

5. Type **20** in the X text box in the Property inspector, type **110** in the Y text box, click the **Opacity list arrow**, then drag the slider to **25**.

6. Click a blank part of the Document window twice, then compare your image to Figure 17.

7. Save your work, then close rainbowtea.png.

You compared the sizes of the original files and files scaled through batch process, and imported a scaled file.

Sending files via e-mail
You can easily include a copy of your open document as an e-mail attachment using one of the Send to E-mail commands on the File menu. You can choose Fireworks PNG, JPEG Compressed, or Use Export Settings, which attaches a file in the currently selected file format on the Optimize panel. Fireworks opens a new e-mail window, saves your document in the attachment format, and then attaches the file to the blank message.

INTEGRATE FIREWORKS
WITH OTHER APPLICATIONS

What You'll Do

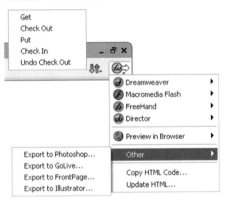

 In this lesson, you will learn about the Quick Export and file management features, and about working with Fireworks documents and library items in Dreamweaver.

Working with Files for Use in Other Applications

Before you begin work on a document in Fireworks, chances are that you know which application will eventually use the file. In addition, you will usually need to edit a file that you've already placed in a Web site in Dreamweaver. Figure 18 shows the options available for both of these jobs.

Using Quick Export

You can use the Quick Export button in the upper-right corner of the Document window to export your document using the most common export options for the application of choice.

If the application into which you want to export is part of the Macromedia suite, you'll find that the program drop-down list contains export options specific to that program. For example, Dreamweaver options are HTML-based, such as exporting or updating HTML or copying it to the Clipboard. Similarly, Macromedia Flash options allow you to export your document

as a Flash SWF file (published Flash movies that can play independently of Flash), or to copy selected objects as vector objects.

You can also export your document to other popular applications, as shown in Figure 18. The Export dialog box opens and provides the relevant options for the program you've selected. For example, if you choose Export to Photoshop, you can select how the exported file will accommodate appearance, layers, objects, effects, and text. If you choose Export to FrontPage, an HTML editor, the export choices are HTML-based, or the same as exporting HTML to Dreamweaver.

Each of the Macromedia application options also includes a Launch command for that particular program. The application opens a new document; it does not open active Fireworks documents. However, you can easily import the file or edit a file created in Fireworks from the other application.

Using the File Manager

You can use the File Manager button in the upper-right corner of the Document window to Get, Check Out, Put, Check In, or Undo Check Out a file used in a Studio 8 site folder and published on a remote server. In Dreamweaver, you must define the folder where the file is located as a Local Root Folder. Checking a file in or out allows you to protect it from or release it to everyone who could access it on the FTP site. Get and Put allow you to transfer a file from or to a remote server. All are versatile options that help you easily connect to an FTP site and manage your files after they've become part of a Web site.

Launching Fireworks from Dreamweaver

When you export a Fireworks document to Dreamweaver, you're actually exporting two files. In addition to the file exported in your chosen format, Fireworks creates a Design Notes file (.mno), which Dreamweaver uses to reference the source PNG file. This allows Dreamweaver to edit the image file in Fireworks from Dreamweaver.

You can use the Launch and Edit tab on the Preferences dialog box, shown in Figure 19, to specify whether and how to use the source PNG file for editing and optimizing.

You can choose one of the following options:

- **Always Use Source PNG**— Automatically launches the source PNG file referenced in the Design Notes and updates changes in both the PNG file and the exported file.
- **Never Use Source PNG**—Automatically launches and updates the exported file only.
- **Ask When Launching**—Prompts you to indicate if you want to launch the source PNG file.

QUICKTIP

Fireworks must be set as the primary external image editor in the Dreamweaver Preferences dialog box.

FIGURE 18
Quick Export and file management options

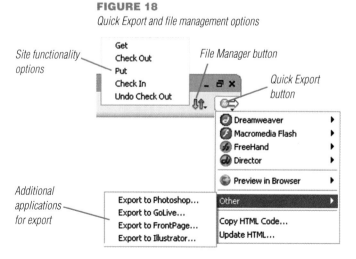

Site functionality options

File Manager button

Quick Export button

Additional applications for export

FIGURE 19
Launch and Edit settings in the Preferences dialog box

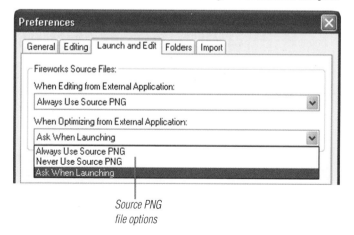

Source PNG file options

Saving Time with Dreamweaver Libraries

Editing and updating frequently used Web site elements, such as logos, graphics, or navigation bars that appear on many pages of a site, can become tedious and time consuming. To speed this process, you can export Fireworks documents as Dreamweaver library items. A **library item** is a piece of HTML (and JavaScript, if you're exporting files with rollovers) that's inserted into a Web page in Dreamweaver and can be updated automatically. Exporting a Fireworks document as a library item saves you time because you can then make changes to the document in Fireworks, and automatically update every instance of the library item throughout the Dreamweaver site.

Inserting a Library Item

To insert a library item (a file with the extension .lbi), simply drag it from the Dreamweaver Assets panel to any page in your Web site. A library item can't be edited directly in the Dreamweaver file, but you can edit the master library item. In this way, you can have Dreamweaver update every copy of that item on many pages throughout your site.

QUICKTIP

Dreamweaver library items do not support pop-up menus.

Exporting a Library Item

Dreamweaver doesn't recognize Library items unless they're located in a folder named Library (which is case sensitive) in your Dreamweaver site root folder. If your Fireworks document contains links to other pages in your site, as in a navigation bar, you need to make the URLs relative to the Library item. For example, if you create a navigation bar with a Contact button, and you want to link to contact.htm, type the link as ../contact.htm. When the Library item is inserted in a Web page, Dreamweaver automatically adjusts the link relative to the page on which it's being used. To export a Fireworks document as a Dreamweaver library item, choose Export from the File

---

Using Flash to create a Fireworks command

You might be surprised to learn that many of the various Command panels in Fireworks are actually Flash (.swf) files. For instance, the Align panel is simply a set of instructions generated in Flash for use in manipulating elements in Fireworks. In fact, advanced users can create their own Flash panels to help them accomplish specific, project-related tasks. For example, a company might create a Flash panel that simplifies the process of inserting its logo into a Fireworks document. To learn more about creating a Fireworks panel using Flash, visit: *http://www.macromedia.com/devnet/mx/studio/articles/fw_command_in_flash.html.*

menu, then select Dreamweaver Library from the Save as Type pop-up menu. See Figure 20. You must also select, or create, the Library folder in your Dreamweaver site as the location in which to export the files. If your image contains slices, you can also choose slicing options, and you can specify that Fireworks place the image files in a subfolder within the Library folder. After the document has been exported, open Dreamweaver. The Library items are shown in the Assets panel.

QUICK TIP

To learn more about exporting files as Dreamweaver Library items, search for "Dreamweaver Library items" in Fireworks Help. To learn more about using Dreamweaver Library items, search for "About library items" in Dreamweaver Help.

FIGURE 20

Exporting a Dreamweaver library item

UNDERSTAND INTELLECTUAL PROPERTY ISSUES

What You'll Do

World Intellectual Property Organization

About WIPO News & Information Resources

About Intellectual Property Activities & Services

New! Message from the Director General

 In this lesson, you will learn about intellectual and copyright property law and online privacy issues.

Understanding Intellectual Property

By definition, using multimedia in Web design involves combining content from several media: graphics, text, illustrations, HTML code, photographs, and other creative expressions of your ideas. The use and reproduction of all of these may be protected under one or more areas of law generally referred to as intellectual property. You can think of **intellectual property** as an idea or creation of a human mind. It also must have commercial value. Intellectual property is like any other property, except that instead of being *tangible*, like a DVD, it is *intangible*, like the songs or movie on the DVD. For comprehensive information on the legal aspects of intellectual property law, visit the Electronic Frontier Foundation Web site at *www.eff.org*, shown in Figure 21.

In the United States, intellectual property law involves four main categories.

Copyright law. A copyright arises upon an expression of an idea and thought, such as a Web page design or a new logo. Matter that is protected by copyright is referred to as a **work of authorship**, which includes the following:

- Literary works (everything from mystery e-books to sports manuals, and from clothing catalogs to computer source code)
- Musical works and sound recordings
- Dramatic works
- Artistic and architectural works
- Pictorial, graphic, and sculptural works (physical and digital)
- Motion pictures, video games and tapes, computer and other audio-visual works
- Broadcast and online transmission

Patent law. Under this "industrial" branch of intellectual property law, an inventor can apply for the protection of new, useful and "nonobvious" inventions and processes. For example, you can apply for a patent if you have devised a gene splicing technique for cancer, but not if you have developed a general idea of what gene splicing entails. The laws of natural science, such as gravity and physics, are not protected. The practical application of natural law, such as a roller coaster design, is protected.

Trademark law. Trademark law involves the protection of commercial identities and symbols. A **trade name** is the name of a business, corporation, company, and so on, which distinguishes one business entity from another. It can be a word, name, symbol, logo, or any combination thereof. A trademark must be adopted and used by an entity to identify their goods and to distinguish them from goods manufactured or sold by others. A *service mark* identifies the source of services instead of the source of goods, such as a restaurant chain.

Trade secret law. This branch of the law protects information created by the expenditure of (often considerable) time or money. Trade secrets are naturally held confidential and not generally known in the trade.

QUICKTIP

Copyright protection extends to original work, such as a digital image, as soon as it's created.

One of the most important areas of general intellectual property is the idea of a public domain. **Public domain** indicates the status of any work or creation that was never protected by some form of intellectual property, or had protection that was lost through time or by legal events. You can use or copy public domain works at will. The prevailing assumption is that using works that are in the public domain should be encouraged because such use promotes competition.

In contrast, copyright infringement is taken very seriously. For example, you might recall one or two news items about Internet music file-sharing or radio sites. The penalty for infringement of a registered copyright is up

FIGURE 21
Electronic Frontier Foundation Web site

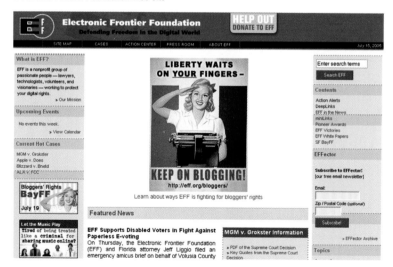

to $150,000 for each infringement. Even inadvertent infringement can lead to penalties, though not as strict.

The assumptions and burdens of proof governing copyright infringement are based upon civil law, not criminal law. The difference between the two is significant. In civil law, there is never the need to show infringement beyond a reasonable doubt, and there may even be an assumption of guilt, or liability as it is known in civil law. For example, U.S. copyright law specifically prohibits removing a watermark from a photograph. If you are charged with removing a watermark, the attempt itself is viewed by the court as your intent to violate the owner's copyright. The assumption is that you are liable and the burden of proof is on you to prove that you're not.

Copyright protects the particular and tangible *expression* of an idea, not the idea itself. If you wrote a story using the facts and idea about aliens crashing in Roswell, New Mexico, no one could copy your story without permission. However, anyone could write a story, make a music video, or post a blog using a similar plot or characters—the idea of aliens crashing in Roswell is not copyright-protected.

One limitation to copyright is **fair use**. Fair use allows consumers to copy all or part of a copyrighted work in support of their First Amendment rights. For example, you could excerpt short passages of a film or song, or parody a television show. Determining if fair use applies to a work depends on the purpose of its use, the nature of the copyrighted work, how much you want to copy, and the effect on the market or value of the work. Fair use is used as the defense in many copyright infringement cases, and is determined on a case-by-case basis.

For information on international intellectual property law, visit the World Intellectual Property Organization (WIPO) at *www.wipo.org*, shown in Figure 22.

FIGURE 22
WIPO Web site

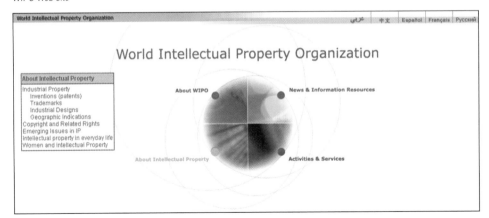

Original multimedia works are protected by copyright law and patent law. Other areas of law that intersect multimedia design are communications law and computer law. The products of the Web are literally intangible property operating in an intangible medium. As a result, the laws governing Web-based design are evolving.

Privacy as It Impacts Advertising and Marketing

Web advertising contains cookies and Web bugs, which are used to track your browsing behavior, sometimes down to the keystroke. The essential questions about online privacy concern how information is gathered, the extent to which information is collected, and with whom it can be shared. For example, if you respond to a banner ad, your surfing history through that site can be stored, resulting in a browsing profile that can be sold to several buyers. When combined with other data, such as credit card purchases or surveys

you've filled out, an aggregate profile of you is formed. That profile might or might not be accurate and might contain information you never thought would be disclosed. Privacy advocates are concerned that this information is collected, sold, reassembled, and used to evaluate an individual without their knowledge or consent.

For information on cookies and Web bugs, visit the educational organization, Privacy Foundation, at *www.privacyfoundation.org*, shown in Figure 23.

FIGURE 23
Privacy Foundation Web site

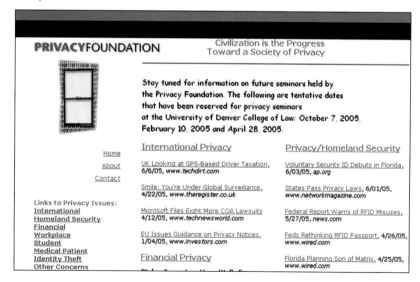

Create a duplicate keyboard shortcut set and custom shortcut.

1. Open fw8_2.png, then save it as **wrapit.png**.
2. Open the Keyboard Shortcuts dialog box from the Edit menu (Win) or Fireworks menu (Mac).
3. Duplicate the current shortcut set and change the name to **MM Standard Copy 2**.
4. Expand the File menu in the Commands section, then select Batch Process.
5. Add a new shortcut to the Press Key text box: Shift+Q.
6. Click OK.

Undo a step in the History panel.

1. Open the History panel.
2. Select the Wrap It text on the canvas. (*Hint*: Make sure that slices and hotspots are not visible.)
3. Delete the Inner Bevel on the Property inspector.

4. Drag the Undo Marker up in the History panel to undo the delete.
5. Save your work.

Replay a step in the History panel.

1. Add a Drop Shadow to the Bubbles bitmap with the following attributes: Distance: 5, Color: #000099, Opacity: 55%, and Softness: 6.
2. Select the Set Live Filter step in the History panel.
3. Select the Hot Deal text on the canvas.
4. Replay the Set Live Filter step.
5. Save your work.

Save the step as a command.

1. Verify that the Set Live Filter step is still selected in the History panel.
2. Save the step as a command. (*Hint*: Use the Save steps as a Command button on the bottom of the History panel.)

3. Name the command **Blue Drop Shadow** in the Save Command dialog box, then close the dialog box.
4. View the new command on the Commands menu.

Find and replace text.

1. Open the Find panel.
2. Search the document for Bobble and replace it with Bubble.
3. Replace all instances, then close the dialog box.
4. Save your work.

Run a batch process.

1. Import box2.gif to the upper-left corner of the canvas, then delete the object. (*Hint*: Look in the packing folder.)
2. Press [Shift][Q] to open the Batch Process dialog box.
3. Select and add all the files from the packing folder, then click Next.

4. Add Scale as the Batch Process, select Scale to Percentage, then set the percentage to 15.

5. Click Next, verify that Same location as original file is selected in the Batch Output section, and that Overwrite existing backups is selected as the Backups section.

6. Click Batch.

7. Save your work.

View the results of batch processing.

1. Open the file management tool on your computer, then compare the sizes of the original files to ones that were batch processed.

2. Import box2.gif at the top of the Layer 1 layer, move it beneath the title, then copy it to Frame 2.

3. Compare your image to Figure 24.

4. Save your work, then close wrapit.png.

FIGURE 24
Completed Skills Review

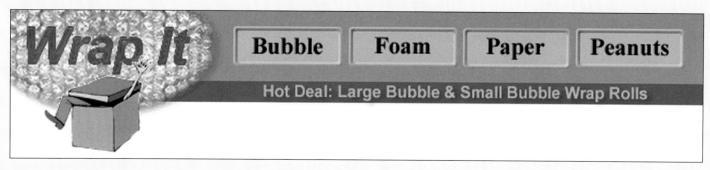

Your company has initiated a campaign to increase efficiency, and has promised to give employees half a day off each week if the goals are met. To do your part, you've identified some ways to work more quickly in Fireworks. You want to save steps that you perform frequently as commands, to save time. To complete this project, you can retrieve any solution file you created from previous Project Builders or Portfolio Projects.

1. Open the document of your choice, then save it as **mydocument.png**.
2. Think of a few sets of steps you perform often, that you could create commands for in this document.

3. If desired, obtain additional images to use in working through the steps you've decided to create commands for. You can obtain images from your computer, from the Internet, from a digital camera, or from scanned media. You can use images from the Web that are free for both personal and commercial use (check the copyright information for any such file before downloading it).
4. Add additional features, then save steps as commands and create additional keyboard shortcuts as desired.
5. Use the Find feature as necessary.

6. Add a new layer that you will use to record the names of the commands and shortcuts, then change the name of the layer to **commands**.
7. Use the Text tool to list the name of each command and shortcut, then hide the layer.
8. Optimize slices as necessary.
9. Save your work, then examine the sample shown in Figure 25.

FIGURE 25
Sample Completed Project Builder 1

You're helping an art gallery highlight their new exhibition on shapes and forms. So far, the shape photographs and images at the Web site don't do justice to the exhibit. They've asked you to design three picture frames in Fireworks that they can use to help accent the images on their Web page. You can pick the shape or form of your choice.

1. Obtain images that will reinforce your shape and form theme. You can obtain images from your computer, from the Internet, from a digital camera, or from scanned media. You can use images from the Web that are free for both personal and commercial use (check the copyright information for any such file before downloading it).

2. Create a new document and save it as **myframe.png**.

3. Import the images and create buttons or a nav bar as desired.

4. Create three or more frames for the shape images, saving the frame steps as commands.

5. Use the Find feature to change font and font color.

6. Add a new object on a layer that you will use to record the commands you created for each frame, then change the name of the object to **commands**.

7. Use the Text tool to describe each command, then hide the object on the Layers panel.

8. Save your work, then examine the sample in Figure 26.

FIGURE 26

Sample Completed Project Builder 2

Intellectual property enters our lives from the moment we wake up and hear the custom sound we programmed into a clock, or smell the coffee that our coffee maker made at a preset time after automatically grinding the beans.

1. Select a product, process, or other intellectual property entity. (*Hint*: Just go through your normal day and notice something that fits the definition of intellectual property. Chances are, something you enjoy or use every day is someone else's intellectual property.)

2. Open a new Fireworks document, then save it as **ip_law.png**.

3. Identify your product or process, then obtain images of it. You can obtain images from your computer, from the Internet, from a digital camera, or from scanned media. You can use images from the Web that are free for both personal and commercial use (check the copyright information for any such file before downloading it).

4. Create an image of your selection, and identify as many components as you can that are eligible for for some type of protection under intellectual property law.

5. Use the Text tool to categorize the elements you identified in Step 4 by copyright, trademark, patent, or trade secret of your product

or process affected by intellectual property. Split them into categories, and discuss each one. (*Hint*: Your precise categorization need not be necessarily correct.)

6. Save your work, then examine the sample shown in Figure 27.

FIGURE 27
Design Project

Patent: Studio recording equipment & processes, jewel box, outer seal and packaging, CD manufacturing

Copyright: Music, lyrics, liner notes, videos, song info that displays in player, photos, artwork, cover & liner design, CD design, concerts, t-shirts

Trademark: Record label, recording studio

Trade Secret: Encryption code to prevent copying (could also be trademark)

Your group can assign elements of the project to individual members, or work collectively to create the finished product.

Your group has been assigned to create a Fireworks document that contains many features and filters. You can choose the topic of your choice that celebrates nature.

1. Obtain images of the topic you've chosen. You can obtain images from your computer, from the Internet, from a digital camera, or from scanned media. You can use images from the Web that are free for both personal and commercial use (check the copyright information for any such file before downloading it).
2. Create a new document and save it as **celebrate.png**.
3. Copy or import the files into your document.
4. Add multiple features, then save steps as commands or create additional keyboard shortcuts as desired.
5. Add a new layer, change the layer name to **commands**, then use the Text tool to identify the commands from steps, shortcuts, and find commands you performed in the document.
6. Save your work, then examine the sample shown in Figure 28.

FIGURE 28
Sample Completed Portfolio Project

Chapter 8   Enhancing Productivity

Read the following information carefully!

Find out from your instructor the location where you will store your files.

- To complete many of the chapters in this book, you need to use the Data Files on the CD at the back of this book.
- Your instructor will tell you whether you will be working from the CD or copying the files to a drive on your computer or on a server. Your instructor will also tell you where you will store the files you create and modify.

Copy and organize your Data Files.

- Use the Data Files List to organize your files to a USB storage device, network folder, hard drive, or other storage device if you won't be working from the CD.
- Create a subfolder for each chapter in the location where you are storing your files, and name it according to the chapter title (e.g., Chapter 1).
- For each chapter you are assigned, copy the files listed in the **Data File Supplied** column into that chapter's folder.
- If you are working from the CD, you should store the files you modify or create in each chapter in the chapter folder.

Find and keep track of your Data Files and completed files.

- Use the **Data File Supplied** column to make sure you have the files you need before starting the chapter or exercise indicated in the Chapter column.
- Use the **Student Creates File** column to find out the filename you use when saving your new file for the exercise.
- The **Used in** column tells you where in a chapter a file is used.

Macromedia Fireworks 8

Chapter	Data File Supplied	Student Creates File	Used In
1	fw1_1.png		Lesson 1
	pool.png	my_blue_heaven.png	Lesson 2
	fw1_1.png		Lessons 3 & 4
	fw1_2.png elbow.gif		Skills Review
	none	crystal.png	Project Builder 1
	none	meandering_paths.png	Project Builder 2
	none	rocknroll	Design Project
	none	emoticon.png	Portfolio Project

Chapter	Data File Supplied	Student Creates File	Used In
2	none	fish.png	Lesson 1
	fw2_1.png		Lessons 2–5
	fw2_2.png		Skills Review
	none	remember_me.png	Project Builder 1
	none	impact_potions.png	Project Builder 2
	none	yoakum	Design Project
	none	classic_buckle.png	Portfolio Project
3	fw3_1.png rocket.gif saucer.png book.eps		Lesson 1
	galaxy.jpg		Lesson 2
	astrocat.jpg		Lesson 3
	none		Lesson 4
	fw3_2.png smbottle.jpg sweet.png jelly_beans.eps rings.png gumballs.tif		Skills Review
	button1.ai button2.gif	mybuttons.png	Project Builder 1
	none	roadtrip.png	Project Builder 2
	none	mountainclimb	Design Project
	none	mybug.png	Portfolio Project
4	fw4_1.png		Lessons 1,2, & 4
	fw4_2.png		Lessons 2 & 5
	leaves.png		Lesson 5
	fw4_3.png		Lessons 6 & 7
	fw4_4.png fw4_5.png fw4_6.png		Skills Review
	ship.jpg	treasure_hunt.png	Project Builder 1
	none	myproduce.png	Project Builder 2
	none	shorebank	Design Project
	none	imports.png	Portfolio Project

Chapter	Data File Supplied	Student Creates File	Used In
5	fw5_1.png		Lesson 1
	fw5_2.png		Lesson 2
	fw5_3.png		Lesson 3
	fw5_4.png		Lesson 4
	fw5_5.png fw5_6.png fw5_7.png fw5_8.png		Skills Review
	picture.jpg	geekchic.png	Project Builder 1
	none	maskgallery.png	Project Builder 2
	none	interactive	Design Project
	none	mytech.png	Portfolio Project
6	fw6_1.png		Lesson 1
	fw6_2.png		Lesson 2
	fw6_3.png		Lessons 3 & 4
	fw6_4.png fw6_5.png fw6_6.png		Skills Review
	cake.gif candle.gif	birthdaycake.png birthdaycake.gif	Project Builder 1
	none	readbooks.png readbooks.gif	Project Builder 2
	none	animation	Design Project
	none	mymoneymyth.png mymoneymyth.gif	Portfolio Project
7	none	none	Lesson 1
	fw7_1.png	gmparts.css gmparts/gmparts.htm gmparts/mm_cs_menu.js gmparts/assets/ folder gmparts/images/folder	Lesson 2
	fw7_2.png	recipes/desserts.htm recipes/entrees.htm recipes/recipes.htm recipes/starters.htm recipes/images/ folder	Lesson 3

Chapter	Data File Supplied	Student Creates File	Used In
	fw7_3.png	litcat/literary_cat.css	Skills Review
		litcat/literary_cat.htm	
		litcat/mm_css_menu.js	
		litcat/images/ folder	
	fw7_4.png	techno/programming.htm	
		techno/technodude.htm	
		techno/techsupport.htm	
		techno/tutorials.htm	
		techno/images/ folder	
	box.jpg	stuffomonth.png	Project Builder 1
		stuffomonth/mm_css_menu.js	
		stuffomonth/stuffomonth.css	
		stuffomonth/stuffomonth.htm	
		stuffomonth/images/ folder	
	none	trash2cash.png	Project Builder 2
		trash2cash/archives.htm	
		trash2cash/contactus.htm	
		trash2cash/join.htm	
		trash2cash/trash2cash.htm	
		trash2cash/viewhow.htm	
		trash2cash/images/ folder	
	none	navigation	Design Project
	none	desktop_theory.png	Portfolio Project
		desktop_theory/aboutus.htm	
		desktop_theory/blotters.htm	
		desktop_theory/desktop_theory.css	
		desktop_theory/desktop_theory.htm	
		desktop_theory/discussion.htm	
		desktop_theory/funlinks.htm	
		desktop_theory/lamps.htm	
		desktop_theory/mm_css_menu.js	
		desktop_theory/ourstore.htm	
		desktop_theory/pens.htm	
		desktop_theory/trays.htm	
		desktop_theory/images/ folder	

Chapter	Data File Supplied	Student Creates File	Used In
8	fw8_1.png		Lesson 1
	tea_photos/teahouse.jpg tea_photos/teapot.jpg tea_photos/teapourer.jpg tea_photos/teatable1.jpg	tea_photos/teahouse.jpg tea_photos/teapot.jpg tea_photos/teapourer.jpg tea_photos/teatable1.jpg tea_photos/Original Files/ folder	Lesson 2
	none	none	Lesson 3
	none	none	Lesson 4
	fw8_2.png packing/box1.jpg packing/box2.gif packing/box3.jpg pakcing/box4.jpg	packing/box1.jpg packing/box2.gif packing/box3.jpg packing/box4.jpg packing/Original Files/ folder	Skills Review
	none	mydocument.png	Project Builder 1
	none	myframe.png	Project Builder 2
	none	ip_law.png	Design Project
	none	celebrate.png	Portfolio Project

Absolute URL
A fixed URL starting with http:// used when linking to a Web page outside of your Web site.

Action
A response to an event trigger that causes a change, such as text changing color.

Additive colors
The primary colors of red, green, and blue that combine to form white in emitted light.

Alpha channel
The opaque area of the object.

Alternate text
Text that appears when you position the mouse pointer over a slice or hotspot.

Anchor points
Points that connect path segments in vector objects. They delineate changes in direction, whether a corner or a curve.

Animation
The illusion of movement, created by rapidly playing a series of still images in a sequence.

Animation handles
Handles on the animation path of an animation symbol: green (start), blue (frames), and red (end).

Animation symbol
An animation created from an object or instance on the canvas and stored in the Library panel. It has properties such as frame count, scale, opacity, and rotation.

Anti-aliasing
Blends the edges of a stroke, text, or pixel selection with surrounding pixels so that the edges blend into the background.

Behavior
A preset piece of JavaScript code that can be applied to a slice, hotspot, or button.

Behavior handle
A round icon that appears at the center of a slice or hotspot.

Bézier curves
The two-dimensional curves in a vector object.

Bitmap graphic
Represents a picture image as a matrix of dots, or pixels, on a grid.

Bitmap mask
A bitmap object used to mask an other object.

Blend mode
A feature that blends the pixels in a layer with the pixels in the layer beneath it to create special effects.

Canvas
The area where you draw and manipulate objects and images.

Client-side scripting language
Computer code that runs within a Web browser.

CMY
Cyan, magenta, yellow.

CMYK
Cyan, magenta, yellow, and black.

Color depth
The number of colors in the exported graphic.

Color ramp
Creates and displays the range of colors in a gradient, including their transparency.

Composite path
The path created by the Join command when two or more open or closed paths are joined to form a single object.

Continuous path
The path created by the Join command if the two objects in the path are open.

Control point
A yellow diamond that appears when you select an Auto shape; displays a tool tip on how to adjust the shape when you roll the mouse pointer over it.

Corner points
The square points of a path that has angles or is linear, such as a square, star, or a straight line.

CSS
Cascading style sheet.

Disjoint rollover
A rollover that swaps an image in a different part of the screen than where you triggered it.

Documents
The files you create in Fireworks.

Electromagnetic spectrum
The range of frequencies or wavelengths from long gamma rays to short radio waves.

Event trigger
An event, such as a mouse click on an object, that causes an action.

Fill
The color category (such as solid, gradient, or pattern) applied to an object, as well as its type and amount of edge.

Frame-by-frame animation
An animation process in which you copy objects into different frames and then modify the objects in each frame.

Frame control buttons
Buttons you use to preview animation in the document window.

Frame delay
The display time for an animation frame measured in hundredths of a second—the default frame delay in Fireworks is 7/100 of a second.

Frames
Individual static images that make up an animation.

GIF
Graphics interchange format.

Gradient
Two or more colors that blend into each other in a fixed design.

Histogram
A graphic representation of the color values in an image, from darkest on the left to brightest on the right.

Hotspot
An area in your document that initiates a specific action, such as linking to a Web page or displaying an e-mail message pop-up window. A hotspot can also initiate a behavior in a browser, such as a swap image pop-up menu.

HSB
Hue, saturation, and brightness.

HTML
Hypertext Markup Language; HTML marks up the text in your Web page so your browser can read it.

Image map
The graphics and HTML containing information about hotspots and their URL links. Fireworks creates an image map when you export a graphic with hotspots.

Instance
A symbol on the canvas; a shortcut to its symbol.

Interactivity
Allows visitors to your Web site to affect its content.

Interlacing
Allows a file to download from the Internet gradually from low to high resolution.

JavaScript
A Web-scripting language that interacts with HTML code to create interactive content.

JPEG
Joint photographic experts group.

Kerning
Adjusts the spacing between adjacent letters or a range of letters.

Layers
These divide and arrange the elements of your document in a logical front to back order. A layer can contain multiple objects, all of which are managed on the Layers panel.

Leading
The amount of space between lines of text.

Library item
Fireworks-generated HTML or JavaScript code that can be inserted in to a Dreamweaver file.

Library panel
Stores symbols for the current document.

Live Filters
Filters that are editable.

Looping
The number of times an animation will play after the initial playback in a Web page.

mailto URL
Opens an e-mail address window in a Web page.

Marquee selection
A flashing perimeter or dashed line around selected pixels.

Mask
Modifies the shape and transparency, including gradients, of an underlying image.

Mask object
A bitmap or vector object that masks another bitmap or vector object.

Mask thumbnail
Appears next to the object thumbnail on the Layers panel when you add a mask to an object.

Motion path
The animation trail in a document, consisting of animation handles. You can drag the handles to change the path of the animation.

Navigation bar
A group of buttons that link to different areas inside or outside the Web site.

Nested button symbol
A button symbol within a button symbol.

Objects
The individual elements in your document that are stored and managed on layers in the Layers panel.

Onion skinning
Allows you to view one or more additional animation frames while in the current frame.

Opacity setting
Determines if your image is completely opaque (100%), completely transparent (0%), or somewhere in between (in 1% increments).

Open standard
Computer code, such as HTML, whose specifications are publicly available.

Optimize
The process that matches the format best suited for the type of graphic with the smallest file size that maintains acceptable image quality.

Path
An open or closed vector line consisting of a series of anchor points.

Patterns
Bitmap images that have complex color schemes and textures.

Pixels
Discrete squares of color values that can be drawn on a computer screen.

Plug-in
Adds features to an application. In Fireworks, plug-ins appear on the Filters menu and the Property inspector.

PNG
Portable network graphics, the default file format in Fireworks.

Point handle
Corresponding to each anchor point, point handles are visible when you edit a curved path segment, but not when you edit a straight path segment. Also called a Bézier handle.

Pop-up menu
A menu that appears when you move the pointer over a trigger image in a browser.

Property inspector
Panel where you modify selected objects and set tool properties and other options. Depending on the activity or action you are performing, information on the Property inspector changes.

Relative URL
A link based on its location as it relates to the current page in the Web site's folder; used to link to a page within your Web site.

Resolution
The number of pixels per inch in an image; also refers to an image's clarity and fineness of detail.

RGB
Red, green, and blue.

Rollover
A graphic element in a Web page that changes appearance when you point to it with the mouse.

Sample
The color of a pixel or range of pixels picked up by the Eyedropper tool.

Slice
Used to attach a link or behavior to the image beneath it, which is how you create interactivity.

States
The four appearances a button can assume in response to a mouse action. They include Up, Over, Down, and Over While Down.

Storyboard
A visual script you use to show the action. It consists of a series of panels that plot the key scenes and illustrate the flow of the animation.

Stroke
A border applied to an object's edge consisting of attributes, including color, tip size (the size of the stroke), softness, and texture.

Styles
Preset attributes, such as size, color, and texture that you can apply to objects and text.

Styles panel
Where Fireworks manages pre-designed graphics and text styles.

Subselection tool
Tool used to move points on a path, or to select objects and paths within a group or composite path.

Subtractive colors
The primary colors of cyan, magenta, and yellow that combine to form black in print and pigment.

Symbol
Any text, graphic, button, or animation object saved in the Library panel. A way to reuse graphic objects, animations, and buttons in a document.

Tags
Pieces of code that determine how the content in HTML should be formatted when a browser displays it.

TIFF
Tagged image file format.

Tolerance
The range of colors the tool will select. The higher the setting, the larger the selection range.

Tools panel
Houses the tools you can use in the Fireworks work environment.

URL
Uniform resource locator, an address that determines a route on the Internet or to a Web page.

Vector graphics
Mathematically calculated objects composed of anchor points and straight or curved line segments, which you can fill with color or a pattern and outline with a stroke.

Vector mask
The vector shape through which the underlying object is viewed.

Web Dither
A fill that approximates the color of a non-web-safe color by combining two web-safe colors.

Web Layer
The topmost layer on the Layers panel. It is a shared layer, meaning that its content appears in all frames that contain the Web elements.

Web-safe colors
Colors that are common to both Macintosh and Windows platforms.

White light
Visible light from the sun that is made of red, orange, yellow, green, indigo, and violet; combined equally, it appears white.